1 & 2
SAMUEL

Text copyright © Harry Mowvley 1998

The author asserts the moral right to be
identified as the author of this work

Published by
The Bible Reading Fellowship
Peter's Way, Sandy Lane West
Oxford OX4 5HG
ISBN 1 84101 030 8

First edition 1998
10 9 8 7 6 5 4 3 2 1 0

Acknowledgments
The New Revised Standard Version of the Bible, copyright ©
1989 by the Division of Christian Education of the
National Council of the Churches of Christ in the USA.

Revised English Bible copyright © 1989, by permission of
Oxford and Cambridge University Presses.

A catalogue record for this book is
available from the British Library

Printed and bound in Great Britain
by Caledonian Book Manufacturing International,
Glasgow

1 & 2
SAMUEL

THE PEOPLE'S
BIBLE COMMENTARY

HARRY
MOWVLEY

A BIBLE COMMENTARY FOR EVERY DAY

The Bible Reading Fellowship
OPENING THE BIBLE

Introducing the
People's Bible Commentary
SERIES

Congratulations! You are embarking on a voyage of discovery—or rediscovery. You may feel you know the Bible very well; you may never have turned its pages before. You may be looking for a fresh way of approaching daily Bible study; you may be searching for useful insights to share in a study group or from a pulpit.

The People's Bible Commentary (PBC) series is designed for all those who want to study the scriptures in a way that will warm the heart as well as instructing the mind. To help you, the series distils the best of scholarly insights into the straightforward language and devotional emphasis of Bible reading notes. Explanation of background material, and discussion of the original Greek and Hebrew, will always aim to be brief.

- If you have never really studied the Bible before, the series offers a serious yet accessible way in.

- If you help to lead a church study group, or are otherwise involved in regular preaching and teaching, you can find invaluable 'snapshots' of a Bible passage through the PBC approach.

- If you are a church worker or minister, burned out on the Bible, this series could help you recover the wonder of scripture.

Using a People's Bible Commentary

The series is designed for use alongside any version of the Bible. You may have your own favourite translation, but you might like to consider trying a different one in order to gain fresh perspectives on familiar passages.

Many Bible translations come in a range of editions, including study and reference editions that have concordances, various kinds of special index, maps and marginal notes. These can all prove helpful in studying the relevant passage. The Notes section at the back of each PBC volume provides space for you to write personal reflections, points to follow up, questions and comments.

Each People's Bible Commentary can be used on a daily basis, instead of Bible reading notes. Alternatively, it can be read straight through, or used as a resource book for insight into particular verses of the biblical book.

If you have enjoyed using this commentary and would like to progress further in Bible study, you will find details of other volumes in the series listed at the back, together with information about a special offer from BRF.

While it is important to deepen understanding of a given passage, this series always aims to engage both heart and mind in the study of the Bible. The scriptures point to our Lord himself and our task is to use them to build our relationship with him. When we read, let us do so prayerfully, slowly, reverently, expecting him to speak to our hearts.

CONTENTS

PBC 1 & 2 Samuel: Introduction

The two books of Samuel form part of a much larger work which includes 1 and 2 Kings. They take their name from the person who dominates the first fifteen chapters, though after that Samuel recedes and eventually disappears. The rest of the book is concerned with the beginnings of monarchy in Israel. First Saul was anointed king by Samuel. His reign was not an unlimited success and he was followed by David, whose rise to power is described. The second book of Samuel then outlines the reign of David almost to his death and deals with the problems encountered within his family. It raises the question as to which of his sons should succeed him and tells what happens to them. Eventually in 1 Kings 1, on David's death, he is succeeded by Solomon. The rest of the books of Kings traces the fortunes of the united Israel under Solomon and then of the two kingdoms of Israel and Judah up to the exile in Babylon in 587BC.

There is a strong possibility that the books of Joshua and Judges also form part of this larger work, in which case we have a long story which extends from the time of the settlement of the tribes in the promised land to their exile from it. It is important to see 1 and 2 Samuel as part of this larger whole.

Date

It is obvious that the final form of this long account cannot have been written until after the final event it records. Since it closes with the note that King Jehoiakin was released from prison in Babylon in the thirty-seventh year of the exile, that is, in 562BC, the whole book was not completed until after that. This means that the Jews were still in exile when it was written.

Purpose

Not all the Jews were taken into exile. In fact, Jeremiah 52:28–30 provides us with some numbers of those carried off—3023 in 597, 832 in 587 and 745 in 582—a total of 4600. If these figures are correct it means that only a relatively small proportion of the population of Judah went into exile. The land and its capital were not left uninhabited. Those who were taken to Babylon were the élite, the leaders of the nation, so that there was little danger of an uprising in Judah. However, most of the peasant farmers continued to live in

Judah and to work their land, but without any effective leadership.

There was much activity among the exiles as they sought to understand and come to terms with what had happened to them. To many it seemed that God had deserted his chosen people or else he was no longer capable of protecting them. In either case, the temptation to abandon faith in the Lord and to worship the apparently superior gods of Babylon must have been very strong. But there were those in exile who interpreted events differently. Ezekiel, himself a priest as well as a prophet, understood the exile to be the result not of weakness or lack of concern on the part of the Lord, but of the sin of the people of Judah. Between 597 and 587BC he spent his time warning the people in exile that there was worse still to come because the disloyalty to the Lord was still continuing. Once Jerusalem had fallen in 587 he regarded the judgment of God as complete and could encourage the exiles with the news that they would soon be free to return. God would restore them. The prophet writing in Isaiah 40—55 also saw the exile as due to the judgment of God but at the time he was writing, say 550BC, the judgment had been carried out and they could look forward to God leading them home again (Isaiah 40:2ff).

It is also almost certain that at some point during the exile the story from creation to the point of entry to the promised land was written, with the needs of the exiles in mind. It was intended to encourage them to maintain their own identity and their own traditions in an alien culture. This writing was one of the sources of the first five books of the Old Testament, although tradition has attributed it to Moses.

The writer of 1 and 2 Samuel, and indeed of Joshua through to 2 Kings, was engaged in a similar task of trying to come to terms with and to explain the destruction of Jerusalem and the exile of the Judean leaders. Although we may speak of 'a writer' it may well be that the book is the work of more than one person, sometimes called a 'school' of writers. Whether these people were in exile in Babylon or had been left behind in Judah is hard to decide, and opinions differ. It doesn't make much difference to our understanding of the books. What is important is to understand that they were written for the benefit of people during that time of exile, to help them to make sense of what had occurred and still to believe in the Lord and worship him alone.

The nature of the books

The books of Samuel and Kings are often referred to as the 'historical books', though in the Jewish tradition they are known as the Former Prophets. The term 'historical books' is not wrong but it can be misleading. If what we have said above is correct, then the purpose of the books was not simply to provide a detailed, impartial account of events from the past; it was to teach a lesson.

It is, of course, exceedingly difficult, if not impossible, to write a history of anything which is purely factual and neutral. Even neutral observers write from the point of view of their neutrality. Suppose we were to try to write a history of Britain from 1979 to 1997. There are certain events which we should certainly be compelled to include—the miners' strike, the Falklands War, the Gulf War, various pieces of legislation, to mention a few. But first of all we should have to decide which events were important enough to warrant inclusion, because it would be absurd to think that we could write about everything that happened to everybody. In other words, there has to be a process of selection. We have to decide what is important, not only to us but to those who will read what we have written. However, what we regard as important may not be the same as what someone else would want to include. The choices we make are bound to be somewhat subjective.

Not only what we include but what we say about the events we do include will depend on our point of view. A history written by a Tory would be different from that written by a Labour or Liberal Democrat supporter, because history requires not just a recounting of events, but some assessment of them, some evaluation. In our modern world the use of tape recorders and careful records places some limit on our freedom, but they still leave room for subjective judgments.

In fact, of course, many writers dealing with this period may well be doing so to make a point either supporting or criticizing what happened during those years. Then, while keeping to the facts, the interpretation of those facts will vary according to the purpose of the writer. In such a case impartiality is not a prime consideration.

Now, imagine a writer and a group of supporters who wish to write a history of Israel and Judah from 1000 to 582BC. First they will have very few written sources and those they have will not be neutral. Any oral sources, stories passed on by word of mouth for many generations, may well have been coloured over the years by the beliefs and prejudices of those who have told them. Further, the writer's intention is not to write a history as a sort of academic exercise for the Jewish national curriculum. Nor is he writing out of general interest. He is writing with a purpose and that purpose is to help his people to come to terms with what has happened. Why are the chosen people in exile? What does this say about God? What does it say about human behaviour? What does it say about national politics? What can we learn from it about the future?

Only with certain qualifications may we call these books 'historical books'. They deal with events in history, but their manner of doing so is determined by their intention.

The author(s)

There is a strong likelihood that the books of Samuel went through a number of 'editions' before they reached their present form and therefore to speak of *an* author is slightly misleading. However, those who shared in the project had a common aim. It is quite impossible to give a name to the authors or editors of these books, but it is possible to say something about the group to which they belonged. It is widely believed that they were 'Deuteronomists'. By this is meant people who were immersed in the teachings of the book of Deuteronomy. This book reflects the views of a group of people from northern Israel who lived there just before the end of that kingdom in 722BC and moved to Judah after that. Whether they wrote it before they moved or after is uncertain and doesn't matter much from our point of view. The book presents a picture of a restored, united Israel with one religious centre where people worship only the Lord. It speaks of the Lord's love for his people, his choice of them, his deliverance of them from Egypt and his settlement of them in the promised land. It calls for obedience to him from those he has chosen. If that is forthcoming they can be assured of his blessing and continued prosperity, but if they disobey they will be punished. The relationship between the Lord and his people is defined as a 'covenant' which demands obedience and exclusive worship in response to his love. The heart of the book, in chapters 12—26, sets out the way in which Israel is to express its obedience and to fulfil its obligations within the covenant. It is not so much a 'law code' as a book of instruction as to what it meant to respond to God's love and so keep the covenant.

The Deuteronomic 'school' fostered these beliefs but during the early part of the seventh century there was no opportunity to spread them in Judah because the nation was dominated by the Assyrians, who insisted on their subjects adopting Assyrian religious beliefs and practices. King Manasseh, who reigned for more than fifty years, had little option but to comply with their demands. Whether he did so willingly or reluctantly, it is hard to say. His death coincided with a weakening of Assyrian control and the opportunity arose for Judah to return to traditional religious worship of the Lord. We are told that King Josiah began the process of reform and that a book was found in the temple in Jerusalem which gave clear direction to the reforms (2 Kings 22). The things he did, such as removing all shrines except the central one in Jerusalem, correspond so closely to the teachings of the book of Deuteronomy that very many scholars believe that the reforms were actually based on that book. The reforms have often been called the 'Deuteronomic Reforms'.

This reform movement soon came to an end when Josiah was killed in battle and Judah reverted to its former ways. The Deuteronomic group still existed and when Judah eventually fell to the Babylonians they felt that their warnings had been justified. While others were shocked and shattered by what had happened, they believed this was the just reward for persistent disobedience and unfaithfulness to the Lord.

The books of Joshua through to 2 Kings therefore set out to show, from this point of view, the reasons for the defeat and destruction of Jerusalem and the exile in Babylon. It is this 'theology' which undergirds the books with which we are concerned here, 1 and 2 Samuel, as well as the rest.

Sources

But where did the writer find all the information? The only source he mentions is the book of Jashar. In 2 Samuel 1:18 we are told that the lament which David sang over the death of Saul and Jonathan was recorded in the book of Jashar. The same source is mentioned in Joshua 10:13, where the poem about the sun standing still on Gibeon's hill is attributed to it. We can only guess from this that it probably contained a collection of poems. In the book of Kings we are told that more information about a king may be found in the 'Book of the Annals of the Kings of Israel' (2 Kings 14:28). This suggests that there were some court records available to the writer which he was able to draw on. Beyond these two sources we know of no others.

But court records were hardly likely to contain the actual words of people in conversations or the words of prayers. So, if they were not recorded, were they really passed on by word of mouth for several hundred years, from one generation to another? It may be that we have to admit that the writer himself wrote what he believed the various speakers might have said. For instance, in 1 Samuel 2, Hannah sings or recites a psalm. The psalm she sings refers to the king (v. 10) and so it can hardly have been used in this form by Hannah, for at that time there was no king. The song she is said to have sung must have come from a later time. What seems to have happened is that the writer felt it to be right and appropriate that Hannah should sing a song of thanksgiving for her baby son and so he used a song which was familiar to him in the sixth century, but which was also appropriate to Hannah's situation. This is not to cast doubt upon the incident itself. After all, some expression of thanks would be absolutely natural. It is simply to suggest that the description of the incident is couched in the writer's own language and perhaps coloured by his beliefs. After all, we have already seen that the writer was not interested in an accurate, neutral account of events, but in helping his contemporaries to learn from the past.

Some of the events described can be confirmed or otherwise by external sources. This applies more to 1 and 2 Kings than to 1 and 2 Samuel, but if there is agreement between 1 and 2 Kings and external sources, this surely adds credibility to what is written in 1 and 2 Samuel. Though the story may be told in the writer's own words and in order to fulfil his aims, there is no reason to doubt the outline of the story itself.

Sometimes it looks as though the writer had at his disposal more than one account of the same event. In 1 Samuel 8—12 there seem to be different attitudes towards the monarchy. In some places Samuel appears to be eager to anoint a king; in others he is reluctant. Again, there seem to be two accounts of the way David entered the court of Saul. In one he was a skilled musician who could calm Saul when he was attacked by bouts of madness; in the other he fought against Goliath and was taken on by Saul as his armour bearer. There is little point in arguing which is correct. The author has done his best to bring his different sources together and make a consistent story out of them. If we think we can sometimes 'see the joins', so be it. But the author intended his book to be read as it now stands. He was no fool who just included stories because he happened to have them. He was a skilled storyteller who could weave his sources together in such a way as to make a coherent whole. However much we may analyse them, we must always look at the story as it now stands, because that is what the author intended us to do.

His skill is shown in other ways, too. His characters are carefully drawn so that they come over to us as real people. There are goodies and baddies but mostly they are a mixture of the two, and this is so true to life. There are ambiguities about Samuel. David himself is full of ambiguities, sometimes selfish, often generous. His motives are never very clear but are always mixed. Joab is a hard man, cruel and heartless, yet unfailingly loyal almost to the end. It is all very real and all very human.

He knows how to get the best out of a story, often saving the 'punch-line' until the most telling moment. He introduces a person or an event some time before the main story, so keeping us in suspense. He holds contrasting pictures before us, for instance Saul and Jonathan, so that one offsets the other and the contrast is heightened. Indeed our author is a very skilful storyteller.

Inspiration

There are those who find all this talk of sources irrelevant. The book which we possess has been written by someone who was 'inspired' by God. By this, some mean that God told the writer what to write and he wrote it. So God knew all about the conversations, some of them very private, and told the writer exactly what had been said by whom to whom. Those who take this view have no difficulty over sources, but there are difficulties when two parts of the story seem to conflict. Ways have to be found to overcome this problem. While respecting these views, the present writer has a different understanding of inspiration. The author of 1 and 2 Samuel was certainly inspired by God and when we read the books we too are inspired by the same God. But divine inspiration does not mean that human characteristics are suspended. The author was using the gifts God had given him to tell the story of his people in such a way that it might help them to understand and to deal with their situation. The interpreter is using the gifts God has given him or her to show the relevance of that message for today. So God is involved in the whole process but he does not override us in such a way as to lift the responsibility from our shoulders. The author had to use his skills to tell his story in a way that would help his readers, and trust that God would use what he had done. The interpreter must do the same, relying on God for help, but recognizing that, because of his or her humanity, the interpretation may be flawed.

The succession narrative

There is one large section of the book which the writer seems to have taken almost without adaptation from an existing source. 2 Samuel 9 to 1 Kings 2 is often referred to as 'the succession narrative' for reasons which are fairly obvious. The chapters trace the fortunes of David's family, especially his sons. Since David was only the second king and was no relative of Saul his predecessor, there was as yet no tradition within Israel itself of sons succeeding fathers as king. Other nations, as well as some Canaanite cities, had kings and so Israel would not be ignorant of what happened there when a king died. It was probably assumed that one of David's sons would succeed him, but which? Indeed, in the story of 2 Samuel as we have it, God had promised that David's sons would reign after him for as far into the future as could be seen (2 Samuel 7). The succession narrative tells of David's adultery and then of the birth to Bathsheba of Solomon, and it hints strongly that Solomon would succeed David for it says that 'the Lord loved him'. However, there were other sons who may be thought to have a prior claim since they were older, some born to David while he was still king of Judah only at Hebron, and others born after he had captured Jerusalem. The narrative tells of the struggles of some of these sons to stake their claim to the throne when David died.

These quarrels within the family are explained as a consequence of David's adultery with Bathsheba and the 'murder' of her husband. Yet she was the mother of Solomon. The whole narrative is an intriguing story. Throughout, the Lord is active but mostly behind the scenes. He is not often mentioned. Things tend to work themselves out according to their own inner dynamic, yet behind it all he is active. This view of God's activity in the world is typical of the so-called Wise Men or sages. In much of the book of Proverbs consequences follow acts in an almost automatic way. If you do this,

this will follow. However, this natural correlation of act and consequence is no accident; it is all part of God's plan and he is behind it.
For this reason it is widely believed that the succession narrative originated among the Wise Men and was used virtually unchanged by the
author of 2 Samuel. The underlying theology of obedience leading to
prosperity, and disobedience leading to adversity, was congenial to
him.

We are then led to ask how the intimate details of David's family
life, especially his affair with Bathsheba, came to be known to the
wise men. These were not events which would be talked about
openly by the king or his wife. Nevertheless, such secrets have a habit
of leaking out within court circles, of which the wise men were almost
certainly a part. (See the commentary for further discussion.)

If we are right in saying that the purpose of the writer was to show
how the downfall of Jerusalem and the exile in Babylon were due not
to the failure of the Lord but to the persistent sin of his people, and
especially in high places, then here was a rich source for the writer to
use.

Text and translation

The earliest Hebrew manuscripts that we possess come from the
seventh or eighth century AD, that is, over a thousand years after the
book was first written. Since during that time all copies were made by
hand, there was ample opportunity for error, either accidental or
deliberate. Against that, we know that the copyists were extremely
careful and they had various devices for ensuring that their copies
were accurate. The discovery of the scrolls near the Dead Sea has
shown us just how accurate the copying was. Therefore, nowadays we
are reluctant to assume an error has been made simply because we
cannot fully understand the Hebrew. There are places where, on other
grounds, it seems wise to read a different sequence of letters, but this
must be done rarely and carefully.

The texts were read in the synagogues and there are some places
where the rabbis felt unable to pronounce a certain word and so
read something slightly different. When they came across the letters
YHWH they always read the word 'Lord'. Most modern translations
follow their example and have 'LORD', spelled in capitals. Similarly,
they preferred not to read the word Baal and often read *bosheth*
instead, which means 'something shameful'.

Further, the texts were translated first into Greek and then into Syriac and Latin for the benefit of those who could not read Hebrew. The Greek translation, known as the Septuagint, was probably made about 300BC for Greek-speaking Jews in Alexandria in Egypt. There are places where the Greek translation differs significantly from the Hebrew text. Then we have to decide whether the Greek translators had a different text before them, or whether they mistranslated the Hebrew, or whether they couldn't understand it and so wrote something which they thought made sense. The footnotes in the New Revised Standard Version draw attention to these differences and to the way in which the modern translators have handled them. Occasionally we shall refer to these in the commentary.

The most significant difference between the Greek and the Hebrew texts occurs in the story of David and Goliath, where no less than nineteen verses of the Hebrew are missing from the Septuagint (1 Samuel 17:12–31). Opinions differ as to whether the longer Hebrew text is the original and for some reason or other the Greek translators omitted the verses, or whether the shorter Greek text was original and later Hebrew copyists added the verses to reconcile the two accounts of the way David entered Saul's court. Most English translations print the longer text. (See the commentary for further information.)

Modern translators, therefore, sometimes have difficult decisions to make. There are other problems too. Some Hebrew words are used only once, or maybe twice, in the whole Old Testament and, since there are hardly any other Hebrew documents from this period, we have few means of deciding their meaning. Sometimes there are similar words in other ancient languages; sometimes we have to rely on the early translations; sometimes we can only guess the meaning from the context in which the word is used. But it has to be said that these occasions are rare.

Translation is a difficult art and various modern translations sometimes show significant differences which affect the meaning of a story. A word in one language is rarely the exact equivalent of a word in another. Or rather, a word in one language has all sorts of associations which are different from the associations its equivalent has in another. Moreover, the precise meaning of a word is often determined by the way it is used and the company it keeps. It is always a good idea, therefore, to look at more than one translation. However, in order to avoid too much confusion the present commentary is based on the New Revised Standard Version (NRSV) with reference from time to time to the Revised English Bible (REB).

It would be useful to have a map of Palestine to hand as you read. Plate 6 in the Westminster Bible Atlas or Map 3 in the New Revised Standard Version would be appropriate.

Harry Mowvley

AN UNHAPPY FAMILY

A childless woman

The story begins with a family. There is a man with his two wives, one of whom is unable to have any children. Elkanah means something like 'God has acquired', but, though names are sometimes significant, this one does not seem to have any special significance. We know nothing of his ancestry other than what we are told here. He was an Ephraimite and Ephraim was the most important of the twelve tribes, descended from one of the two sons of Joseph and settled in the central part of the land of Canaan, west of the Jordan.

Then, as now, childlessness was regrettable but for slightly different reasons. It meant that there would be no one to care for the husband and wife in their old age. Moreover, it wasn't just that Hannah wanted a baby to fulfil her maternal instincts. Children, in those days, were a sign of God's blessing and the highest blessing was to have no less than seven sons. To be childless was therefore a sign of God's disfavour. It was difficult for Elkanah also. The Israelites had no belief in a life after death. The most they could hope for was that their name would live on, especially in their children, but if there were no children then death was the end of everything. For both man and wife childlessness was a severe misfortune. Therefore, sometimes a kind of surrogacy was practised. In the same situation Sarah offered her maid to Abraham so that he could have children (Genesis 16: 1–6). In the present case Elkanah had a second wife and already had children by her but not by his favourite wife. Monogamy was not the rule in those days. Kings and well-to-do people could have several wives. Imagine these two women living under the same roof. There was bound to be jealousy. Peninnah made fun of Hannah but the story has nothing to say about Hannah's attitude to Peninnah.

The family at worship

Things came to a head when they all went up to the shrine at Shiloh to make their sacrifice (v. 3). Shiloh was an important place of worship. It was where the ark of the covenant was kept and this was regarded as the throne of the invisible God who had led them through the wilderness after bringing them out of Egypt. Some sacrifices were burned completely on the altar, the whole offered to God as an expression of homage to him. Others were part-burned and the rest of the meat was shared between the offerer and his family. So Elkanah shared the meat with Peninnah and Hannah but offered twice as much to Hannah (v. 5). This favouritism only increased Peninnah's anger and she taunted Hannah. The Hebrew actually says she 'thundered' at her. To her credit, in the story, Hannah made no active response. She wept and went off her food. It was no comfort to be told by Elkanah that she always had him (v. 8).

Hannah's prayer

Hannah not only wept; she also prayed, but she did so silently. The prayer as recorded is a remarkable one (v. 11). She promised that if God would give her a child she would dedicate him to God's service at the shrine. So it wasn't so much that she wanted the joy of bringing up a child. She was prepared to forgo that if her disgrace of childlessness could be removed. The child would be a Nazirite, a term not much used in the Old Testament which means 'dedicated to God'. In Numbers 6 there are set out regulations which Nazirites should follow. They were to drink no wine (see Amos 2:11–12) and they were not to cut their hair, as in the case of Samson who was also a Nazirite and whose mother had also been unable to have children (Judges 13:2–5).

There is a recognition here that childen are a gift from God. They belong to God and are given to parents on trust. Hannah's willingness to give up her son is echoed in Mary's acceptance of God's will for her son (Luke 1:35–38). It is a reminder that children are not a possession to be enjoyed selfishly. They belong to God and are held on trust, a trust to be discharged faithfully.

A PRAYER

Lord, keep us free from jealousy when others have things which we long for and have not. Help us to receive your gifts with gratitude as you entrust them to our care.

GOD'S GIFT RETURNED

Eli may be forgiven for thinking that he had a drunken woman on his hands. Hannah was obviously distraught and her lips were moving. Eli couldn't hear anything because she was praying silently. He couldn't see what she was saying, although he was watching her lips, because his sight was already poor. She would probably have been swaying with the intensity of her prayer. He therefore accused her of coming to worship drunk (v. 13).

However, when she explained herself, he accepted her explanation. She had been pouring out her 'soul' (v. 15). This is a word which sometimes means 'appetite' and expresses the idea of 'desiring' or 'longing'. Once he understood this and realized how urgent her prayers had been he pronounced a priestly blessing over her and promised the fulfilment of her prayer. The change in her demeanour is striking (v. 18). It shows how seriously the priest's words were taken because he was seen as God's mouthpiece. In many of the psalms there is a similar change of mood from lamentation to thanksgiving (e.g. Psalm 6:8) which may have been brought about by a priest's pronouncement.

Answered prayer

When they returned home Elkanah and his wife had intercourse again and this time Hannah became pregnant (v. 19). The verb 'to know' is often used in this sense in the Old Testament. God 'remembered' her. This does not mean that it had slipped his mind and then suddenly he thought of her again. The word 'remember' nearly always means that the person who does so *acts* in accordance with what is remembered. The son who was eventually born was given the name Samuel. This name means something like 'the name of God', but it was chosen bcause it sounds very much like the word which means 'to ask'. Quite often in the Old Testament, names given to people and places depend upon their sound even more than upon their actual meaning. So, Hannah had 'asked' for a child and she was given 'Samuel'.

Shiloh revisited

The Old Testament Law demanded that all males should visit the sanctuary three times a year for the three main festivals, the feasts of Passover, Weeks and Tabernacles (Exodus 3:17; 34:22; Deuteronomy 16:16). However, the journey to Shiloh was apparently an annual one and the women went too. While Samuel was a baby he and his mother were not expected to make the journey to Shiloh. The process of weaning him would take two or three years and so some time elapses between verses 23 and 24. Elkanah agreed to the delay but, according to the NRSV translation, makes a strange comment. Why should he wish for God to 'establish his word' when he had already fulfilled his promise by giving them a son? It is more likely that he would encourage Hannah to fulfil her promise to dedicate her son to the Lord. There is some evidence to suggest that we should read 'your word' rather than 'his word'. The REB understands it in this way. Perhaps he was afraid that she might go back on her promise and be tempted to keep Samuel for herself.

He need not have worried, for as soon as Samuel was old enough she took him to Shiloh and left him there (v. 24). To make the fulfilment of her vow she took a bull for sacrifice as the Law laid down in Leviticus 22:17–25. It didn't have to be a bull; it could have been a sheep or a goat. So either Elkanah and Hannah were quite well-to-do or they were making a considerable sacrifice in our modern sense of the word as well as in the literal sense.

The NRSV translation of verse 28 says that Hannah 'lent' Samuel to the Lord, but the dedication of him as a Nazirite suggests more than a loan. Actually there is another play on that word 'to ask'. The Hebrew word used here could be translated literally as 'she caused to ask', but in the few other places where it is used it seems to mean something like 'to hand over'. It surely has this meaning here. The writer has chosen this rather unusual word because of its similarity to the name Samuel and because Hannah had 'asked' for him.

For REFLECTION

How often do we make promises to God and then, when we have received what we asked for, forget all about it? Do we sometimes promise more than we are prepared to give?
Vows are meant to be kept.

HANNAH'S SONG

The instinct of the author is absolutely right. What his story requires here is a song of thanksgiving from Hannah. The birth of a baby is usually an occasion for expressing joy and giving thanks, especially if the parents have longed for a child over a period of time. The joy can still be seen on the faces of those mothers who thought they could never have a baby but have been enabled to do so by fertility treatment or some other technological means. For them it is a 'miracle'. So it was for Hannah and it was right that she should show her happiness and thanks in a song. But, almost certainly, the author did not have a copy of the words she actually sang. So what was he to do? He could make up a song which would be appropriate, or he could use an existing song which seemed to suit the occasion. He seems to have chosen the latter course, probably using a psalm which had been sung in the temple at some later time, though it has not found its way into our book of Psalms.

A royal psalm

If we read this psalm on its own, forgetting for the moment that it was sung by Hannah, we can see that it is a psalm sung by a king in thanksgiving for a victory. As he rejoices in his victory he may now make fun of or gloat over his enemies. Although the NRSV has 'my' victory, the Hebrew text has 'your' victory (v. 1). This is more likely to be correct in view of the way the following verses speak of the king's natural weakness and the strength given to him by God. Victory cannot be achieved by human srength alone; it is given by God. This is a common Old Testament view and we shall have to refer to it again and again as we read on. So, God is all-powerful and exalts the weak, the poor and the disadvantaged. This in itself makes it appropriate to Hannah's situation for, if she was not actually poor, she certainly had been disadvantaged.

The psalm on Hannah's lips

The passage in the psalm which makes it even more immediately appropriate for Hannah is, of course, the second half of verse 5. It is not an exact description of her because so far she has had only one son. It is a more general statement about the power of God. Seven sons, as we saw in an earlier passage, was a sign of the greatest blessing from God.

The psalm addresses God as the Holy One (v. 2). This is a title which came to be used frequently, especially in the book of Isaiah. It sets God apart from human beings, stressing his divinity. Moreover, there is no other god like him (see also Isaiah 40:25). This does not deny the existence of other gods, but it means that for Israel no other god was to worshipped or served.

As applied to Hannah, the enemies to gloat over would be Peninnah and any who sided with her. The song goes on to praise the Lord as the one who has the power both to give life and to take it away (v. 6). The birth of a child is not something achieved by human activity alone; it is a gift from God.

By the end of the psalm we have clearly gone beyond Hannah's situation into a more general song in praise of the Lord's power. Even the king is dependent on it (v. 10). Of course, there was no king in Hannah's day (Judges 21:25) although Samuel will eventually anoint Saul as king and, later, David. However, there is sufficient in the psalm to justify the choice of it as Hannah's song.

An Old Testament Magnificat

It is scarcely possible to read this song without being reminded of another. Mary, the mother of Jesus, was also surprised and overjoyed when she knew she was pregnant. She also sang a song, which is recorded in Luke 1:46–55. She also praised God and sang of the disadvantaged being raised and the mighty being brought low. The child she bore was not just a priest or prophet like Samuel. He was the king, the anointed, the Messiah.

A PRAYER

God, we thank you that you still perform wonders.
Increase our faith in your power and your love.

SLEAZE *in* HIGH PLACES

We're bound to feel some sympathy for Eli. He had given his life in service at the shrine at Shiloh and now he was getting on in years. His consolation would be that his sons would carry on his work as priests. Unfortunately they had proved to be disappointments. They had let their father down but, more importantly, they had let his God down. They had turned out to be 'scoundrels' (v. 12). Literally it says they were 'sons of Belial' and perhaps the writer wanted to draw out the contrast between them and Hannah, for in 1:16, when Eli had mistakenly thought she was drunk, she had assured him she was not a 'daughter of Belial'. His sons had turned out to be what she was not.

Cheating at the altar

Their position as priests should have been regarded as a great privilege. Priests were there to enable people to meet with God. They were responsible for teaching the Law and so helping people to live their lives according to the will of God. They were also responsible for making sacrifices on behalf of people or else supervising them. They therefore stood between God and the people, representing each to the other. They were not a barrier separating God from the people, but a link joining them together. To take advantage of that situation was therefore a terrible thing. It amounted to a misuse of their privilege.

Some rules for sacrifice are set out in Leviticus 1—7 but this does not tell us all we should like to know about how the sacrifices were offered. In any case, the practice probably changed somewhat over the centuries. Certainly some sacrifices were burned whole on the altar, but others were part-burned and the rest eaten by the worshipper and his family. The peace-offering described in Leviticus 3 is of this kind and this seems to be in mind here. Two parts of the procedure are mentioned: in verses 13–14 the meat was boiled and the priests' servant plunged a fork into the pot. Whatever he brought out was for the priests. The Hebrew leaves it uncertain whether this was the usual, correct procedure (so REB) or whether it was an abuse (so NRSV). Certainly what follows in verses 15–16 was malpractice.

In any sacrifice the blood and the fat were regarded as God's. The blood represented the life of the animal (Leviticus 17:14), and so belonged to God already. It was not offered on the altar but was sprinkled round it. The fat was burned along with certain parts of the meat and only then could the communal meal take place. At this time at Shiloh the priests sent their servants to demand the meat while it was still raw and before the fat had been burned on the altar. Eli's sons wanted it raw so that they could roast it, presumably using the fat, rather than make do with boiled meat. Since this was contrary to correct practice, the offerer might object, but he was then threatened. If he did not hand over the meat, the servant took it by force.

We may sympathize with their desire for roast instead of boiled meat but that is not the point at issue. It is not their greed that the writer condemns. It is the misuse of their privileged position and their disrespect for the things of God. How often does familiarity breed contempt!

By contrast, Samuel, still a boy, was acting as a member of the priestly family at Shiloh (v. 18). Already he was wearing the linen ephod, which was a priestly garment. We shall hear a good deal about ephods and their use later on. His mother, who had handed him over to God, still cared about him and brought him a new robe each year. Eli, in return, blessed her and consequently she went on to have more children, three boys and two girls, of whom we hear no more. The story now focuses on Samuel himself. He grew up 'in the presence of the Lord', that is, at the shrine in Shiloh alongside Eli and his wicked sons.

MEDITATION

Think of the privileges God has given you.
Have you used them well? Have you been tempted to abuse them?
Have you abused them? If so, now is the time to tell God and to
make a fresh start.

DIRE CONSEQUENCES

Notice that throughout this chapter the story of the downfall of Eli's sons is interrupted by passages which describe the development of Samuel. In this way the writer cleverly brings out the contrast between them.

Disturbing rumours

It would seem that Eli was too old to see for himself what was happening at the shrine and had to rely on what he heard. What he heard didn't please him. Not only were his sons misusing the sacrifices; they were also having sexual relations with the female attendants (v. 22). On the strength of these rumours Eli took his sons to task. He made an interesting distinction between wrongs against another person and wrongs against God. In the former case God could intervene to put things right, but in the latter this was not possible. The New Testament, of course, sees sins against another person as equivalent to sins against Jesus. 'Inasmuch as you did it not... you did it not to me' (Matthew 25:31–40). Disobedience to their father on this occasion is said to have been brought about by God whose will it was that they should die for their sins at the sanctuary. Their fate had aleady been sealed.

By contrast, Samuel was gaining in favour with both God and the people (v. 26).

The sons' downfall

Persistence in sin can only bring retribution, for God is just. Here the judgment was passed by a 'man of God'. This term is sometimes used of prophets and his 'thus the Lord has said' is the common formula by which a prophet introduces his speech. Other than that we have no idea of his identity. The judgment was all the more severe because of the abuse of their priestly privilege. The 'ancestor in Egypt' (v. 27) may refer to Aaron, Moses' brother, who traditionally was known as the forefather of the priests. But, more likely, here it refers to Levi. Moses was of the tribe of Levi and in the story of the journey through the wilderness the Levites were chosen as priests because of their almost fanatical loyalty to the Lord (Exodus 32:25–29). Unlike their ancestors, Eli's sons had been disloyal, especially with regard to sacrifices they were supposed to offer on behalf of people. They treated the things of God with contempt and so judgment must surely follow. Not only would Hophni and Phinehas die, but other descendants of Eli would also die young, a threat which was made twice. Long life was a great gift, a blessing from God. That blessing was now withdrawn from this family and anyone who did manage to live a bit longer would be poor enough to envy other people's prosperity. Instead of Hophni and Phinehas, God would raise up a new priest, Samuel.

A new priesthood

What follows in verses 35–36 does not seem to fit the immediate context. The founder of a 'house' or dynasty cannot refer to Samuel for there is no record of his sons following him as priests. This priest and his sons who 'went in and out before the anointed one' seems to refer to Zadok and his descendants who later officiated at the royal sanctuary under David and his successors. The descendants of Eli, the Levites, would beg from them. Although he was dealing with events at Shiloh, the writer seems to have had at the back of his mind the later situation in the priesthood when Levites were reduced to a secondary position, responsible for teaching the Law and for the temple songs, but not for sacrifice. This was reserved for those descended from Zadok the priest appointed by David in Jerusalem (see 1 Chronicles 6). The situation at Shiloh has given the author an opportunity to explain this later situation.

Divine justice

Sometimes Christians have been tempted to concentrate so much on the love of God that they have forgotten that he is also just. Stories like this in the Old Testament remind us that justice and love are not contradictory. Contempt for God is a serious matter and brings its own consequences which have to be faced. This saves the love from being regarded too sentimentally.

A MEDITATION

'It is... only when one sees the anger and wrath of God hanging like grim realities over the head of one's enemies that one can know something of what it means to love them and forgive them.'

Dietrich Bonhoeffer

ARE YOU LISTENING?

This must surely be one of the best-known stories in the Old Testament and it is a fairly straightforward account which needs little explanation. Perhaps the best way to approach it is to look first at the setting for the story and then to examine the two characters involved.

The setting

Verse 1 mentions two things. Samuel was already serving at the shrine but, at this stage, his service must have been of a routine kind, perhaps a bit like a choirboy in a modern cathedral. He did not yet know the Lord (v. 7), which means that he had no personal experience of God. He was therefore unable to recognize what was happening when God called to him. Second, we are told that the word of the Lord was rare, a word which also came to mean 'precious' because the rarer things are, the more precious they become. Words and visions belong together as the ways in which God communicated with his people, especially through his prophets. The book of Isaiah opens with the statement that this was the 'word' which Isaiah 'saw'. It doesn't mean that God was not wishing to reveal himself to his people; rather it means that there were few people who were able to receive his revelation. They were deaf to his voice and blind to his presence. People like the 'man of God' in the previous chapter were few and far between.

Verse 3 says that the lamp had not yet gone out. In Exodus 27:20 we read that a lamp was to be kept burning in the tabernacle throughout the night and this practice was followed at Shiloh. The text says that there was a temple there, and there may have been some kind of building, but the writer is probably influenced in his choice of words by the fact that a lamp was kept burning in the later Jerusalem temple. It was probably early morning, before daylight, when this event took place.

The elderly priest

We have already seen that Eli was losing his sight as he grew older. This is meant quite literally but is there not also a suggestion that he was blind to God's presence and unable to see visions? We are bound to feel some sympathy for Eli. He himself seems to have done little wrong except that he failed to discipline his sons when they committed the sins described in chapter 2. However, to that extent he also was guilty and must share in the judgment which would fall on his whole family.

God's voice is not always easily recognized and sometimes it takes a person with experience to make known what he is saying. It was Eli's experience which enabled him, in spite of his failings, to recognize what was happening when God called to Samuel. He was not afraid to hear the truth, unpleasant though it was. He could only accept the judgment and take his punishment.

The young successor

Storytellers often use threefold repetition and this one is no exception. It was only on the third occasion that Samuel, advised by Eli, was able to recognize that it was God who was speaking to him. This constituted him as a priest in his own right but the call also resembled that to prophets and the later Samuel seems to combine the two roles. Moreover, as is often the case with prophets, he was given a distasteful message to pass on and was reluctant to do so. The message was intended not for the people in general but for Eli and his family. It was a threat of punishment for Eli's weakness and for his sons' misconduct with the sacrifices. In verse 14 it is not that the sons' sins could not be expiated by sacrifices and offerings, as the NRSV suggests. Rather, the text means that their sins in respect of the sacrifices and offerings, as suggested in 2:29, would not be forgiven because they persisted in them.

Samuel's future

The closing verses, of course, simply sum up the period of Samuel's youth and young manhood. He was highly respected as one who faithfully passed on the message God had for his people. All this prepares us for the events which follow later.

A PRAYER

Speak to us your word, Lord, and open our ears that we may hear and recognize your voice. Then make us faithful so that we may share what we hear with others.

WAR *with the* PHILISTINES

The Philistines had invaded the land of Canaan by sea, coming from Crete. They had intended to settle in Egypt but had been repelled by the Egyptians, so instead they settled on the coastal strip in the south-west of Canaan (the modern Gaza Strip). They were more advanced militarily than those nations which had attacked Israel during the earlier part of the period of the Judges, and their intention was to take possession of the whole land. In fact, they gave their name to the land, for 'Palestine' is derived from the word 'Philistine'. They were to be the main enemies of Israel for many years.

Who began the battle?

It is not altogether clear who started the war. The Hebrew text suggests that it was the Israelites, as the footnote in NRSV makes clear. If so, they must have been anxious to stop the Philistines from encroaching further on their land. The early Greek translation, the Septuagint, has another introductory clause which suggests that the Philistines were the aggressors, wishing to extend their territory. Both the NRSV and the REB have followed the Greek text, assuming that the clause has been omitted from the Hebrew text by accident by a scribe as he copied it. The battle was in the best interests of both and it matters little who started it.

In those days battles were well-organized affairs, the opposing armies being drawn up facing each other. This was done somewhere between Ebenezer and Aphek, some ten miles inland at the southern end of the plain of Sharon.

The first round

The first clash resulted in an overwhelming victory for the more powerful Philistines. A 'thousand' is a military unit, not a precise number. For the Israelites the defeat raised the question, 'Why?' Since the Lord had promised this land to them and had brought them into it, he was expected to give his people victory over anyone who sought to rob them of it. Did the writer see the defeat as a punishment for the wrongs done by Hophni and Phinehas? Was this the 'something to make the ears tingle' threatened by Samuel in 3:11? The elders of

Israel saw it differently: it was because they had not taken the Ark into battle with them. It is noticeable that Samuel is not mentioned in all this. Hophni and Phinehas were still in charge of the shrine at Shiloh, attending the Ark. Obviously Samuel had not yet gained any authority there and probably could not do so until the two priests were dead.

The Ark

The Ark represented the presence of the Lord. In the earliest days it had been a wooden box carried on wooden poles. Israel had been forbidden to make any image of their God (Exodus 20:4) and so the Ark was probably understood to be his throne on which he was seated, although invisible. Wherever the Ark went, the Lord was there. When, during the wilderness journey, the Ark was lifted up to go on the next stage the people would cry, 'Arise, O Lord,' and when it settled down for the night they would say, 'Return, O Lord' (Numbers 10:35–36). Later it was situated in the Holy of Holies in the Jerusalem temple and was embellished with gold. The cherubim at each end were the Lord's attendants. Deuteronomy says that it contained the tablets of stone on which the ten commandments were written (Deuteronomy 10:2) and so it became known as 'the Ark of the Covenant'. The title 'Lord of hosts' is often associated with the Ark, the 'hosts' being either the heavenly armies or, as here, the armies of Israel.

The presence of the Ark on the battlefield not only encouraged the Israelites but greatly worried the Philistines. They are credited with knowing how God had delivered the Israelites from the Egyptians (v. 8). It wasn't the Ark itself which worried them; it was the presence of the Lord which it represented. For both sides, and for the storyteller himself, this made all the difference. We may agree that the presence of the Lord with us in our ventures is important and that without him our chances of success are diminished. But it is not true that God always gives us success simply because we who ask for help are his chosen people. It depends whether our wishes conform to his will. Even then, apparent failure may have to precede success, just as Jesus' suffering and death preceded his victorious resurrection.

A REFLECTION

We often ask for the presence of God because we know how important it is. But do we want him for himself or for what we can get out of him?

The GLORY DEPARTED

Neither the fears of the Philistines nor the hopes of the Israelites were fulfilled. In spite of the presence of the Ark the Israelite armies were defeated. The writer records this in a very matter-of-fact way, first the flight of the Israelites, then the huge losses sustained by them, then the capture of the Ark and finally the death of Eli's two sons as foretold by Samuel.

Eli's death

The main focus of the story is not on the battle but on the Ark. Eli was already anxious about it. Had he perhaps questioned the wisdom of taking it in the first place? Even if he had, he would have had little say about it, for his sons were in complete control. It is a sad picture, with the messenger running into Shiloh in mourning but unseen by Eli because of his blindness. It was only when he asked the cause of the people's agitation that the messenger reported events to him. He did so in a slightly different order from verses 10 and 11. He saved the news that the Ark had been captured until the end and it was this, rather than the news of the defeat or of his sons' deaths, that caused Eli to fall over backwards and break his neck. Already old and blind, this was the last straw.

The lesson which the storyteller wishes to draw out from this event is clear enough. God cannot be manipulated by human beings. The Israelites had decided upon their course of action and when things did not go as they had planned they sought to bring God into their plans on their side, confident that he must help his own people. Perhaps Eli himself had realized that God could not be 'used' in this way and this accounted for his anxiety as he waited for news. He had been prepared for the death of his sons and was reconciled to it (3:18), but the capture of the Ark was another matter. Had God been defeated? Had he allowed himself to be captured? Was he now separated for ever from his people?

Such questions were relevant also to the writer in his own day. By then the belief had grown up that Jerusalem and the temple, where the Ark was kept, were the city and the dwelling-place of God (Psalm 48) and therefore could never be captured. When they were, by the

Babylonians, questions were raised about God's ability to defend himself and his people or his willingness to do so. This story provides him with an example from the past of a similar situation which Israel had had to face. Self-reliance is no substitute for reliance on God.

The temptation to try to 'use' God in this way is never far from us and the story reminds us of our dependence on God and of the need to allow him to control us rather than seeking to control him.

Ichabod

The news affected Eli's daughter-in-law, causing her to go into labour (v. 19). This time the first item of news was about the capture of the Ark, followed by news of the death of her father-in-law and her husband. She died giving birth but before she did so she named her son Ichabod (v. 21). This name is made up of two parts. 'Chabod' means 'glory' and this is preceded by a small and rare word meaning 'not'. So literally the name means 'glory is not'. The explanation of the name which is given, 'the glory is departed', uses the word which was commonly used to denote exile—the glory has gone into exile. Since this book was written during the exile in Babylon, the word would have special resonance for its readers. This time God and people are separated by the people being taken into exile. 'Glory' may perhaps be best defined as 'that much of God's holiness as humans are able to see'. So it was not just a symbolic object which had been carried off. It was as though the God who had appeared to them on Mount Sinai in his holiness (Exodus 19) and the God who had spoken face to face with Moses so that his face shone (Exodus 33 and 34) had been taken from them, leaving them totally deserted.

A PRAYER

Help us to understand, God, that we cannot control you but are dependent on you. May we do your will and not just seek your help with our plans.

POOR OLD DAGON!

How the writer must have enjoyed telling this story! The Philistines certainly got more than they bargained for. If they were afraid when the Israelites took the Ark into battle, these subsequent events terrified them. We may wonder, of course, how the writer or indeed anyone else in Israel came to know what happened in the Philistine cities. To ask the question, however, is to miss the point of the story, which is intended to show the superiority of the Lord over other gods.

Dagon's downfall

The Philistines occupied five cities on the south-west coastal strip of Palestine: Ashdod, Ashkelon, Ekron, Gaza and Gath. Since it was a sacred object, the Ark was given a place in the sanctuary at Ashdod alongside Dagon (v. 2). The Philistines had more than one god and another one would do no harm. Not much is known of the religious beliefs and practices of the Philistines. They had come from Crete (Caphtor). They had iron weapons and were skilled warriors. They did not practise circumcision and so came to be described in the Bible as the 'uncircumcised'. Dagon, the god responsible for grain, was one of their chief gods.

In the eyes of the Philistines the first collapse of the image of Dagon may have been an accident or a coincidence. He fell 'on his face to the ground', a phrase which is often used of a person making obeisance to a superior. When it happened a second time, and this time the image was broken, it was realized that something more serious had occurred and the catastrophe was attributed to the God of the Ark. In mythology, combat between the gods is a common feature, but here there was no contest. There could be no doubt about the power of the Lord over Dagon. Decapitation of conquered enemies was quite usual and the hands, representing power, were severed. Dagon was completely defeated. It appears that the Philistines avoided treading on the threshold of the temple of Dagon and the reason given here is that his head and hands fell there.

To make matters worse, an epidemic of 'tumours' broke out (v. 6), possibly haemorrhoids as a result of dysentery. The word written in the text must have been regarded as indelicate, for the rabbis consistently read a different word when they came to this word in the text, though the dictionaries give the meaning 'tumour' for both. It was certainly something very unpleasant. The writer recognizes this as due to 'the hand of the Lord' and so, eventually, do the people of Ashdod. Remember that Dagon had lost his hands! The only remedy was to get rid of the Ark on which the Lord was enthroned.

Other Philistine cities

A council of the rulers of the five cities met to consider what to do and the ruler of Gath offered to take the Ark there (v. 8, so NRSV). The text here is a little uncertain. The Hebrew suggests that the decision to move it to Gath may have been taken jointly by the rulers rather than Gath having volunteered (so REB). When the same epidemic broke out there, it was moved to Ekron amid the complaints of its inhabitants. So, it was agreed that the only course was to get rid of the Ark altogether and send it back where it belonged, to Israel.

For readers

Readers of the story in the days of the exile when this book was written would have been greatly encouraged by it, since it sought to reassure them how far superior their God was over any other gods. What happened to the Ark during the exile, we are not told. It may have been taken to Babylon with the rest of the temple furniture and vessels and lost for ever. The God enthroned upon it was not lost; he was with his people there, as Ezekiel (ch. 1) made clear, and he could be relied upon to overthrow all opposition. Isaiah 46 portrays the Babylonian gods as needing to be carried in procession whereas the Lord carried his people.

We may have our doubts about a God who afflicts people with a plague of haemorrhoids to show his power. Such a view of God needs to be modified in the light of the New Testament with its stories of Jesus. Yet this story is intended to give us confidence in God who can never be defeated, can never be captured and caged, but whose universal authority and power are to be celebrated.

A PRAYER

God, we thank you that Jesus could not be held captive even by death, the last enemy. You raised him from the dead and so we acknowledge your power and look forward to your universal reign.

GETTING RID *of the* PROBLEM

By the time the ark had been round all five Philistine cities with the same result each time, it became clear that the plague was connected with its presence, but by then seven months had passed.

The problem was how to get rid of the Ark. Obviously there was something special about it. It was a sacred object and the God it represented was powerful, so great care was needed. The question was probably not what to send away with it (as NRSV suggests, v. 2), but by what means could they do so (so REB). It would be too risky to try to destroy it. It must be sent out of the country but how could this be done safely? The religious authorities who were supposed to know about these things were consulted. Like other nations, the Philistines had their priests and diviners who could be consulted on difficult questions and whose answers were thought to have divine authority.

The precautions

They advised that if it was to be sent back to where it belonged, two precautions were necessary. First of all, some compensation must be paid (v. 3). The word translated 'guilt offering' is not used here in the technical sense it has in the sacrifical laws in Leviticus 6. The Philistines would have been unaware of this and it is unlikely that the writer would represent them as knowing about it. The offering was not to the Lord, but was a payment to the Israelite people. In Leviticus 6 any guilt offering has to be accompanied by twenty per cent compensation for the wrong done, and that is what is meant here. The Hebrew text doesn't mention a 'ransom'. It says that if they followed these instructions they would be healed and then they would know why God had laid his hand upon them (so REB). NRSV has followed the early Greek translation and suggests that the payment of compensation would set them free of the plague. The compensation was to take the form of gold images of the 'tumours' (it would be interesting to see what golden haemorrhoids looked like!) and of the mice or rats, one for each of city. This is the first we have heard of the mice or rats, though in 5:6 the phrase 'both Ashdod and its territories' appears in the early Greek translation as 'its territories swarmed with rats' (so REB). At any rate we must assume that a plague of mice accompanied the haemorrhoids. By making these golden images and sending them back with the Ark, they would be honouring the God of Israel whose presence it represents. How far the Philistines would be aware of the stubbornness of Pharaoh and the subsequent release of the Israelites, we have no means of knowing (v. 6). It doesn't seem very likely. It may be that the writer has attributed his own knowledge of it to them.

The second precaution concerns the vehicle on which it was to be sent away (v. 7). For such a sacred object it was important that the cart should be a new one and that the cows should already have calved and be giving milk, but not have been used for work before. They should be mature cows, but new to wearing a yoke, so avoiding the risk of defilement.

The departure

The cart should then be sent on its way leaving the cows to go wherever they would. Beth-shemesh was about twenty miles to the east of Ashdod in Israelite territory. If the cows took it back there it would confirm that the epidemic and the plague had been caused by Israel's God. If not, then it could be put down to an accident or coincidence. The advice was followed; the Ark returned to Beth-shemesh, so proving that the Lord had been responsible for the defeat of Dagon and for the plague. Later on, the story of the Ark will be taken further (2 Samuel 6) and we shall see again the need to take extreme care because of its sacred nature.

On the face of it, this whole story of the capture of the Ark, the plague upon the Philistines and the elaborate precautions taken to send it away seems far removed from the view of God as revealed by Jesus. Perhaps we should allow the storyteller to have his bit of fun at the expense of the Philistines and to see his story in that light. Nevertheless, we shall keep coming across the fact that the Old Testament view of God is different in some respects from the New Testament view. Some people have therefore thought that we should abandon the Old Testament altogether. Yet there are valuable insights into both divine and human nature which we need to see. We shall understand the New Testament better if we read and understand the Old.

A PRAYER

Save us, Lord, from that familiarity which breeds contempt and from the arrogance which denies that you are indeed the Holy One.

The 'GLORY' RETURNED

It was springtime when the Ark was sent back. The immediate reaction of the people of Beth-shemesh is described with great reserve. We are not told how they recognized a cart loaded with a box and pulled by cows to be the Ark. We might have expected a more dramatic description of its arrival.

A proper reception

However, the Ark was dealt with in an entirely proper way. A stone in the field served as an altar. The cart was used as fuel for the sacrifice and the cows were offered as a burnt offering (it was more usual to offer bulls) (v. 14). The Ark itself was handled by some Levites who lived there, just as it should be in the eyes of this writer. As we saw in the Introduction, the writer of the books of Samuel was steeped in the traditions of Deuteronomy. In Deuteronomy 10:8 the Levites were set aside as carriers of the Ark and in Deuteronomy 18 they lived in the various towns, having no territory of their own. So, for him, it was perfectly right for Levites to be living in Beth-shemesh and for them to unload the Ark from the cart. As far as the golden models of the tumours and mice were concerned, we are not told what happened to them. Verse 17 explains what the situation was in the writer's own day. It suggests that they remained with the Ark and were known to have been with it when it was presumably carried off into Babylon in 587BC. The stone, still there in the writer's day, marked the spot where the Ark had stood and the sacrifice had been offered.

The Philistines had followed to see what happened. When they were satisfied by what they saw they returned home, doubtless glad to be rid of the dangerous Ark (v. 16).

An improper reception

So far so good; but then there is a radical change in the story. Something happened to cause the Lord to kill seventy men and this made the people of Beth-shemesh as anxious to get rid of the Ark as were the Philistines. What they had against the people of Kiriath-jearim which made them invite them to fetch the Ark, when it had caused them so much trouble, we do not know! Nor do we know exactly what caused the problem. According to NRSV and REB, which follow the Greek text, the family of Jeconiah did not rejoice (v. 19). Unless this is a remarkable understatement for something more serious, the death of seventy men seems a very harsh punishment indeed. However, the Hebrew text, followed by RSV, does not mention the family of Jeconiah. It says that the people of Beth-shemesh looked into or perhaps 'inspected' the Ark. This might well have involved touching it to open it and look inside, and we learn from the later story in 2 Samuel 6 that to touch the holy object was highly dangerous and led to death. In cases like this it is always difficult to decide whether or not the Greek translators had before them a different text. On the one hand, words may have dropped out of the Hebrew text accidentally after the Greek translation had been made. On the other hand, the Greek translators may have been trying to make better sense of a text which they found difficult to understand. Whatever happened at Beth-shemesh God's reaction still strikes us as odd and distasteful. The passage can be understood only against the background of a strong belief in the danger of contact with anything 'holy', that is, belonging exclusively to God, by those who are not authorized to do so, as the priests and Levites were.

Again the story serves to remind us that God is not to be approached casually as though he were another human being. Though he welcomes our approach to him, his very nature demands that we do so carefully, thoughtfully, humbly and with proper respect.

The people of Kiriath-jearim were perhaps more welcoming or less inquisitive. At any rate the Ark remained there until the time of David and they suffered no ill effects.

A REFLECTION

Holy, holy, holy, though the darkness hide thee,
Though the eye of sinful man thy glory may not see;
Thou alone art holy, there is none beside thee,
Perfect in power, in love and purity.

Reginald Heber, 1783–1826

'HERE I RAISE MY EBENEZER'

This section is a summary of the period during which Samuel 'judged' Israel. The shrine at Shiloh where he was brought up had evidently been destroyed by the Philistines (Jeremiah 7:15) and the Ark had been captured and then returned to Israel. There is no suggestion that Samuel sought to renew his association with the Ark and he now lived at Ramah, which is several miles to the south of Shiloh. Precisely what his duties were as a judge is unclear (v. 6). As a priest he would be expected to give rulings in matters of the law as it applied to individuals, possibly in difficult cases which could not be easily dealt with by the local elders. He is said to have judged 'Israel' but the three centres which he visited for this purpose (v. 16) are all situated fairly close together in an area some ten miles north of Jerusalem, in the territory occupied by the tribes of Benjamin and Ephraim. It may be, therefore, that his influence was limited to this central area. As we shall see, it was the area from which Israel's first king came.

The return to the Lord

Samuel called for a return to the worship of the Lord alone (v. 3). It would appear that, as often happened in the book of Judges, the people had turned to worship other gods. Baal was one of the gods of the Canaanites, responsible for rain and fertility, and the plural can be used of the various manifestations of him at the various places throughout the land. Often associated with him is the goddess Astarte. The plural can be used of her in exactly the same way. The temptation for Israel to worship these local gods was very strong. It persisted for a very long time after this. The prophets called for a rejection of them and Samuel does the same here. It would appear that the people were ready to do this. The phrase 'lamented after' is rather curious and the Hebrew verb is used only twice elsewhere. It does seem to mean 'to lament' and we should probably take it to indicate that the people were lamenting over their circumstances, threatened as they were by the Philistines, and were prepared to follow the Lord. Samuel's plea therefore fell on open ears.

The Philistines again

The threat of the Philistines served as a spur to this return to the Lord. The assembly at Mizpah is said to be of all Israel (v. 5). Probably this means that leaders from various places gathered together, probably from towns in Ephraim and Benjamin. Instead of a sacrifice, as we might expect, they drew water from the well and offered it to the Lord. Water was a very precious commodity since no rain at all fell during the six months of summer. Along with their offering they confessed their sin. Such a gathering of the clans was too good an opportunity for the Philistines to miss and they prepared to attack. This time Samuel did make a sacrifice and sought the Lord's help (v. 9). 'The Lord thundered with a mighty voice' refers to an actual thunderstorm and a violent one at that. It wasn't the thunder itself which frightened the Philistines; it was what it represented, namely, the voice of God. The result was that they fled back to their own territory where they were to remain for some time (v. 11).

Ebenezer

The word Ebenezer (v. 12) means 'stone of help' and the monument was there to remind the people of the help that the Lord had given them once they had returned to worship him alone. The defeat of the Philistines is presented as complete, though we shall soon discover that it was not. There may be a suggestion here that Israel could manage very well without the king which they were going to demand in the next chapter.

The whole section reflects the belief of the writer that Israel is to have one God and one God alone (Deuteronomy 5:7) and that they should love him with heart, soul and might (Deuteronomy 6:4–5). Any deviation from this was likely to bring disaster. What had befallen Judah and Jerusalem in his day could be put down to a failure in this crucial matter and what was needed now was for them to return to this central belief.

A REFLECTION

What are the 'baals' and 'astartes' which we are tempted to worship in place of the God and Father of Jesus? Do we need to confess our deviation from the worship of him alone?

'GIVE US *a* KING'

The next five chapters are concerned with the beginnings of a monarchy in Israel. This shows how important a matter it was for the writer. Until now Israel had had no permanent leader. 'Judges' had arisen from the various tribes to deal with crises. In the previous chapter the leadership of Samuel had been sufficient to rid them of the Philistine threat. Now it had resurfaced and the people felt that something more was needed. The pressure from the Philistines was very intense and the obvious answer was to have a king as their permanent leader, like other nations. In the following chapters, two responses to this question can be found. In some places God, and Samuel, seem to be in favour of a monarchy; in others they are opposed to it. Some have thought that this latter view was that of the writer in the light of what happened later and that he has included the story of God's reluctance to make his point to the people of Judah in the days of the exile in Babylon. On the other hand, it may be that both views could be found among the Israelites and the inclusion of both shows the dilemma which faced Israel. Common sense suggested they needed a king, but this could be understood as an act of disloyalty to the Lord, their true King. To do without a king left them exposed to danger.

Samuel's successors

Naturally as he got older Samuel appointed his sons to succeed him (v. 1). He had exactly the same problem as Eli had had before him. His sons were not fit to follow him. They lined their own pockets by taking bribes to allow the guilty to escape justice. They could not be relied upon to save Israel as their father had done. A rather curious feature here is that they operated from Beer-sheba which is some fifty miles south of Ramah where Samuel still lived (v. 2). It is on the very southern border of the territory usually thought of as Israel and so was an inappropriate place from which to judge the whole people. We are given no reason for this but it indicates their limited authority and the gap between them and their father.

The request for a king

A delegation from the various towns came to Ramah to make their request (v. 4). They would be familiar with kings from the way in which other nations were governed and from their Canaanite neighbours, each of whose cities had a king. Uneasy about this, Samuel prayed about it. He may have thought they were dissatisfied with his leadership but God assured him that it was a rejection of his own authority and not Samuel's. This was nothing new. They had been disobedient again and again, ever since leaving Egypt. Nevertheless Samuel was to 'listen' to them, which implied that he should agree. God would allow them to have their own way if they persisted. They had that freedom.

The danger

At the same time Samuel was to warn them of the dangers of having a king (v. 9). The men would be conscripted into the army or other court duties, the women would also have to serve at court, the land would be stolen by courtiers, slaves and animals would be commandeered and they would virtually become slaves. For people set free from slavery in Egypt, that would be intolerable. It is possible that Samuel, instructed by God, was able to foresee all these things, but it is more likely that the details were written with hindsight. The writer knew all these things had happened towards the end of Solomon's reign and had led to a revolt by the Northern tribes. They had continued and had been condemned by prophets like Amos and Isaiah. He therefore had plenty of evidence on which to base his account. So if they decided to go ahead after such a warning the consequences would be their own fault. They had chosen their own future.

It may seem odd that the advice of such a trusted leader as Samuel should be disregarded. In the account as we have it, he had been a good and reliable judge and he had already seen off the Philistine threat once. We might have expected that the people would listen to him and follow his advice. But not even Samuel could divert them from their decision to be like other nations.

A PRAYER

Lord, we have been led astray too often by the example of others.
Make us firm in our loyalty to you and ready to listen to your
warning and advice.

The CASE of the MISSING DONKEYS

Here for the first time we are introduced to Saul, Israel's first king. Both his ancestry and his appearance marked him out for his future role (v. 2). His ancestry could be traced back through several generations and so his was a family of some standing in the community. We know nothing about the individuals mentioned in his family tree but we are told that it was a Benjaminite family. The word Benjamin literally means 'son of the right hand' or perhaps 'son of the south', seeing that directions were given looking eastward. The tribe of Benjamin, traditionally descended from the youngest son of Jacob, had settled in the southern part of the territory occupied by the tribes which had been brought out of Egypt. Ephraim and Manasseh, descended from the sons of Joseph, had settled just to the north. Judah, further to the south, does not seem to have been regarded as part of Israel at this time. Although, geographically, Benjamin was a small area it was an important tribe and closely related to Ephraim.

Saul's father, Kish, was a wealthy man and had considerable standing in the area. Saul himself is described as handsome and tall. 'Head and shoulders above everyone else' refers primarily to his size but the writer wishes to show, too, that he was a born leader. Whatever happened later, the potential for a good king was already there in his family and his personal gifts.

The search for the donkeys

We are not told what the profession of Kish was. Clearly he owned some donkeys which one day strayed out of the enclosure in which they were kept (v. 3). Saul and his servant were despatched to look for them. The area in which they searched extended northward into neighbouring Ephraim, though the precise locations aren't known. Zuph is mentioned in 1:1 either as a place name or a personal name and is associated with Ephraim. The journeying between Ephraim and Benjamin suggests that their search was somewhere along the border between the two. You may have noticed that although there were two of them, Saul and his servant, sometimes the account speaks of one person, 'he' not 'they'—that is, Saul. This shows where the focus of the writer's attention lies. The main interest is in Saul.

The search was unsuccessful and Saul was about to give up when his servant had a bright idea. They should go and consult the 'man of God' (v. 6). This would cost money and Saul had none with him. The great man was not ashamed to take advice—and money—from his servant, just as later the Syrian Naaman was ready eventually to take the advice of his Israelite servant girl (2 Kings 5).

The man of God

Initially, to increase the suspense, the name of the 'man of God' is withheld. Then the writer includes an explanatory comment of his own in verse 9, which has been the subject of much scholarly discussion about the origins or early days of prophecy in Israel. This 'man of God' is also a 'seer' (v. 11). The seer sometimes expected to be paid for information and that seems to be the opinion of Saul and his servant. The prophet as we know him later proclaimed the word of God without payment and usually without being asked to do so. However, the writer obviously sees some connection between the seers and the later prophets. It has been suggested that 'seer' is a northern term which was later displaced by the southern term 'prophet'. Be that as it may, by the time of the exile, when this writer was at work, the two had become synonymous, even if they had separate origins. The function of the man of God here is clearly priestly as well as prophetic. He must bless the sacrifice before the people can share in it. Later, as we shall discover in chapter 13, Saul is rebuked for making a sacrifice before going into battle without waiting for a priest to do so.

Now at last the identity of the man of God is revealed (v. 14). It turns out to be Samuel and for the first time Saul and Samuel meet. It will be a stormy relationship.

A PRAYER

Grant us the humility to accept advice even if it comes from someone least expected to give it.

NEVER MIND *the* DONKEYS

In this account there is little to give the impression that the Lord and Samuel were reluctant to provide Israel with a king, as appeared to be the case in chapter 8. Here they seem to take the initiative in doing so. But it is not so simple as that. Even if the writer was using a different tradition about the beginnings of monarchy, he was not so incompetent as to leave obvious contradictions in his story. So, once the decision had been made, however reluctantly, that Israel's wish for a king should be granted, there was no further need to express that reluctance again here.

Instructions for Samuel

Samuel was prepared in advance for the meeting which was to take place between him and Saul. It was revealed to him by the Lord (v. 15). Just how this revelation took place, we are not told. Sometimes it was done through a dream, but more often than not in the Old Testament we are simply told that the Lord spoke to a person. He had done so already to Samuel when he was a boy in the temple. Then Samuel had not been able to recognize him; now he could. Later on we are often told that the word of the Lord came to the prophets and we have already seen how Samuel may sometimes be regarded as a prophet as well as a priest. God can reveal his will to all kinds of people and it is by no means easy to describe how he does it. When people say they are called by God to some specific task, they often find it hard to say how they can be sure that it is a call from God. They just know it is.

It may be significant that the writer avoids using the word 'king' even though he speaks of anointing. Instead he uses the word 'ruler' (NRSV) or 'prince' (v. 16). Does this suggest that the reluctance is still there? The purpose of the anointing was to provide the people with someone to save them from the Philistines just as the Judges had earlier been raised up as 'saviours' from other peoples. Also, the last part of verse 16 reminds us srongly of the Lord's call to Moses in Exodus 3:7. This idea that God is aware of his people's needs and is ready to save them is prominent throughout the Old Testament.

When the two met, Samuel, who had been forewarned, recognized

Saul, but Saul remained unaware that the 'man of God' was Samuel (vv. 17–18). The location of the donkeys, which was the reason for Saul approaching Samuel, was put into the background. There is obviously something much more important to be done than finding lost donkeys. The question in verse 20 really means, 'To whom does all that Israel desires belong?' But what was it that Israel desired? It may simply refer to the wealth and prestige such as was found in Saul's family and the respect in which they were held. But may it not perhaps refer to the kingship which Israel had asked for in chapter 8? This would now belong to Saul and his house. Saul's reply contradicts what we were told in verse 1 and must be seen as an example of eastern humility in the presence of someone as important as Samuel.

The meal

Together they went up to the shrine, which was on top of a nearby hill as was usual, ready for the sacrifice (v. 22). It was a regular feast day for the people of the town, which is not identified. Some thirty of them gathered there to share in it. Then, the sacrifice having been made, they sat down to a meal. As a result of what Samuel had been told, Saul and his servant were given the chief places and the best cuts of meat. Samuel had been so sure of what was to happen that he had set the latter aside for his special guest. The footnotes in NRSV indicate that there is some uncertainty about the precise meaning of verse 24 but there is no doubt that this translation conveys what was intended. Having eaten, they descended to the town below where they stayed the night, and were awakened next morning by Samuel so that he could send them off and tell them where the donkeys were.

For THOUGHT

Consider how God prepares the way before we ourselves are aware of it.

SAUL *a* PROPHET?

After all, it wasn't about the donkeys that Samuel wished to speak to Saul. To keep the real matter secret, the servant was sent on ahead, and then Samuel anointed Saul as prince or ruler over Israel (v. 1). This was not just a human decision. Samuel makes it clear that it is really the Lord who has anointed Saul. He himself has only been acting on behalf of the Lord. He would receive a sign to confirm this; though, in fact, there seem to be three signs.

The donkeys

First they will meet two men who will tell them where the donkeys are (v. 2). In Genesis 35:20 and 48:7 Rachel was buried at Ephrath, which is identified with Bethlehem in Judah; here her grave is in the territory of Benjamin although the exact location of Zilzah is not known. Apparently someone else had found the donkeys and reported it to Saul's father.

The food

Next they would meet three men with food (v. 3). They would be on their way to 'go up to God at Bethel'. Presumably the food they would have with them was meant for sacrifice there. The oak of Tabor, which is apparently near Bethel, is not to be confused with Mount Tabor which is much further north. Saul did not really need the food but he was to accept two loaves, perhaps to avoid giving offence. It was part of the sign.

The prophets

These would appear on a hill, at the foot of which there was a Philistine garrison (v. 5). Shrines were often built on hills near towns or villages. The word Gibeah means 'hill' and may not be a place name. It may simply mean 'hill of God'. Things happened just as they had been promised The picture is a very vivid one. A band of prophets came down from the shrine preceded by a group of musicians. What were the prophets doing? They were prophesying! This can hardly mean the same kind of activity as that engaged in by people like Isaiah or Jeremiah later, whose task was to declare to the

people the word of God. More likely it refers to a frenzied dance practised in a highly emotional state of mind, induced and helped by the
music. If all this was accompanied by words from God, then we are
told nothing of those words. It was the event which was important
and not any message from the Lord. It was a communal rather than
a personal experience and anyone coming into contact with it might
well be caught up in it as Saul was. The links between these bands of
prophets and the later classical prophets are still not clear. We do
know that such groups were still active in the days of Elijah and
Elisha (1 Kings 18; 2 Kings 2:15 etc). They were known as 'sons of
the prophet' and their leader was addressed as 'father'. It may well be
that out of these groups there arose certain individuals to speak the
word of God and eventually some were called independently to do
so. In this present story their appearance to Saul is simply a sign to
confirm what Samuel had done.

Naturally people who saw it were surprised at what had happened
(v. 11). They knew Saul and knew that his father was Kish, but who
was the father of the prophetic band to which he had become
attached? The experience seems to have been a one-off; it didn't
happen to him again. His later madness was something different.

The fact of his being anointed was still kept a secret even from his
uncle, who was told only about the donkeys.

Gilgal

There is a verse in the middle of this story which seems out of place.
Verse 8 tells of a command to Saul to go to Gilgal and wait. This looks
forward to the events described in chapter 13 (v. 8). Some think the
verse has been misplaced from there accidentally but it is difficult to
see how such a mistake could have been made. Perhaps it is included
here as a reminder that even the anointed king must always do as
God says, especially when he speaks through Samuel. So it places a
limit on the king's powers from the outset.

A PRAYER

*Give us the courage to accept your call and the wisdom to read the
signs which confirm it.*

A KING ACCLAIMED

The question that arises when we read this passage is: why did Samuel have to cast lots to find out who was to be king when, according to 10:1, he had already anointed Saul as king? The answer which is usually given is that the writer has included in his book two separate and differing accounts of the way Saul became king. These present verses depict the reluctance of both the Lord and Samuel to agree to the people's request for a king. This was the situation also in chapter 8, and indeed 10:17 could almost follow directly on from 8:22. The intervening story depicts Samuel, directed by the Lord, as taking the initiative to anoint Saul. As indicated earlier, the writer may have wished to show how both views existed among the people. However, it is not likely that he deliberately left two opposing views in his story which he surely intended to be read as a whole. We have already seen that there may be some hint of reluctance in chapter 9. If, then, we interpret the story as it now stands, as a consistent narrative, we may say that the casting of lots in the present passage (vv. 20–22) was to convince the people of what the Lord had already told Samuel and Saul privately—that it was to be Saul who was to be king.

Israel's rejection of the Lord

The request for a human king to save them from the Philistine threat was seen as an act of treachery, seeing that it was the Lord who had saved and protected them until now (v. 19). Nevertheless, the Lord would not force them to be obedient and faithful to him. God does not force his will upon people. If they decide to go their own way he not only allows it but continues to work out his purposes even in the situation created by their disobedience. So Israel was allowed to have the king they wanted and from now on God's activity on Israel's behalf will always take account of the monarchy for as long as it lasts.

The National Lottery

The events described in this section took place at Mizpah, the town where Ebenezer, the stone of help, had been erected following the defeat of the Phlistines (ch. 7). Casting lots was a lengthy business. The 'lot' could provide only one of two answers to a question, yes or no. Possibly it consisted of a bag containng two stones, one indicating 'yes' and the other indicating 'no'. The name of the tribes would be brought forward in turn until one was found where the lot said 'yes'. In this case it was the tribe of Benjamin. Then the name of each family within that tribe would be subjected to the 'lot' until again it came up with a positive answer, as it did with the Matrites. The process was next repeated with individuals within that family until a 'yes' response was given to one of them. It turned out to be Saul. This equivalent to tossing a coin may seem to us to leave it to pure chance. In the Old Testament, when it was done in a genuine attempt to discover the will of God, it was regarded as a legitimate and reliable method.

Saul, however, was nowhere to be seen. It turned out that he was hiding among the baggage (v. 22). But why? Was he embarrassed, or frightened, or unwilling? Or was it because he knew how the lot would fall already and didn't want to show this in any way? This story, like the one in chapter 9, says he stood head and shoulders above everyone else. So he was not only chosen by God but was now also acclaimed by the people.

Reactions

In order to limit the powers of the king, Samuel produced a constitutional document setting out what the king was entitled and obliged to do (v. 25). This was to be stored in the sanctuary for future reference. Precisely what its terms were is not stated but the important point was that there were both prescriptive and restrictive regulations. The monarchy, however, was not universally welcomed. The 'men of valour' or warriors who supported Saul are contrasted with the 'men of Belial', the worthless men who opposed him. The seeds of discontent were already there.

A REFLECTION

God's will can be resisted and disobeyed. He does not enforce it against our wills. But can it ultimately be thwarted?

SAUL *as* KING—AGAIN!

If, for the moment, we forget what has happened in the three previous chapters and read this chapter on its own, we find a story which is very similar to those found in the book of Judges. There, when one tribe is under attack from a neighouring state, its people appeal to the Lord for help. The spirit of the Lord falls upon a man who then rallies the other tribes to answer the appeal. This 'saviour' defeats the enemy and delivers the people who are threatened. The difference lies in what follows. Whereas in the book of Judges these 'saviours' drop out of the story once their task is completed, here Saul is made a permanent leader and king. The chapter can therefore stand as yet another account of the way Saul became king. Once we take the preceding chapters into account we see this in a rather different light. Saul was anointed privately in 10:1. He was publicly acclaimed king in 10:24. Now his leadership is to be tested and affirmed by military success against an enemy.

A serious threat

Jabesh-gilead was situated in the territory of Manasseh on the east of the River Jordan. Later the whole area was known as Gilead. It was bordered to the south by the Ammonites. The Ammonites had troubled Gilead before (Judges 9) and would continue to do so until they were defeated by David (2 Samuel 12).

The passage in 10:27 beginning 'Now Nahash...' and continuing to the end of the chapter, has been included by NRSV although it is not found in the standard Hebrew text or in any of the early translations into Greek or Latin or Syriac. It is found in a manuscript among the Dead Sea Scrolls. It is lacking in most of the English translations, including REB. Whether it was in the original version or not makes little difference. All it does is to give a reason for the siege of Jabesh-gilead, described in chapter 11.

Jabesh under siege

What follows seems a very peculiar way of waging war. It seems most odd for the attackers to grant a seven-day period for the besieged to call up reinforcements if they could be found. War in those days was a rather civilized affair in spite of the claims of huge numbers slaughtered. On the other hand, the idea of gouging out the right eye of 7000 men in the added passage is pretty gruesome. It would not only incapacitate them but would humiliate them as well.

The spirit for Saul

Gibeah, Saul's home, was some forty-five miles from Jabesh, so seven days was not long for messengers to reach Gibeah and then for the other tribes to be called out and make their way to Jabesh. Although he had already been made king, Saul is still found coming in from the field where he had been looking after his cattle! The spirit of the Lord seized him (v. 6) as it had done Othniel (Judges 3:10), Gideon (Judges 6:34), Jephthah (Judges 11:29) and Samson (Judges 14:6, 19; 15:14). This 'spirit' was the power of God which enabled a person to do whatever the Lord called him to do. It was not a power that could be used for any purpose, but only for the purpose for which God had given it. It was not thought of as the third person of the Trinity in the Old Testament, for there was no such doctrine then; that didn't arise until the end of the New Testament period. It does, however, have something to tell us about the Holy Spirit who is given to Christians to enable them to live their Christian lives and to perform their Christian service. The Holy Spirit cannot be used for selfish ends. Saul's method of calling out help from the other tribes was unusual. It was obviously meant to put pressure upon people to turn out and help their 'brothers' in need.

The kingship reaffirmed

In 10:27 we were told that some were not enthusiastic about Saul's kingship. Others were now anxious to get rid of these people whom they regarded as potential threats. Saul resisted the temptation on the grounds that his victory was due to God. He made no claim for himself.

So the act of making Saul king at Gilgal is seen as a renewal of what had happened earlier in 10:24. The military victory was a confirmation that the choice of Saul had been correct.

A PRAYER

Fill us with your spirit, Lord, so that we may do your work.

SAMUEL'S CHALLENGE

This writer has a pretty good idea of what goes on in the priesthood. Sleaze is nothing new. As far as this story is concerned, Eli and his sons have already been tainted with it and were therefore removed from the priesthood. Probably it still went on in the writer's own day, for the prophets often complain of bribery and corruption in the judicial system (Isaiah 5:23). Samuel, we must remember, was both priest and judge. Indeed, right down to the writer's own day priests formed a kind of court of appeal. When disputes could not be settled by the leaders meeting in the gateway of the town, the matter was to be referred to the temple officials for a judgment (Deuteronomy 17:8ff). In this story Samuel is presented as innocent of all wrong-doing. He wishes to establish his right to criticize his people and so challenges them to prove him guilty if they have any complaint against him (v. 3). The solemnity of his claim is underlined by his calling on the Lord as his witness. By doing this he was inviting God to punish him if he was not telling the truth. It was, therefore, a very serious and solemn defence of his own probity. It is, of course, easy for us to be critical of corrupt priests and there can be no excuse. At the same time it has to be said that people in such a position have greater opportunity and face stronger temptation to do wrong.

Recalling the past

We have already met a few long songs or speeches in this book and have discussed how they came to be recorded. Here is another. It is highly unlikely that anyone kept a copy of what Samuel said on this occasion. Unless we take the very literalist view that God told the writer exactly what he had said, we have to say that the writer composed the speech himself but did so because the character of Samuel in the story required something like this from him at this juncture. In fact, the speech is in many ways similar in style to many passages found in the book of Deuteronomy and we have seen that this writer was immersed in that tradition.

The speech begins by reaffirming what God has done for his people in the past (vv. 1-11). As a counsel for the prosecution in court Samuel opens his case by going over the well-known events of the past in which God acted on behalf of his people. The familiar pattern which formed the framework for the book of Judges is retraced. God acted to save his people; once saved, they either forgot or rebelled against him, worshipping other gods; God gave them into the hands of their enemies; they cried to him for help; God sent a saviour to rescue them; and the process began again (see Judges 2:11–23). It demonstrated the incredible patience of God.

The plea for a king

Once again the Israelites had been threatened by the Ammonites. This time they had asked for a more permanent ruler to deliver them. They had not been prepared to rely on God their King; they wanted a human king (v. 12). Now we have already met this before in chapter 8 when they were faced by the Philistines, and that request had been granted. Saul had already been anointed at Mizpah and his kingship had been reaffirmed at Gilgal. Here, then, we have yet another account of the beginnings of the monarchy in Israel. As it stands in the whole story, it now rounds off the founding of the monarchy with this confirmatory speech by Samuel in which he calls again for obedience to the Lord.

The judgment

As in chapter 8, God, through Samuel, allowed the monarchy but made it dependent on the obedience of both king and people. If they were obedient Israel would prosper; if they were disobedient they would suffer disaster at God's hands. The promise and the threat were accompanied by a sign (v. 17) which would make it abundantly clear who was really in control. The result was that the people came to be in awe of God.

A REFLECTION

Are we too quick to condemn those in high places who do wrong?
Do we overlook the fact that often their opportunities
present them with stronger temptation to do wrong?
Does this apply to politicians, business leaders, clergy,
people who handle large sums of money?

POPULAR RESPONSE

The thunder and rain which damaged the wheat harvest (v. 18) were sufficient to convince the people of their sin, and they confessed that their desire for a king was wrong. Samuel had the ear of God and so they asked him to present their confession to God. This did not alter the situation. Their plea for a king had been answered positively, though reluctantly. This chapter, taken on its own, doesn't actually record any anointing of the king. That has already been described in the earlier chapters and there is now no going back on it. This whole chapter acts as a summary of the previous ones and rounds off the narrative of the institution of the monarchy.

The grace of God

Although their act of crowning a king was an act of rebellion, for which they deserved to die, Samuel now directed their thoughts to the future. The past was past; what was done could not be undone. The future lay open to them and they were called into it. There is no mention here of God's forgiveness. Possibly we should assume it, though perhaps even more likely the idea is not even considered. Against God's will they had chosen to be ruled by a king and they would have to live with the consequences of that, whether or not they were forgiven. But as they did so they would not be abandoned by God. This promise had certain demands attached to it. The people were to be unswervingly obedient to God; they were to serve him fully and sincerely and this would include worship (v. 20); they were not to be seduced by things which promised much but which could deliver nothing (he was probably thinking of idols) (v. 21). To assist them in this they would have the prayer of Samuel, the man of God who had the ear of God, and he would teach them how to live in accordance with God's will. Again they were to recall, perhaps in worship as well as elsewhere, what God had done for them. That should reinforce their will to serve him.

All this, however, was not merely for Israel's sake. God had chosen them as his own people and if they were to cease to be his people that would be a blot on his reputation. What he was about to do was 'for his name's sake' (v. 22). It was to safeguard his reputation. However, this could not go on for ever and it must not be taken for granted that God would be at their beck and call when they were in trouble, irrespective of their behaviour.

What's in it for the writer?

We must now try to imagine that we are Israelites reading this in, say, 580BC. The king and people have been 'swept away' (v. 25) because they have not listened to or obeyed the word of God as it has come to them through Samuel and then later, through his successors, the prophets. God's patience has been exhausted and the long-promised judgment has befallen both Israel, a century and a half earlier, and now Judah. The writer has spent five long chapters dealing with this question of the monarchy. This shows how important a question he believed it to be for himself and for his readers. Later in his work, in the book of Kings, he goes on to describe how all the kings of Israel and nearly all the kings of Judah, with very few exceptions, have led the people astray and the people have allowed themselves to be misled. Now both king and people have been 'swept away'. What now? It needed people like Ezekiel the prophet to say again that 'for his name's sake' God would call his people into being again (Ezekiel 36:22ff), just as 'for his name's sake' he would have kept them in being if only they had been obedient (v. 22).

For Christians, God's patience is shown even more by the fact that he sent his Son into the world to call into being a new people of God, to bring forgiveness for our disobedience and to help us, by his Spirit, to live in obedience.

A PRAYER

Help us, Lord, to be sincere in our confession, to accept the forgiveness you offer through Jesus, to live with the consequences of our sin and to lead lives more acceptable to you by the help of your Holy Spirit.

A Clash *of* Authority

The opening verse of this chapter is curious in the extreme. The Hebrew actually says that Saul was one year old when he became king and that he reigned for two years! The early Greek translation omits the verse altogether and there is a strong likelihood that the verse was added later to make it conform to the pattern which is used throughout the books of Kings to introduce the reign of a new king. Even so, this doesn't explain the figures. Some numbers have been missed out and it is difficult to guess what they should be.

Ready for battle

It is helpful to know where the different places are in relation to each other. Michmash was some seven or eight miles north-east of Gibeah. Geba was about half way between the two. Gilgal was about fifteen miles to the east. Clearly the Philistines had penetrated well into the territory of the tribe of Benjamin. The garrison may have been quite a small one since it was reduced by Jonathan and his one 'thousand' (v. 3). This is the first we have heard of Jonathan and here we are not told that he was Saul's son. We have not even heard that Saul was married. Yet by now he has a grown-up son capable of leading a group of soldiers. Jonathan's victory was the prelude to a more significant battle near Michmash.

The striking thing about the story in NRSV is that Saul refers to his people as Hebrews. This is a term which is usually used by other peoples such as the Egyptians in Exodus and the Philistines in 1 Samuel 4:6, 9, and 14:11. Some translators again turn to the Greek which says, 'The Hebrews have revolted' and then move the phrase so that it is spoken by the Philistines: the Philistines heard of it and said, 'The Hebrews have revolted' (REB). This makes excellent sense. The term is used again in verse 7 by the writer himself. This is very unlikely and REB has read 'some of them' instead. Alternatively, 'the Hebrews' may have been a third force of mercenary troops, like the Habiru who are known from certain letters found at Tel-el-Amarna in Egypt. The Habiru, also known as the *'apiru*, were distinct from the Israelites or Hebrews. They were not an ethnic group, but a social class, active throughout the Middle East from the sixteenth to the twelfth century BC. If this was the case, Saul summoned them to help him, but in verse 7 they deserted when they saw the Philistine army.

The sacrifice

The minor victory of Jonathan sparked off the much larger conflict. The size of the Philistine army is enormous. No wonder the Israelites were afraid, either hiding or fleeing across the Jordan for safety. Saul was now stationed at Gilgal with his army. Before going into battle it was regarded as important to ensure God's help by offering a sacrifice and so Saul waited for Samuel to arrive and offer it as he was instructed to do in 10:8. He waited the full seven days and still Samuel didn't come (v. 8). Meanwhile his troops were drifting away home. This left him in a very difficult position. In the end Saul decided to offer the sacrifice himself. As soon as he had done so, Samuel appeared suddenly without giving any reason for the delay. Where he had come from, we do not know. Poor Saul then got a dressing-down for taking over Samuel's job, and the promise of a dynasty to rule Israel for ever was withdrawn. The question of the relation between the religious and the secular authority is an ancient one and still concerns us today.

So Samuel and Saul parted, Samuel disappearing as quietly as he had come and Saul, with the army, going to meet the Philistines near Gibeah. It is difficult not to feel considerable sympathy for Saul. True, he had been disobedient to God's word given to him by Samuel; true, he had assumed responsibilities which were not his; true, he might have waited another day; but the impression left by the story is that this was almost a deliberate ploy by Samuel. He had not been in favour of a king in the first place and he had warned the people about the dangers of a monarchy. Now he is able to withdraw his support for Saul. For the writer, however, it showed the importance of obedience on the part of the king, an obedience which continued to be lacking down to his own day.

A QUESTION

Can the different roles of church and state be so clearly divided?

The PHILISTINES *in* CONTROL

Samuel, then, departed as mysteriously as he had arrived. Where he went we are not told. His part in the story is over for now. He has censured Saul and so his work is done, for the moment. We have come a long way from the boy left at the shrine in Shiloh who couldn't recognize the Lord's voice, to the mighty figure who can anoint kings, criticize and unmake them.

Saul's army had already dwindled away as he said. In verse 2 he had two thousand men at his disposal. Now the number is down to six hundred (v. 15). He didn't count them, as NRSV suggests; he reviewed them. The Hebrew word used here is often translated as 'to visit', but in military contexts it means 'to pass in review' or 'to number' or 'to muster' (so REB). We are not told how many of Jonathan's thousand remained with him. Clearly the Israelites were in an extremely weak position at Gibeah. The Philistines, on the other hand, with their huge army at their base in Michmash, were able to send out raiding parties into all the surrounding district, to the north, west and south-east respectively. In other words they were in control of the whole territory occupied by the tribe of Benjamin, with the Israelite population subdued. The situation painted here is very bleak for Israel.

Israel unarmed

The weakness of Israel is underlined in the second half of this passage. The Philistines had brought with them implements and weapons made of iron. Until now the Israelites had been able to use only bronze. Moreover, at this particular time Philistine control was so strong that the Israelites were not allowed to work with metals at all (v. 19). (Here, used by the Philistines, the word 'Hebrew' does refer to the Israelites.) The manufacture of arms was therefore non-existent. Indeed, so rigidly was the prohibition enforced that they were not even allowed to sharpen their own farming implements. The only arms available were the personal weapons of Saul and Jonathan. The threat to Israel's continuing existence in the area was therefore very strong indeed.

The writer of 1 Samuel is no doubt here describing the situation as he understood it to have been. But perhaps there is more to it than that. In many places in the Old Testament there are stories which suggest that the weakness of his people and their vulnerability is intended to remind them of God's own power. Caught between the Egyptians and the Reed Sea they had only to stand still and see the deliverance which God would accomplish for them (Exodus 14:13f). Gideon was deliberately left weak with only the least alert troops and the rest sent home (Judges 7:2ff). We shall meet the same idea again in the life and work of David. It anticipates the saying of the apostle Paul in 1 Corinthians 1 that God chose what is weak to shame the strong so that no one should be able to boast of his own achievements but only of what God had done. We cannot say, of course, whether this writer had this in mind when he wrote this passage but the lesson is there for us to see.

A PRAYER

Lord, in our foolishness grant us our wisdom; in our weakness fill us with your strength. Take away our fears and renew our faith. In our success keep us humble. To you be the glory.

JONATHAN *the* HERO

There was now a lull in the fighting. Saul, apparently unwilling to rely on Samuel any longer, had with him as priest Ahijah, who was descended from the priestly line of Eli which had been discredited (v. 3). He was carrying the ephod, the short priestly garment in which the sacred lot was carried. Clearly Saul had every intention of calling on him to discern God's will when it was necessary, in spite of the fact that he was no longer entitled to do so.

The fight at the Michmash pass

The story reads like a good Western movie! Without Saul's knowledge, Jonathan decided to carry out a bold personal attack on a detachment of Philistine soldiers holding the pass in the mountains (v. 6). It ran between two rocky crags named Bozez and Seneh. The name Bozez is connected with a word which means 'mire', while Seneh has something to do with 'thorns'. Neither of the names seems to have any special significance here. The Israelites were always at their best in this kind of terrain (1 Kings 20:23ff). Also we meet here once again the belief that God may accomplish his purpose through weak and apparently ineffective agents. But it was important for Jonathan to know that such a raid was what God wanted him to do. It is never easy to discover God's will and here Jonathan was uncertain. He needed a sign from the Lord in order to be sure. The response of the Philistines, when he and his armour bearer made their first move and came out into the open, would provide the answer (v. 10). Jonathan did, of course, need to be ready and willing to accept whatever God required, though no doubt he was hoping for a positive answer and was glad to have a go at the Philistines. As always in these situations, the surprise factor was important. The Philistines, thinking that they were some of the Israelites who had hidden in caves and rocks (13:6), invited them into their camp with disastrous results. This was the sign to proceed with the plan. So the two of them scrambled over the rocks and when they reached the detachment they killed the twenty men who were there. The phrase 'within an area about half a furrow long in an acre of land' is odd, to say the least. The Hebrew text begins with the word 'like' and we should probably understand the phrase to describe the manner of the attack and not the location: say, 'like the cutting of a furrow in an acre of land' (compare REB). The main Philistine army heard it and, thinking this was the prelude to a full-scale attack, were thrown into a panic.

Saul's reaction

Saul also heard the noise and, realizing that some of his men had attacked the Philistine detachment, he took a roll-call to see who was missing and therefore who might be responsible (v. 17). Jonathan was missing. Saul was going to ask the Lord what to do next. The text says he consulted the Ark (v. 18) but this is almost certainly wrong. The Ark was never used as a means of discovering the will of God and it had been left at Kiriath-jearim. The REB is doubtless correct in following the Greek translation and reading 'ephod' in place of 'Ark' in both places. It was the ephod that was used for this purpose and it was the ephod which Ahijah carried (v. 3). Before Ahijah could get the ephod ready, Saul heard the noise increasing and decided not to bother with it. He made up his own mind to go and see what was happening.

As he approached, he found the Philistines in total confusion, fighting among themselves. When they saw him some Hebrews who had been with the Philistines deserted and joined Saul, so we are told. But the term 'Hebrews' is generally used only by Egyptians and Philistines and maybe we should understand it here to mean 'those who had deserted to the Philistines two or three days earlier'. We have seen, however, that the Hebrews here may refer to a third force of mercenaries (see on 19:3). These now rejoined Saul while others came out of hiding. Even with these additions it is doubtful if Saul's six hundred men suddenly increased to ten thousand as is said in verse 23. In fact, this is not in the Hebrew text and the phrase should be omitted from NRSV. The whole point of the story is that by two men with slender resources the Philistines were routed, because it was the Lord who gave Israel the victory. It reminds us that, important as resources may be, they are not in themselves a guarantee of success. God can use even our limited resources to achieve more than we often imagine. Five loaves and two fish may feed a multitude (Mark 6:30–44).

A PRAYER

Help us, by your Spirit, to discern your will and give us the courage to do it. In all our success, to you be the glory.

WHO ATE *the* HONEY?

Already Israel's first king is beginning to go off the rails. He had offered sacrifice instead of waiting for Samuel. He had accepted the descendants of Eli who had been disqualified from the priesthood. He had gone to see what was happening in the Philistine camp without bothering to consult God. In the latter part of this section (v. 36) he was going to pursue and destroy the Philistines without reference to the Lord until he was reminded of the need to do so by the priest. When he did he got no answer and so realized that something was amiss.

A foolish vow

How easy it is to make vows thoughtlessly, vows which cannot or will not be fulfilled. Saul made a vow that both he and his men would abstain from food until he had secured victory over the Philistines. The writer calls this a 'rash act' (v. 24). Nevertheless, the keeping of a vow was so important that his men refused to eat even the most alluring honey when they came across it. Later, when he sought guidance from God and obtained no answer, he realized that the vow had been broken. But by whom? We know about the vow but Jonathan didn't. He had been absent when it had been made, doing his bit against the Philistines. So when he saw some inviting honey he had a taste and was greatly refreshed by it. When told of his father's vow he was critical of Saul for making it in the first place. The army would have been better able to fight if they had been properly fed, he argued (v. 30).

Saul did not know who had broken the vow and the only way to find out who was responsible was to cast lots. Once again the ephod would be brought out and the sacred lot cast. How this worked we described in 10:20ff. Urim indicated a negative answer and Thummim a positive (v. 41). The culprit was eventually shown to be Jonathan. Now vows were taken very seriously (see Deuteronomy 23:21–23) and even though it was Jonathan who was guilty Saul was prepared to put his son to death, just as Jephthah had been ready to kill his daughter in Judges 11. However, the popular protest persuaded him not to. After all, God had been with Jonathan when he had destroyed the Philistine detachment and thrown their army into confusion.

The meat-eaters

In the middle of this story there is another one which not only breaks the continuity but seems out of place (vv. 31–35). Whereas in verse 36 Saul contemplates defeating and despoiling the Philistines, here he has done so and his men have eaten some of the captured livestock. It is hardly likely that they would have done so so blatantly in view of Saul's vow and later it is not the eating of meat which is the issue but the tasting of the honey by Jonathan. Even in these verses it is not simply the eating of meat which is the issue but the eating of meat with the blood still in it. This was forbidden in the Law because the blood belonged to God. It was drained from the meat before the carcase was sacrificed. It couldn't be offered to God because it was his already (Leviticus 17:10ff and 19:26). Later, when the Jerusalem temple became the only place where sacrifice could be offered, it was permitted for people to eat meat without it being sacrificed so long as the blood had been drained off. This was the situation with which the writer would be familiar from his knowledge of Deuteronomy 12:15–16. Therefore Saul built an altar so that animals could be sacrificed and their blood be properly dealt with. There is no suggestion, however, that Saul's vow is being broken. Indeed he himself is helping them by building the altar. It seems safe, then, to assume that this story originally had a different setting and has been placed here as a kind of interlude between Jonathan's mistake and his father's discovery.

Saul's entourage

These last verses simply record Saul's achievements and the names of his family and his commander. Of these Michal, his daughter, and Abner, his commander, will feature prominently in future stories. The final verse prepares the way for David's entry into his court.

A REFLECTION

How careful should we be when we make promises to God?
Are there circumstances in which they may be broken?

25 1 SAMUEL 15:1–33

A Demand *for* Obedience

This story, stressing the need for obedience, bothers us by the way the lesson is taught. The destruction of the Amalekites, its ferocity and the fact that God commanded it and disapproved when it wasn't properly carried out, seem to conflict with all we have learned about the love of God. There is no way of lessening its impact. We can only try to understand it from the Old Testament point of view. The Israelites believed that Israel's enemies were also God's enemies and that those enemies must be eliminated. Since there was a solidarity between men and their possessions, those possessions, including wives and children, must be destroyed. Before we condemn them we should recall that the Allies, after two thousand years of Christian teaching, killed thousands of people, including women and children, in Hamburg, Dresden, Nagasaki and Hiroshima, all in the cause of a 'just war'. We need to recognize the importance of the positive lesson about obedience, remembering that Jesus also required this (e.g. in John 15:10).

The Amalekites

For the moment, the Philistines are forgotten and a new enemy takes their place. The enmity between Amalek and Israel goes back a long way. When Moses and his people were in difficulties in the wilderness, the Amalekites attacked them from the rear. Joshua eventually defeated them, and the Lord promised, 'I will utterly blot out the remembrance of Amalek under heaven' (Exodus 17). The incident is recalled in Deuteronomy 25:17–19 and the threat is repeated word for word. Saul is now charged with the task of carrying out this promise. The Amalekites lived in the Negev, the area to the south of Judah towards Sinai. The command to 'utterly destroy' in verse 3 is a technical term often translated 'put them to the ban'. Since this, like many other wars, was seen as the Lord's war against his enemies, the spoils of war should be 'devoted' to him and this very often meant their complete destruction so that they could not be used by anyone else. This was therefore a religious obligation (Leviticus 27:28–29).

Saul raised a very large army for this war. The ten thousand soldiers of Judah are mentioned separately, which indicates that Judah was not regarded as part of Saul's kingdom at this stage.

The Kenites lived among the Amalekites (Judges 1:16) but they had been helpful to Israel. In particular, Jael, the wife of Heber the Kenite, had killed Sisera, the Canaanite general (Judges 4:17ff and 5:24ff). For this they were to be spared.

The promise half-fulfilled

Saul won the battle against the Amalekites (v. 7) and partially carried out the 'ban'. Everyone except the king and everything except the best of the sheep and cattle was destroyed. Common sense dictated that he should spare what could be of use to him and his army. But obedience must overrule common sense, especially when common sense serves selfish ends. (The Carmel of v. 12 is not the mount where Elijah met the prophets of Baal. It was a town a few miles south of Hebron.)

Nothing could be hidden from God, who then told Samuel in the way messages were given to prophets (v. 10). It was not a welcome message but it is not clear whether his anger was directed against himself, or against Saul or even against God. Saul, now confronted by Samuel, compounded his disobedience first by lying, saying that he had carried out the 'ban', then by blaming others for not having done so and then by claiming that he had spared the animals so that they could be sacrificed. How true it is that one lie leads on to another.

Samuel as prophet

Samuel's response is given in the kind of rhythmic prose, almost poetry, which the later prophets used (vv. 22–23). His words are, in fact, echoed by Hosea (6:6). The climax of it is the rejection of Saul as king. That is the consequence of disobedience. Coupled with this is the threat of his replacement by another. Although unnamed, David is already in the frame. The title 'Glory of Israel' for the Lord is unique. It is a different word from the 'glory' that departed when the Ark was captured in chapter 4. It simply means 'illustrious'. The rejection of Saul as king is final—God will not change his mind—but Saul's plea that he may return with Samuel and worship the Lord is answered positively. Samuel's killing of Agag is chilling (v. 33) but has to be seen in the context of the 'ban'. What Saul failed to do, Samuel does.

A PRAYER

Thank you that our disobedience may be forgiven through the death of Jesus. Help us not to seek revenge but to love even our enemies.

A SURPRISE ANOINTING

Both the Lord and Samuel were disappointed with Saul on account of his various failures to do as he was told. Samuel 'grieved' (v. 35). This is a strong word usually used of mourning for the dead. The form of the verb suggests that he went on grieving for some time. The Lord 'was sorry'. The writer is not afraid to describe God as having feelings common to humans, or as having made a mistake. Yet it is not as simple as that. It was not really a mistake; rather it was human pride and self-will which thwarted the will of God and made it necessary for him to take a different course. On the face of it there was nothing that Samuel could do about a replacement until Saul died. To have anointed a successor while Saul was still alive would have been tantamount to treason and therefore punishable by death. No wonder he was reluctant. God, apparently, was not prepared to wait for this to happen. A successor must be anointed at once, even though he couldn't immediately take the throne.

The visit to Bethlehem

It must, however, be kept secret. So Samuel went to Bethlehem on the pretext of a priestly visit for the purpose of sacrifice. Just why Jesse and the elders were uneasy is not clear (v. 4). Had they heard about Samuel and his activities and were afraid of him? Or was it because he came from the territory of Benjamin and they lived in Judah, an area which seems to have had only a loose connection with the tribal areas to the north? In any case, Samuel set their minds at rest and they accepted his priestly authority.

Gathering for sacrifice

The story never tells us that the sacrifice took place. Presumably it did, but this is not where the point of the story lies. Although Samuel knew he was to anoint one of the sons as king, he didn't know which one. So when they were all assembled he had to rely on the voice of God inside him. It was natural to start with the eldest and he was surprised that this was not the one (v. 6). If it had been down to Samuel he would have been, but the Lord had other ideas. Not only was that a surprise; there was a greater one in store. Although he had been told to anoint one of the sons, he now heard the voice telling him that none of them was the one chosen. Surely there must have been a mistake somewhere along the line. Samuel was sufficiently certain about what he was to do that it dawned on him that there may be another son who was not present. It turned out to be so.

The anointing

Samuel had been told not to rely on outward appearances because the inner disposition was more important (v. 7). Yet when David was brought in from the fields he was seen to be attractive, rosy-cheeked and bright-eyed, even if young. Presumably the Lord did not choose him for these reasons, although they are mentioned here. Apparently his disposition was good, and the Lord knew the potential that was in him. So he chose him and Samuel anointed him. We are told that the 'spirit' of the Lord came upon him (v. 13) but there is no sign of odd behaviour as there had been in the case of Saul. It meant that he would be provided with the gifts that he would need to be king. But they were not to be used yet. Saul was still king and would remain so. David was the king in waiting.

The anointing took place in full view of the brothers, so apparently they and Jesse knew of it but said nothing at this stage. In some of the subsequent stories they seem to be unaware of it or to have forgotten it. But from now on David's life is directed towards his becoming king. Once more, as in earlier passages, it is the person with least to offer who is chosen. It is not his own natural gifts which fit David for his task; it is the spirit of God which gives him the qualities needed for kingship.

A THOUGHT

"Tis not the habit that makes the monk' (Thomas Fuller, 1732).
It is the character of the person which is important.

MUSIC THERAPY *for the* KING

If David was eventually to become king then it was necessary for him to be introduced into the royal court. These verses give us one account of how that happened. There will be a different one later. If we are to take this story at face value it would appear that Saul had some authority in Judah, since he could summon David to his court (v. 19). We saw in 11:8 that the Judean forces who helped attack Jabesh-gilead are mentioned separately from the Israelite forces and this might suggest the independence of Judah. There are other grounds for thinking that Judah was never fully a part of Saul's kingdom, but it may well be that the relationship between them was a close one.

The spirits

We find all this talk about spirits difficult because we think of a spirit in personal terms and, indeed, in some biblical passages that seems to be the case. The Hebrew word for 'spirit' also means 'wind' and if we think of the wind as powerful and yet unseen that may help us to understand what is often meant by 'spirit'. It is an unseen power whose presence can be discerned only by seeing its effects.

In verse 13 we were told that the spirit of the Lord came upon David. Now, some time later, it was removed from Saul and replaced by an evil spirit from the Lord. Literally, the Hebrew says that just as the spirit went 'from with' Saul, so the evil spirit came 'from with' God. To our modern ears this exchange of spirits may seem strange, though in some cultures it would still be quite natural. We have already seen how the phrase 'the spirit of the Lord' denotes the God-given power to do successfully any task which God may require. So here the gifts needed for successful kingship were withdrawn from Saul and given to David. From now on, Saul's fortunes will decline while David's will improve.

But what about the evil spirit? Did God really send an evil spirit to torment Saul? From now on, Saul suffered intermittent bouts of madness which, in biblical terms, was attributed to evil spirits (v. 23). Such spirits needed to be exorcised and there are numerous examples of this in the New Testament (e.g. Mark 5). Demon possession is still recognized by some people as the cause of madness or mental aberration. Others describe these disorders in more scientific or medical terms, regarding the references to evil spirits as outmoded but graphic ways of explaining them.

What makes it more difficult here is the fact that it came from the Lord. Does God really send evil spirits upon people? If we believe in a personal Devil opposed to God, then it will be perfectly natural to attribute evil spirits to him. But for the Old Testament writers there was only one God who was responsible for all that happened. Therefore madness, permanent or intermittent, must come from him as a power which has these effects. In the present story it is all part of the divine plan which will ultimately see David installed as king of all Israel.

The music maker

The soothing, calming influence of music was clearly recognized (v. 17). How the young courtier had come to know about David's ability, we are not told. But was David also already a man of valour, a warrior? (v. 18). Perhaps this fuller description of David's many gifts is due to the storyteller's knowledge of his later achievements. For the moment it was the musical skill which was important. It led to David being described as 'the sweet singer of Israel' in 2 Samuel 23:1 and being associated with the singing of psalms in the later temple worship.

What Jesse thought when his youngest son was summoned to Saul's court, we can only speculate. He knew of the anointing and so probably he saw this, with mounting excitement, as a first step towards David becoming king. Along with his son, he sent other gifts to the king, including a 'donkey of bread' which means a donkey-ful of food, not so much to pay for David's keep as to express his gratitude and loyalty (v. 20). So David got his foot on the first rung of the ladder.

A THOUGHT

*God can use our simple talents to accomplish
more than we often think. The question is, do we offer them
to him willingly and gladly?*

28

A GIANT'S CHALLENGE

There can't be many people who don't know at least the outline of the story of David and Goliath. It has become proverbial for the victory of the weak over the strong. If we look at it more closely we shall find that there are some awkward questions to be asked, especially when we try to fit it into the whole story of David and his introduction to Saul's court.

The text

To begin with, there is a major difference between this story as told in the Hebrew Bible and that told in the Greek translation, the Septuagint. Often such differences are not important enough to worry about, but here no less than nineteen verses, 12–31, are missing altogether from the Greek. This omission changes the course of the narrative. The discrepancy is unlikely to be just an accident. It is a good idea to read through the whole chapter and then to re-read it omitting the verses mentioned. The fuller form tells us that David's brothers, although Judeans, were fighting alongside Saul and that David appeared on the scene only because he was taking supplies to them. The introduction of David in verse 12 reads as though we had never heard of him before. In the shorter form David is already with the army, though we are not told in what capacity. Since he was just a boy (v. 33) we must assume that he was a servant to one of the soldiers. In spite of the fact that chapter 16 says he became Saul's musician and armour bearer, Saul appears to know nothing about him at all. Whether we read the longer or the shorter form, David was still a shepherd boy in earlier times (v. 34).

The question over which scholars still argue is: which is original? Did the Greek translation omit these verses and, if so, why? Or did some later Hebrew copyist add them to the original after the Greek translation had been made and again, if so, why? If these verses are omitted then we seem to have a story of David's entry into Saul's court which is quite separate from that in chapter 16. If they are included, then it looks as though an attempt has been made to combine the two stories.

Most of the English translations use the fuller version and so we shall comment on that.

The giant

What an extraordinary sight this must have been! Normally the two sides would draw up their battle lines opposite each other but at a distance. They would then wait for the moment to engage, as in chapter 4. Here, however, the Philistines were ready to settle the issue by single combat because they had such a tremendous warrior (v. 4). This method of deciding battles is fairly common in folk stories. Goliath stood nine feet tall. His armour was made of bronze and his weapons of iron, weighing enormous amounts. No wonder the Israelites were terrified and unwilling to accept the challenge. Is there some exaggeration here? Certainly the intention of the writer is to emphasize the Philistine's strength in order to show how much stronger God is.

David

In chapter 16 David was introduced into Saul's court as musician and armour bearer, as we have seen. In this chapter he is with his father, looking after the sheep and taking supplies to his three brothers who were in the army (v. 12). The writer was apparently aware of this, for he introduced a comment to explain that David spent some time with Saul and some time with his father (v. 15). This makes him into a part-time armour bearer and musician! However, as armour bearer we should have expected him to be with Saul at the front.

Visits to the front

On account of the stand-off between the two armies, supplies were needed for the soldiers and these were provided by the families. This gave David the opportunity of meeting not only with his brothers, but also with other soldiers. It enabled him to hear both the giant's challenge and the offer of a reward by Saul to anyone who would accept the challenge (v. 25). His surprise that no one was prepared to do so prepares the way for his own offer.

A PRAYER

Give us, Lord, the courage we need to
meet the challenges which life presents to us in the knowledge that
your grace is sufficient for us.

An UNEQUAL MATCH

This part of the story especially is very familiar and the main point stands out clearly: God is more powerful than anything his enemies can muster.

The impudent youngster

The relationship between David and his brothers is not unlike that of Joseph with his in Genesis 37. Both were shepherds and in both cases the younger is chosen in preference to the elder, leading to jealousy and resentment, which in David's eyes is unjustified. There is no hint here, however, that Eliab had witnessed Saul's anointing of David. This lends some support to the view that in chapters 16 and 17 we have two different accounts of the way David entered Saul's court.

The volunteer

In this story David is introduced to Saul as if they had never met before and this impression is confirmed later in the chapter (vv. 55–58). The 'heart' which failed in verse 32 represents courage, as it sometimes does. The tenses in verse 34 of NRSV suggest that David no longer looks after his father's sheep, though, in fact, at this time he did. In both this verse and the next they point to repeated activity. It would be better to translate, 'I look after my father's sheep and whenever a lion or a bear has come... I have gone after it...'

For David the forces which were at Saul's command were not simply Israel's forces; they were the Lord's (v. 36). They were meant to carry out the promise and purpose of God that the Israelites should occupy the promised land, driving out all counter-claimants. It is this belief which still explains much of Israel's attitude to the land in the present day. Later on, Amos would claim that they had forfeited that right by their unfaithfulness and that they were then in no better position than the Philistines (Amos 9:7). Here the same Lord who helped David overcome the wild beasts would help him do the same to the Philistine giant. To show how this was God's doing he discarded the totally unsuitable armour and used the same weapons as he had used against the lions and bears (v. 40).

The fight

All the odds are on a Philistine victory, but only if we discount the power and presence of the Lord. Goliath made fun of David and threatened him with severe consequences, but David responded with identical threats. Goliath called on his gods and cursed David; David trusted in the Lord whose victory would show that Israel had a God more powerful than the Philistine's gods. It turned out to be no contest. Already the Lord had shown his superiority over Dagon (ch. 5) but either the Philistines had forgotten that or they thought that, with Goliath, there was a better chance of victory this time.

The pursuit

The outcome of the battle had been decided by Goliath's defeat and death (v. 51) and so we might have expected an orderly withdrawal of the Philistine forces. Instead, on the way back to the nearest two of their five cities, they were set upon by the Israelites and many were killed. Verse 54 says that David took Goliath's head to Jerusalem; but Jerusalem was not an Israelite city at this time. It was still in the hands of the Jebusites and was captured only later by David (2 Samuel 5). The storyteller seems to have forgotten this. Further, did David really have a tent to which he could take the weapons? Goliath's sword turns up later at a place called Nob (21:9).

Saul and David

Although in chapter 16 Saul had been told that David, the musician, was the son of Jesse and had sent a messenger to bring him to the court where he played for him, in this story David and his parentage are still unknown to Saul (v. 55). He is introduced to Saul as a stranger, still carrying Goliath's head. The writer of the books of Samuel has tried in some ways to reconcile the two stories in chapters 16 and 17. It is clear, however, that there had been handed down through the years these two traditions relating how David arrived at Saul's court. It was difficult to run them together to make a wholly consistent story but the writer has nearly succeeded.

A PRAYER

*Give us the faith, Lord, to trust in your power and not in our own,
and to know that there is no other God like you.*

A POPULAR HERO

After his victory over Goliath, David was not allowed to go home to look after his father's sheep any longer. He became a prominent member of Saul's court.

A close friendship

In the next few chapters the story of Jonathan's affection for David is interwoven with stories about Saul's jealousy of David, so that each acts as a foil to the other. In this way the writer skilfully brings out the contrast between the two. The friendship between Jonathan and David is almost proverbial. It is exceedingly close, so close, in fact, that it has sometimes been seen as a homosexual relationship. However, both Jonathan and David later married and raised families and the phraseology used in verse 1 is exactly the same as that used in Genesis 44:30 to describe Jacob's affection for his youngest son, Benjamin. It is a pity that close, same-sex relationships have come to be regarded with suspicion by some people. It certainly should not be assumed that they are all homosexual.

So, Jonathan and David became 'soul-mates' (v. 1). Obviously the word 'soul' does not stand for some inner part of a person; here it represents Jonathan's total 'being', his very self. The 'covenant' between them is simply a bond or binding agreement based upon that love.

It is worth noticing that the initiative is with Jonathan at this stage. Jonathan loved David; Jonathan made a covenant with David (this is better than REB which has 'Jonathan and David made a solemn compact'); Jonathan gave him his robe and his armour. As yet there is nothing to suggest that it was reciprocated by David. It looks like a case of hero-worship which developed into a mutual love, even though the worshipper was in a superior position to the hero. The heir to the throne has become committed in love to the young servant.

The gift of his robe, his armour and his weapons to David is extremely generous and indicates the depth of his affection (v. 4). But it may be even more than that, for these were the symbols of his royal status. The gift may have been the surrender of his position as heir.

Had he heard of David's anointing? Probably not. Perhaps it was an acknowledgment that David, with his wisdom and skill, was more fitted to the tasks of kingship than he was. If this is correct it makes the friendship even more remarkable, especially on Jonathan's side, and it is part of the divine plan which will lead to David becoming king.

David the soldier

We are not told what sort of ventures Saul sent David on, but whatever they were he was successful in them (v. 5). We should probably assume that they were military tasks of some kind since, as a result of the success, David is made general in charge of the army. Even the court officials were impressed. They might have been expected to be jealous but instead they welcomed David's appointment.

As the story goes now, all this must have happened between David's victory over Goliath and Saul's return with the army from the pursuit of the Philistines, for in verse 6 we read of the victorious return of Saul and the army, celebrated by the women who had been left behind. The first line of the song would be gratifying to Saul, but the second aroused his jealousy. It was the beginning of prolonged animosity against David.

It would make better sense if, in verse 6, we could read the plural 'Philistines' for the singular. This would then allow some time for the events in verses 1–5 to take place and for David's wider exploits to become known. There is no evidence for such a change but it is just possible that the writer changed the plural which was in the version of the story he received to singular in order to make the account fit with the Goliath episode. In any case, the scene is now set for the long section of narrative which deals with Saul's attacks on David.

These already began in verses 10 and 11 as Saul, in one of his fits of madness, tried to pin David to the wall with his spear, not just once, but twice, without success.

A PRAYER

Help us, Lord, to rejoice in the gifts which you give to others and to be willing, like Jonathan and John the Baptist, to stand aside and give place to another who may gifted in ways we are not.

A ROYAL INTRIGUE

Saul's jealousy turned to fear, not for his life but for his throne. In 16:13–14 it was the spirit of the Lord which was removed from Saul and given to David. Here it is the Lord himself, but there is little or no difference between the two. Saul was fighting a losing battle. If the Lord had given David victory over Goliath then he would surely give him victory over Saul. Yet Saul would fight to keep his throne; he would not let go easily. Jealousy is a destructive force. Once given a foothold, it gains power until it takes control of our actions and demands more and more of us. We are driven to further desperate measures. So now Saul makes three attempts to get rid of David.

Dismissal

All three plans involved using the Philistines in one way or another and the plans became increasingly devious. First, in verses 12–16, David was made commander of the army, which may have looked like promotion. More importantly from Saul's point of view, it got him away from the immediate court where he was the object of popular adulation. He was sent as army commander to deal with the enemy, probably the Philistines, in the field. The hope was that he might get killed. But, the writer reminds us, the Lord was with him. In fact, all it did was to increase his standing with the people.

A proposal of marriage

Next, in verses 17–19, Saul offered David a place within the royal family through marriage to his elder daughter, Merab. The condition was that he should again go and fight the Philistines. Saul's actual words are instructive. First he claimed David's loyalty—'Be valiant for me'—then he used words which made it sound pious—'Fight the Lord's battles.' Who could refuse a challenge like that? David certainly couldn't. But behind the fine words the plot is clear. Saul would get the Philistines to do his dirty work for him. With characteristic humility David questioned his right to become the king's son-in-law, but he didn't refuse the offer. It is not said that David succeeded in his battles but we must assume that he did, for when the time came for Merab to be given to him, the conditions having been fulfilled, Saul broke his promise and gave her in marriage to someone else.

A better proposal

Since another daughter, Michal, had fallen in love with David, Saul repeated his offer (vv. 20–30). Having gone back on his offer of Merab he needed some back-up for this new offer and so he got his servants to tell David how much he thought of him. This time, however, he must bring back the foreskins of a hundred Philistines. The Philistines did not practise circumcision and so, several times, they are identified by this writer as 'the uncircumcised'. Since David could not afford a marriage dowry the foreskins would do instead. David liked the idea, perhaps because the thought of becoming the king's son-in-law pleased him or perhaps because he had himself been attracted by Michal. Anyway, he went and got the required trophy. The Hebrew says he brought back two hundred foreskins and this is probably correct. He went well beyond what was required of him and this time Saul could not refuse him his reward. So David and Michal became husband and wife.

Now, by rights, one of Saul's daughters should have been given to David much earlier as the reward for killing Goliath (17:25). Obviously this had not happened and, as the story now stands, Saul had therefore broken his word twice. We have seen, however, that the story of David and Goliath was probably a separate account which has not been thoroughly integrated into the whole narrative.

Saul's schemes all backfired. They made matters worse, for the more success David had the more popular he became and the more Saul needed to get rid of him.

A COMMENT

Beware of jealousy! If unchecked, it festers until the whole being is corrupted and eventually it destroys not its object, but its subject.

FRIENDS *at* COURT

From now on, David led a charmed life. Sometimes he succeeded when failure seemed more likely, through his own cleverness or skill or through good fortune. For the writer of 1 Samuel, all this success is due rather to the fact that the Lord had chosen him and anointed him as king. Therefore the Lord was with him and nothing could stand in the way of him.

The value of friendship

In this chapter it is his friends who save him, and first, Jonathan. What are friends for and what is love if it doesn't show itself in actions? Both Jonathan and Michal expressed their love by keeping David safe. Having failed to get rid of David by underhand means, Saul now became more open about it. He made the serious mistake of telling Jonathan and his servants what he had in mind. The Hebrew means not so much that he spoke to them *about* killing David, but that he spoke to them *in order to* kill him. In other words, he sought to involve them in his plan. He probably thought that the true heir to the throne would be as keen as he was to get rid of any possible usurper, but he had underestimated Jonathan's affection for David. All this had the opposite effect from what he anticipated. Jonathan was able to warn David to keep out of the way for the time being. He then appealed to his father and did so most eloquently (vv. 4–5). David was innocent of any evil intent against the king and had done nothing but good for him. To kill a traitor would have been permissible but to kill an innocent man was a breach of the sixth commandment and this applied as much to the king as to anyone else. The king was not above the law. According to 10:25 Samuel had set out the rights and duties of kingship and this would include upholding the law.

Jonathan's appeal was successful and Saul agreed to spare David. It is not easy to know whether this was a genuine change of mind or simply an empty promise. The strength of Saul's reply suggests the former and we should give Saul the benefit of the doubt. The oath he swore was validated by reference to the living Lord (v. 6). To have sworn such an oath without meaning it would have been a further breach of the commandments, this time the third, 'Thou shalt not take the name of the Lord thy God in vain.' Saul seems to have been capable of these sudden, genuine changes of mind. Jonathan certainly thought it was genuine since he called David back into the court as before. For a while, normal service was resumed

Saved by the wife

Yet again there was war against the Philistines (v. 8) and after another resounding victory for David, the evil spirit, the black mood of jealousy, returned to Saul. Once again, while David was playing for him he tried to spear him. There had already been an incident like this in 18:10–11 so perhaps David was ready for it this time. It did mean that, once again, he had to get away from Saul.

The king assumed that David would go to his own house which he shared with his wife Michal, and so sent his servants to guard the house and prevent his escape. Why he waited till morning and didn't kill him straight away is not clear (v. 11). Perhaps he wanted to wait until Michal was out of the way. The delay gave David and his wife time to plan the escape. We then have a classic scene, found in many books and films. Michal let him out of the window and put a dummy in his bed. The dummy was an 'idol', a 'teraphim'. Now what was an idol doing in the house of David and Michal? A teraphim was a household god, perhaps meant to bring protection or good fortune to the family. Since there is no criticism of it here it may simply have been regarded as a hangover from the past, a bit like a horseshoe hung over the door, fairly meaningless. The size of the teraphim seems to have varied. Rachel stole her father's when she went off with Jacob (Genesis 31:19, 33–34). She hid them in the saddle of the camel and sat on them, so they must have been quite small! This one was large enough to look like a man in bed. The servants were to take David—in his bed!—to Saul, so that he could kill him. What a disappointment for Saul! Michal excused herself by saying that David had threatened to kill her if she tried to stop him. We've heard that one before! At any rate it meant that David had escaped yet again.

There was no going back now. He would never be safe so long as he was anywhere near Saul. David had to get right away.

A REFLECTION

'They do not love that do not show their love'
William Shakespeare, *Two Gentlemen of Verona*

PROPHETS AGAIN

Now that David was excluded from the court with no possibility of returning, where was he to go? He could have gone home to Bethlehem and resumed his work as a shepherd. Instead he went to Ramah to see Samuel. We are left to imagine how the conversation went. No doubt David reminded Samuel that he had anointed him king some time ago and now wanted to know what was going on. Things had gone well to start with. He'd made an entry into the royal court, forged a friendship with the king's son who had recognized his gifts and his destiny, he had married the king's daughter and all looked set fair. Now it all seemed to have been swept away on the tide of Saul's jealousy. So where did he stand and what was he to do? It often seems the case that circumstances contradict our call to service and we need the confirmation of a trusted friend. Samuel's response was to take him to Naioth. This is the only place where Naioth is mentioned in the Bible and the same is true of Secu. So we have no idea of their location except that they can't have been too far away from Ramah.

Saul on a 'high'

Did Samuel take David there because he knew of the prophetic band who lived there? But why or how should this meeting of Saul with the prophets answer David's questions about his future? The whole story is strange, not least because it is so similar to the story of Saul's meeting with the prophets in chapter 10, and both stories end with the same commonly used saying: 'Is Saul also among the prophets?' It may be, of course, that this is simply a duplicate account of the same event, but even if that is so we still have to ask why the writer included it again at this point. What purpose does it serve in its present context? In chapter 10 the experience was a part of a sign that God had chosen Saul to be king. Was it again meant as a sign that Samuel had the God-given right to confer or to remove the gifts required for kingship?

There are certain obvious differences between the two stories. Here the reason for Saul's visit was to kill David (v. 20). Here Saul first sent messengers—three times—before going himself. This looks like the familiar storyteller's art; it heightens the tension. Here the prophets do not seem to have been overtaken by frenzy until they saw Saul's messengers. This time Samuel appears either in charge of the prophets (NRSV) or simply at their head (REB). The Hebrew is unclear. However, when Saul himself arrived he had to ask where Samuel was. Here there is no mention of a high place. Could it be that the prophets lived at Naioth but, in chapter 10, had gone to the high place at Gibeah to worship there (assuming that they are the same prophets)?

This ecstatic behaviour is brought on by the spirit of God (v. 20). In chapter 10 that same spirit of God had conferred on Saul the gifts required to be king, but that spirit has now been taken from him (16:14) and given to David. In place of the spirit of God the Lord had given him an evil spirit. Now the spirit of God possessed him again. There is no suggestion of a restoration of his gifts, however, and his frenzy takes place in the presence of Samuel as though to show that Samuel is in control of affairs.

In all this there is no mention at all of David beyond the fact that he was at Naioth. Did he see it all from a distance? Was it meant to convince him of Samuel's authority and so to confirm his own anointing? At least Saul's frenzy prevented him from fulfilling what he had come to do, to catch and kill David. Did it show him in this way that the divine spirit was protecting him?

The whole passage leaves us with more questions than answers about its intention. We can only make intelligent guesses as to the purpose it fulfils in the whole narrative of David's flight from Saul.

A PRAYER

Lord, sometimes we cannot understand the things that happen to us. They seem to conflict with our calling. Help us to go on trusting you to fulfil your purpose.

FRIENDSHIP TESTED

Whatever the significance of what happened at Naioth, it wasn't enough to persuade David of his safety and so he fled from there.

Safety or danger

He found Jonathan but we are not told where the meeting took place. It was certainly in a town, for in verse 11 Jonathan suggests they go out into the field or open country. It is most likely that Jonathan would be in Gibeah where Saul had his court. Perhaps David felt free to go back there because he knew that Saul was delayed at Naioth.

In the conversation that follows, Jonathan seems to claim that he knew nothing of his father's determination to kill David, but in 19:1 we were told that Saul had spoken to Jonathan about it and so he must have been aware of it. However, following Jonathan's defence of his friend, David had been restored to favour and so here we must assume that Jonathan meant that he had no recent indication from Saul as to his intention. David recognized that Saul had not confided in Jonathan this time because he knew how close friends they were. Once Jonathan had been persuaded by David's strong oath that the danger was real, he was prepared to help in any way he could (v. 4).

The day of the new moon was a special day (v. 5). It is often associated with the Sabbath as a day to be kept apart (see Isaiah 1: 13–14). Food offerings were presented to God (2 Chronicles 2:4) and, like the Sabbath, it was a day when no work was done (Amos 8:5). All members of the household would be expected to be present. The test would be whether David's absence was noticed and, if it was, what Saul's reaction would be. The excuse of a yearly sacrifice for Jesse's family in Bethlehem was just a white lie!

More solemn promises

In verse 8, NRSV's 'deal kindly' is rather weak. It has more to do with being loyal, often to an agreement which has been made. It is correct, though, in making clear that the agreement or 'covenant' was one which had been initiated by Jonathan (see on 18:3). But it did place David under an obligation to Jonathan as well as vice versa. Moreover, the agreement was a binding one. The Hebrew calls it 'a covenant of the Lord', that is, it was witnessed and validated by him. This is what is implied in the word 'sacred'.

The answer as to who should bring him news of Saul's reaction to his absence is withheld for a while. Instead we have another speech by Jonathan offering his loyalty to David and reminding David of his obligations in return. The Hebrew of verses 12–17 presents a number of difficulties but, though NRSV and REB differ slightly, they preserve the true sense of the passage. The solemnity of the agreement is brought out by the way the Lord appears frequently in the speech so that everything takes place in his presence and by his will. It begins with an oath which invokes the Lord. Perhaps it ought to read something like, 'The Lord is witness...'. Jonathan's pledge to tell David of Saul's intention is accompanied by another oath sworn in the Lord's name. When Jonathan asks for David's loyal love he calls it 'the love of the Lord', that is, love which corresponds to the love which the Lord has for his people.

It is fairly clear from the passage that Jonathan recognized David, and not himself, to be Saul's successor (see on 18:4). 'If I am still alive' in verse 14 almost implies '...when you become king' and the covenant binds David to show his loyal love towards Jonathan's descendants if he himself is dead. As we shall see, David fulfilled this obligation (2 Samuel 9).

This is a moving account of the affection Jonathan had for David, which came to be reciprocated by David so that their lives were bound together. The 'love' which has been mentioned frequently is usually preceded in the Hebrew by the verb 'to do'. It expresses itself in action or it is not love at all. Nor is it a fleeting emotion which prompts action now and again; it is enduring, loyal, faithful. This ought to save us from a shallow and sentimental understanding of the word 'love'.

A PRAYER

We thank you, Lord, for your love to us expressed in the activity of Jesus and revealed by his death. Help us to love you and then to love our friends and our enemies in this way.

'PARTING *is* SUCH SWEET SORROW'

The plan for disclosing Saul's intention towards David is now described. It is a fairly simple one. No one would suspect anything underhand about Jonathan going out for some archery practice. The sign is not to do with the point at which the arrows fell; it is in the words which Jonathan spoke to the boy who went with him (v. 21). Meanwhile David was to return to his hiding-place. As the footnote in NRSV indicates, there are some difficulties in the way of a translation of the Hebrew of verse 19. However, they concern matters of detail which do not affect the interpretation of the passage. David is to go into hiding again—precisely where doesn't matter very much. It was probably some rocky outcrop. From there he could not be seen but he could hear what Jonathan said to the boy. Jonathan rounded off his instructions to David with a reaffirmation of his earlier pledge to him (v. 23).

The absent guest

Why should Jonathan remain standing when the other two were seated (v. 25)? The Hebrew word that is used usually means 'to arise' but that doesn't make much sense either. At any rate, the three of them, Saul, his general and his son, were present, but David's place was empty. On the actual New Moon day, Saul noticed his absence but didn't comment on it. Any uncleanness, that is, accidental ritual impurity, could have prevented him. The arrangements for the following day were the same. On what was probably an ordinary day and not a special feast day, perhaps uncleanness was no longer an excuse for absence. Instead Jonathan made the agreed excuse but Saul was not taken in by it.

We know nothing about Jonathan's mother, Saul's wife. We have not even been told that Saul was married, though we know he was because he had at least three children. If this was a genuine description of his wife then family relationships must have been very strained (v. 30). However, it may just be one of those outbursts which we are inclined to indulge in when fury takes hold of us. We say things we don't mean and regret them afterwards. There is no doubt about Saul's rage. 'Your mother's nakedness' is probably a way of speaking about the whole process by which Jonathan came into being.

If it is a fact that Jonathan had already given up the idea of being king in favour of David, then Saul knew nothing of it. He fully expected Jonathan to succeed him and was surprised that Jonathan didn't share his belief that David was after the throne. When Jonathan defended his friend, his father reacted to him in the same way as he had reacted to David, by throwing his spear at him (v. 33).

The plan executed

The planned method of informing David was put into action and then the boy was sent home so that the two friends could meet for the last time. The description of this meeting is very poignant. It may be wondered how David could bow three times when he was prostrate on the ground! Actually he fell on his knees and then touched the ground with his forehead three times. It was the sort of action you can still see in some parts of the world. The words used sometimes describe an act of worship when it is done before God. Here it expresses David's humble gratitude to his friend.

The feelings expressed are now fully mutual. In fact, David 'wept the more' (v. 41). A literal translation of the Hebrew would be 'until David has made great' and this is usually taken to mean that he wept more than Jonathan, who then recalled the mutual promise. It was one which bound not only them but also their descendants, and it was the Lord's presence with them that made the promise binding. So the friends parted, Jonathan back to face his father, David to begin a period of flight from him. They would meet again only briefly.

A REFLECTION

Promises between parting friends are easily broken. Time wears away the resolve to keep in touch. But sometimes the friendship is so strong that, however far paths may diverge, pledges made are kept. Are there any such promises which we have not kept? Perhaps this is the time to make them good.

The HUNGRY FUGITIVE

David was in a very precarious situation. Driven from court, he could hardly go back home to Bethlehem where he could have been found easily. He was quite alone with no resources of any kind and extremely vulnerable. He had no food and this now became his priority.

Another white lie

We do not know exactly where Nob was. It is listed as one of the towns in the territory of Benjamin (Nehemiah 11:32) and appears to have been not far from Jerusalem (Isaiah 10:32). It was probably on the southern border of Benjamin. It may be that David just happened upon the place but it is more likely that he knew of it and of the priests who ministered at the sanctuary there.

Ahimelek, the leader of the priests there, met him 'trembling' (v. 1), as the elders of Bethlehem had met Samuel (16:4). It was not so much that he was afraid; he was somewhat anxious. He probably recognized David coming from the king's court and therefore wondered what this was all about. It would not be usual for such a person to be alone without any attendant, especially one so renowned as a leader of the army. The situation was distinctly odd.

We shall have occasion to mention David's cleverness several times during this period of his life. By claiming he was on a secret mission from the king he was immediately spared any further questioning (v. 2). His men were not far away, he said, but the secrecy meant he could be vague about their whereabouts. What he needed was rations for them. It's hardly likely that he asked for only five loaves. This was probably a second, ironic question: 'What is there in your possession? Five loaves? Supply me.'

The holy bread

All that was available was the 'bread of the Presence'. Although this is mentioned several times in the Old Testament, its significance is never made clear. In Exodus 25:30 it is to be placed on the table continually (see also Exodus 35:13; 39:36; 40:23; 1 Kings 7:48). Leviticus 24:5–9 gives us a little more information without telling us why it was there. There were to be twelve loaves set out in two rows of six. They were to be made with the best flour. They were to be replaced with fresh ones every Sabbath. Only the priests could eat them and only in a holy place; they were the holiest of holy gifts and they represented a 'covenant for ever'. In Chronicles they are described as two rows of bread and their preparation is the task of the Levites (1 Chronicles 9:32 etc.). Perhaps they were reminders of the bread given to the Israelites in the wilderness and therefore a sign of his unfailing provision for them, but we cannot be sure. We have mentioned the idea of 'holiness' earlier. These loaves are holy, they are set apart for God and can be handled only by people similarly set apart. They could not be made available to David. How was it, then, that David did not die when he received the holy bread? Perhaps it was because he had been anointed as future king and had received the spirit of the Lord. Ritual purity was also important.

In spite of both custom and law, Ahimelek gave the loaves to David on condition that the men who were supposedly with him were ritually clean. Sexual activity was not morally wrong but did involve ritual uncleanness. Since Israel's battles were also the Lord's battles, it was necessary for the men to be ritually clean before engaging in them. Hence David's reply. The text speaks of their 'vessels' being clean. The word used has a very wide range of meaning. It may mean a vessel from which you drink, a weapon with which you fight or an instrument on which you play. Sometimes it almost corresponds to our word 'things'. It was used for David's bag in which he kept his pebbles and for the weapons which Jonathan's lad took home. Here it may mean weaponry as a whole. They had been especially careful about ritual cleanness since it was a special mission they were on. Even twelve loaves would not have been much for a company of soldiers, but it was plenty for David himself.

This is the story to which Jesus referred when he and the disciples were criticized for rubbing corn on the Sabbath day (Matthew 12:4). Necessity sometimes demands unusual, even unlawful, measures.

A PRAYER

Save us, Lord, from putting the letter before the spirit. Forgive both our white lies and our failure to see when need is more important than rules.

A SPY ABROAD

The first verse of this section introduces a note of suspense and danger into the narrative. It seems to have little to do with the story and brings with it all sorts of questions. Its implications will become clear only later. There just happened to be at Nob someone who not only knew David but also knew Saul's attitude to him. We shall have to wait a while before we learn the significance of this. All we're told about Doeg is that he was an Edomite and not an Israelite. The Edomites were supposedly descended from Esau and usually there was no love lost between Edom and Israel. However, this Edomite was a member of Saul's staff. What the chief of the king's shepherds was doing at Nob, we are not told; nor do we know why he was detained there or what detained him. Such information was not thought to be necessary to the story. All the writer wants to do is to build up the suspense. It was not Doeg's presence which made David move on, though it anticipates trouble later on. He had never intended to stay at Nob; he simply needed supplies for his journey.

Goliath's sword

David's excuse for being without a weapon is a lame one indeed (v. 8). Would a soldier like him, or indeed anyone from the court, venture out without a weapon however urgent the business was, especially if he had had time to muster a group of men to go with him, as David claimed? Surely he would also have collected his weapons if the royal commission was so important. Still, Ahimelek didn't see through it or, if he did, he didn't let on. There would be no store of weapons at the shrine but there was the sword which had belonged to Goliath. David had used that once before to kill the Philistine and cut off his head. We were told that Goliath's armour had been taken into David's tent but perhaps that did not include the sword. How it came to be at Nob and what it was doing there remains unknown. Perhaps it had been set up as a trophy of victory. Whether or not Ahimelek recognized David earlier, he certainly knew who his visitor was now, for he recalled the Goliath incident (v. 9). Fortunately—or was it the Lord's will?—David now found himself with food and weapons.

Among the Philistines

He was now able to continue his flight from Saul south-westwards. And where did he go? To a Philistine city of all places! (v. 10). He really was 'between the devil and the deep blue sea'. If he had stayed anywhere in Israel, Saul would have been able to find him. Among the Philistines he was a marked man. Perhaps he thought he would not be recognized there, or perhaps he thought that they would welcome a defector of such standing and a warrior with such a reputation. If these were his hopes he was sadly disappointed. He was recognized immediately and the Philistines recalled the victory songs which the women had sung about him. They even called him the king, although they knew he wasn't king yet. What they knew of him persuaded them that he would be. So he was not made very welcome at Gath. The risk involved in entertaining such a defector was too great.

To get away from there was now the problem. He did so by pretending to be mad (v. 13) and doing it sufficiently well to deceive Achish the king, who decided he had enough fools around him. So he managed to escape, but where to go next?

A REFLECTION

The stories of David can be looked at from two angles. On a purely human level chance plays a considerable part, as do the wit and cleverness of David. Behind that there is the divine will which ensures that all things move forward in such a way that God's will that David should be king will be fulfilled. This mixture of human effort and divine guidance is found in our own lives and it is often difficult to disentangle these two strands in our experience.

ON *the* RUN

The town of Adullam is listed in Joshua 12:15 as one of those captured by Joshua in the south of the country. It fell within the territory occupied by the tribe of Judah (Joshua 15:35). It was situated between Gath and Bethlehem, about fifteen miles north-east of Gath and twelve miles south-west of Bethlehem. The cave must have been somewhere near the town. It was in among the rolling hills which separate the mountains of Judah from the Philistine plain. In and around this area David spent much of the next year or more, hiding from Saul.

David's gang

Somehow David's family learned where he was—maybe someone in Adullam recognized him on one of his visits to the town itself. They went to join him in the cave (v. 2). It doesn't sound as though Jesse himself was with them; he was probably too old. What made the brothers join him? No doubt family loyalty played a part. Did they also remember his anointing? They would certainly remember his fight with Goliath. They probably recognized him as the future king and wanted to help him to achieve that. No doubt he was pleased to have their support.

The news of his presence there spread and there gathered to him all sorts of malcontents. They accepted him as their leader and he found himself no longer alone but with four hundred people under his control. The four hundred may be a round number, ten times forty, but it represents a considerable force. They became a strong and loyal band who supported him in his enterprises.

A thoughtful son

David now realized that his activities placed his mother and father in considerable danger. Saul knew where they lived and could put pressure on them to reveal David's whereabouts, or indeed hold them hostage. Responsibility for parents was recognized in the fifth commandment (Exodus 20:12). He therefore arranged for them to move to Moab, east of the Jordan beyond the Dead Sea. Moab was often at enmity with Israel, but somehow David gained access to the king— perhaps it wasn't as difficult as it has now become to speak directly to royalty—and persuaded him to accept his parents until such a time as his future became clearer.

On the move again

We must assume that among those who joined David was the prophet Gad, who was able to advise David both now and later. He was a most useful addition to the band. Gradually David was acquiring considerable resources. Gad, as God's spokesman, advised him to leave the cave and move into the forest nearby. It sounds like an early version of Robin Hood and later there was a certain amount of robbery of some to help others, though this was not the main aim of the band.

Back at the court

Meanwhile the writer takes us back to Saul's court in Gibeah. The tamarisk tree on the hilltop may have signified a sacred site. Saul seems to have been very fond of his spear, if only to throw it at those of whom he disapproved! (v. 6). Now it was his courtiers that he addressed and accused of collaboration with David. It is not absolutely clear whether it is bribery Saul is talking about or whether he is referring to their expectation of what they would receive if and when David became king. He certainly felt there was a conspiracy against him in which Jonathan was involved and that other members of the court were implicated too. There is almost a whining note to his speech: 'Is no one sorry for me?' Once jealousy takes hold, there is no end to the damage it may do. It impairs judgment and arouses suspicion even when there is no ground for it. Here, of course, there were some grounds, especially where Jonathan was concerned.

Doeg then appears again, back home from Nob, and now we can see why he was mentioned earlier in 21:7. Here he is described as in charge of Saul's servants and not as chief of his shepherds. He sought to prove his loyalty to Saul by telling him what had happened at Nob. He added one other bit of information that we had not heard of before. Ahimelek had actually 'consulted the Lord' on David's behalf, ready to pass on any advice from God to help him on his way.

A PRAYER

We thank you, Lord, that we can turn to you for help when we are in danger and for advice when we are in doubt. Teach us to put our trust in you always.

A KING OUT of CONTROL

Doeg's information was acted upon at once. Not only Ahimelek, but all the other priests from Nob, the whole priestly family, were summoned to appear before the king.

The questioning

Saul began with a command which already contained an element of threat: 'Now you listen to me.' Ahimelek's reply was not a statement of fact. Saul could see he was there! It was a cautious response, something like, 'Yes, master, I'm listening.' Saul was no longer able to stick to the facts of the case. His rage drove him on to make quite false accusations against David (v. 13). David had never 'risen against him', that is, tried to overthrow him. He certainly wasn't lying in wait for him. Just the opposite: he was trying to avoid pursuit by Saul. But this is what happens when people reach this state of jealousy and anger. False accusations come to the lips all too readily.

Ahimelek had two choices. He could have tried to humour Saul. He might have claimed that he hadn't recognized David. Or he might have said that he wasn't aware of David's intentions or the king's feelings and that, if he had been, he would have acted differently. That might just have got him off. Instead, he chose to be honest and straightforward, contradicting Saul's estimate of David. Far from rising against Saul he had been faithful. 'Quick to do your bidding' (v. 14) is an attempt to make sense of a difficult Hebrew phrase. It may mean 'captain of your bodyguard' (REB) but, if so, there is a play on words because the word for 'bodyguard' is derived from the verb meaning 'to hear, to be obedient'. The phrase would therefore again suggest David's loyalty. 'Honoured' means not only 'respected by others', but 'honourable'. Ahimelek gave David an excellent character reference and flatly contradicted Saul's accusations, rightly so. But, with Saul in his present mood it was a dangerous thing to do.

Ahimelek could hardly have inquired of God 'today'. Some time must have passed between David's visit to Nob and the priests' summons to court. The Hebrew translated 'the first time' may also mean 'to profane'. This explains the difference between NRSV and REB. 'On this occasion' is better than 'today'. The matter which he claims to know nothing about is Saul's pursuit of David with the intention of killing him. So he pleads not to be accused of wrong-doing.

The sentence

As far as Saul was concerned the accusation still stood. The priests had helped David get away and must die. But the sentence was not easily carried out. The servants refused to obey Saul's command (v. 17). This was not just because they thought it unfair. That would not have been a good enough reason for their refusal. Even Saul didn't turn on them in anger for refusing. The reasons went deeper. If it was dangerous to lay hands on a holy object such as the Ark (6:19 and 2 Samuel 6:6–7) it was at least equally dangerous to lay hands on a holy person such as a priest. He had been set aside to provide a link between the holy God and humanity and to make it possible for ordinary people to approach God. His position brought him into the realm of the holy. To kill a priest would therefore have been to bring death and destruction upon oneself. So the task was left to Doeg, a non-Israelite, and he was prepared to do it. We are not told that he suffered any ill effects. The picture of eighty priests submitting to death by one person is surprising. Maybe they were unable to run away, or were they just brave? The murder was followed up by the destruction of the town of Nob and everything in it.

The escape

One priest did escape. Abiathar fled and joined David (v. 20). Out of the evil something good had come, as far as David was concerned. He now had a priest with an ephod whom he could consult for advice. Nob served him very well. Not only did he have food and a weapon; he now had a priest to join his prophet and the rest of his band.

A PRAYER

Lord, give us courage to speak the truth even when to do so is costly. Remind us again of your ability to bring good out of evil.

STILL RUNNING

Exactly how David learned of the impending attack on Keilah we are not told. It was just four miles or so south of Adullam and was sufficiently close to Philistine territory to come under attack from them. They seem not to have been intent on occupying the town; it was more of a case of making raids to rob the townspeople of their grain. David's expedition to stop them was the first one undertaken by his men and they were afraid (v. 3). It is a little strange that they should say 'here in Judah' as though the defence of Keilah involved a journey outside Judah. It is highly unlikely that the city was thought to be outside Judah. Obviously it wasn't in Philistine hands and it would hardly be a fully independent town. However, they were afraid to venture out of hiding, even though the enterprise had the blessing of the Lord, and so they asked David to make sure he had heard correctly. Did David undertake this out of the goodness of his heart because he was sorry for the people of Keilah or had he also an ulterior motive? Did he want to get on good terms with Judeans so that they would welcome him as king eventually? We shall have to ask this sort of question again and again.

Where was Abiathar?

By what means David 'inquired of the Lord' we are not told. The usual way would be to consult a priest who would use an ephod, or the sacred lot which he kept in it, to determine the Lord's will. But David had no priest. It is true that Abiathar went to join him but, according to verse 6, he didn't reach David until after they had entered Keilah. However, the Hebrew of verse 6 is difficult. It would be a very unusual way of saying what both NRSV and REB say. It could just about mean something like, 'When Abiathar had fled to David he went down to Keilah carrying the ephod.' It could then be that the priest had joined David earlier, had helped him to decide to help the people of Keilah and then went there with David and the others, taking the ephod with him.

At any rate, David and his men beat off the Philistines and then settled there themselves! It couldn't have been much of an improvement for the people of Keilah. To have six hundred men suddenly added to the population with no obvious resources of their own to offer, other than their protection from the Philistines, could not have been easy. It was perhaps a case of 'out of the frying pan into the fire'. It soon becomes clear that they weren't overjoyed by it (v. 12).

The aborted attack

When Saul heard that David and his men were living in a walled and gated town, it was music to his ears. So long as David was out in the open country, moving about from place to place among the rolling hills of the region, it was very difficult to find him, let alone kill him. But if he was settled in a town which could be besieged, then Saul could cope with that sort of warfare.

There seems to have been a good supply of information in both directions. Saul had heard where David was and David heard that Saul was coming to attack him. How the information was carried is hard to say, but it must be remembered that we are not dealing with large distances. Gibeah and Keilah were only about twenty miles apart.

This time when David wished to consult the Lord he certainly was able to do so through Abiathar and his ephod. To his two questions he received a positive answer. Yes, Saul would come; yes, the lords of Keilah would hand David over to him. There was only one thing to do and that was to move on again. Once more Saul heard what was happening and called off the expedition. David and his men had now no fixed base. They just moved about in the area from one place to another.

A REFLECTION

If only we could always discover God's will as easily as this!
Sometimes when we ask for guidance we may feel sure that we
have received it, but at other times certainty is beyond us.
Then we have to trust that our own judgment has been reached
with God's help.

A LUCKY ESCAPE

The story of Saul's pursuit of David takes place in the area to the south of Judah known as the Negeb (pronounced Negev). It was ideal territory for a fugitive. It stretches roughly from Hebron in the north to the Egyptian border in the south and from the Dead Sea in the east to the Mediterranean in the west. In the north-east of the area are the Judean hills with steep valleys between them. Moving westward through the foothills, we come to the Philistine plain with its five cities. Among the hills and in the foothills where David moved, there were plenty of caves and good hiding-places. The NRSV calls them 'strongholds' but this suggests defended positions. 'Fastnesses' is perhaps a better word, places which were not easy to find and which provided shelter and security. To the south were large tracts of unin-habited territory but in the north, where David was, there were a number of towns and settlements where he may have been able to find provisions. Even so, six hundred men are not easy to hide—or to feed.

A friendly rendezvous

Horesh was one of these settlements. Since Ziph is more than twenty miles south of Gibeah and the territory between was not all that easily accessible, it is unlikely that Saul ventured so far south *every* day looking for David (v. 14). He may have been searching nearer home, of course, but the writer intends the reader to understand that Saul could not rest until he had found David and put him to death. Significantly, the writer claims that it was God who protected David. His purpose in anointing him king must be fulfilled.

Jonathan did make the journey to meet his friend, to tell him of Saul's intention and to encourage him (v. 16). Now he was quite open about the way he saw the future. We saw how the gift of his robe and his armour may have been a sign of his abdication in favour of David (8:4). Now he declared it openly. It is almost a John the Baptist recognition of the anointed one, to whom he must come second. Some people's role in life seems to be to prepare the way for others; it is no less honourable for that. Jonathan and David had already pledged themselves to each other; they did so again here.

The informers

Why the Ziphites took this action and were ready to betray David we cannot say (v. 19). It could have been because they were loyal to Saul, though generally the people of Judah seem to have sat loosely to his authority, if they acknowledged it at all. It could have been that they had some hopes of reward for handing over one who was regarded as a usurper of the throne. Or it could simply be that they found the presence of six hundred reprobates, who infringed their territory and demanded their supplies as a nuisance—the 'not in my back yard' syndrome! Whatever their motivation, they told Saul they were ready to hand over David to him.

Saul acknowledged David's cunning. Was he even suspicious of the Ziphites? Was this why he insisted that they should make sure of David's possible hide-outs?

A near thing

Presumably they took a second look, though we are not told that. Instead the story hurries on to tell of Saul's action. Apparently he was satisfied and set out after the returning Ziphites to find David. David retreated further south to 'the rock'. It sounds almost like a well-known place; rather, it became one later because of what happened here. Saul reached the valley next to the one where David was hiding and it seemed only a matter of time before he was tracked down and captured.

The Philistines came to his rescue, indirectly and unintentionally (v. 27). They made another of their attacks on Israel in some other part of the country. It meant that Saul had to abandon his pursuit of David and deal with it. Again, 'circumstances'—or was it the will of God?—saved David. The rock between the two valleys came to be known popularly as the 'Rock of Division' (NRSV footnote is better) because it kept the two parties apart for long enough for David to be spared.

From there David moved eastward to the caves near En-gedi on the shores of the Dead Sea. Here there would be fresh water and vegetation.

A REFLECTION

We degrade Providence too much by attributing our ideas to it out of annoyance at not being able to understand it.

Dostoevsky, *The Idiot*, 1868

42

An OPPORTUNITY REFUSED

Once the Philistine threat had been dealt with, Saul resumed his hunt for David. En-gedi (v. 1) was a spring on the western shore of the Dead Sea. The 'wilderness' would be the land to the west of this and leading to it. The number of men he took with him is quite extraordinary. Three thousand is three army units and they were picked troops. All this was to chase a fugitive who is said to have had only six hundred men and whose arms and supplies would be strictly limited. It is an indication of how seriously Saul took the threat to his throne. The Rocks of the Wild Goats (v. 2) were a well-known landmark in Old Testament times, now no longer known.

In the cave

What a coincidence that Saul should be taken short at that very spot and go into the very cave where David and his men were hiding! (v. 3). It was a large cave which extended a long way back. Saul stopped fairly near the entrance and did not notice the other occupants in the far recesses. It seems hardly likely that David had all six hundred men with him in this cave. Those who were with him would be his closest companions while the rest would be hidden elsewhere. To his companions this was a God-given opportunity to put an end to the constant pursuit. David, however, refused to make the most of it. They regarded it as the fulfilment of God's promise to David (v. 4). We have no record so far of any such promise in respect of Saul. David believed that it was the Lord who had given Goliath into his hands and similarly with the Philistines. It may be that there was a general promise that the Lord would deliver David's enemies into his hands. In fact, the written Hebrew text has the plural ('enemies') here, though when the rabbis read this passage they read the singular, so making it fit the occasion. So David's men quoted this promise to him as grounds for getting rid of Saul. This David refused. Instead he crept up behind Saul as he crouched down with his cloak spread out round him and cut off a corner of the cloak as evidence that he had had the opportunity to kill him if he had so wished. As soon as he had done it his conscience got the better of him and he wished that he hadn't.

Some scholars alter the order of the words here (so REB) so that David refused to kill Saul because he was the Lord's anointed but had no qualms about cutting off a corner of his cloak. There are no grounds for this except that it is thought to make better sense. It may well be that David regretted damaging the robe because it was a royal garment belonging to the chosen king.

The reason for David's regret was the fact that Saul was the Lord's anointed (v. 6). But was this any longer so? Remember, the Lord had taken his spirit away from Saul and given it to David and Samuel had anointed David king. Strictly speaking, then, David was now the Lord's anointed and not Saul. It would appear that David regarded Saul's anointing as remaining in force until his death and his own anointing as being something for the future, after Saul's death. If, therefore, Saul remained the legitimate king any attack on him would be an attack against God himself. Even damage to the royal cloak might be seen in this light.

If we were to take a more cynical view we could say that, although David knew he was now the Lord's anointed, he also knew that the people saw Saul as this and therefore any attack on him would be frowned upon by his subjects. If David were to kill the one whom they believed was the Lord's anointed they would be less willing to make him king and he would eventually need their support. We shall come across this ambiguity again later.

However, all this happened so quietly that Saul got up and went on his way oblivious of it.

A PRAYER

Lord, our motives are often mixed. We claim that we are doing your will but then our actions also serve our own purposes. We do not know which has priority. Help us always to put your will first.

RECONCILIATION?

The encounter between Saul and David is presented in legal terms, as a court case. David is the inferior party since it is a case against the king—*Rex v. David*, as we might say. So he made proper obeisance before Saul and even addressed him as father (v. 11). Saul was, of course, David's father-in-law but it is not the family relationship which is meant here. David simply recognized Saul as the one who was head of his people, just as a father was head of his family.

Self-defence

So David began by pleading his own case. He was innocent of any treachery and, as Exhibit A, he produced the corner of Saul's robe (v. 11). This was clear evidence that he had no desire to kill Saul, for he had had every opportunity to do so. If anyone had done wrong it was Saul, for he had hunted an innocent man. This raised the question of revenge but David would leave that to God. The second sentence in verse 12 means, 'The Lord may avenge me...but I will not...'. The old proverb which he quoted simply means, 'One wrong leads to another.' As we might put it, 'Two wrongs don't make a right.' Saul's wrong against David might have been expected to have evoked another wrong in response, but David would never allow this to happen. So Paul was not the first to make the point, 'Do not repay anyone evil for evil... never avenge yourselves but leave room for the wrath of God... "Vengeance is mine; I will repay," says the Lord' (Romans 12:17–19).

It was ludicrous to come and search for David with three thousand picked troops. After all, what was he? Not much more than a dead dog or a flea in comparison. A flea can be a nuisance but it doesn't need an army to get rid of it. Saul really was taking a sledgehammer to crack a nut.

So David would leave the matter with God the judge, from whom he expected a verdict of 'not guilty' (v. 15).

A startling response

Saul's response was remarkable. His reply shows the other side of his character, the good side which alternated so violently with the bad.

There is no need to think that Saul was insincere, even though the bad side would shortly return. He responded to David's address as 'Father' by addressing him as 'My son' (v. 16). A proper and healthy relationship was thereby restored with tears of remorse from Saul. 'Righteous' is sometimes a legal term meaning 'innocent'. In court in Old Testament times, a verdict of 'not guilty' would be expressed as 'Righteous is he'. Here it is, 'You are righteous, or innocent' and Saul is making not a comparison but a contrast. David was innocent; Saul was not. Saul had repaid David's service with evil; David had repaid Saul's threats with good. The contrast which Saul admitted is a sharp one. Saul's wish now was that God would repay David with good for sparing his life.

There then followed a surprising admission. Saul, at last, saw the truth and recognized that David was the one to succeed him as king, and not Jonathan (v. 20). He accepted the inevitable. All he could do was to ask that his descendants, including Jonathan and his family, would survive. Sometimes when a king who was of a different line came to the throne it was necessary to put to death the descendants of the late king in order to forestall any rebellion. If this happened then Saul's line would be wiped out and he himself would be forgotten. David agreed not to do this and was true to his promise (2 Samuel 9).

That this was a genuine response of Saul and not some kind of trick is shown by the fact that he now returned home. It would have been possible, with the men at his disposal, to have captured David who was clearly within earshot. He could have pretended to be sorry and then attacked him. Instead he went home and left David safe. David, however, was not foolhardy enough to disband his men and return to Saul's court. He had seen these changes of mood before and so he returned to his hide-out with his men.

A REFLECTION

In taking revenge, a man is but even with his enemy;
but in passing it over, he is superior.

Francis Bacon, *Essays*, 1625

An UNHELPFUL FOOL

Samuel's death and funeral are recorded here in the briefest of notices (v. 1). We might have expected more, but the narrator's interest has now moved on and is focused on David. Still, there is enough here to remind us how much Samuel had meant to Israel in his lifetime. He has not appeared at all since anointing the young David as king. He did not rebuke Saul for his treatment of David as he had done over other matters. Nor did he advise David in the difficulties which he faced. Perhaps he was just too old. It is dangerous to argue from silence. At his death there was a great assembly of people from all over Israel. Although it is not specifically stated, it looks likely that David was among them. The temporary truce with Saul would make it possible for him to join in the mourning, but afterwards he returned to his old haunts in the Negeb.

A fool and his wife

Amid all the drama of David's departure from court and his separation from Jonathan, so eloquently described in chapter 20, one thing is conspicuous by its absence. There is no mention of the fact that he was leaving behind his wife, Michal. She, too, had saved him from Saul's jealous anger. She and David were in love, we are told, but there was no mention of even a goodbye kiss. Again we must be careful not to draw hasty conclusions from the silence. There may well have been a farewell meeting which the narrator has not mentioned because all his interest was focused on Jonathan. Or it may be that the place of women was less important and the matter was thought not worth mentioning.

Be that as it may, in this present chapter David is introduced to another woman whom he is to marry. More than one wife was quite permissible. The woman's name was Abigail, which may mean 'My father is joy'. She was married to Nabal whose name means 'fool'. Their respective characters are described in verse 3.

Nabal was a sheep farmer of some substance and he grazed his sheep and goats in the somewhat barren area where David and his men lived (v. 2). In the rainy season there would be plenty of grass and vegetation even in this area which is described as a wilderness.

In the dry summer months it would be more difficult, but there was enough for the animals to survive. Nabal lived with his wife in Carmel. This town was mentioned earlier in 15:12, but it is perhaps worth repeating that this is not the Carmel range where Elijah confronted the prophets of Baal (1 Kings 18). It is a town a few miles west of the Dead Sea.

The outlaws and the shepherds

This is very much like a Western film script, except that it deals with sheep and not cattle. Nabal's shepherds had come into contact with David's men while they were out on the hills with the sheep. Far from stealing the sheep for food, the outlaws had protected them. Was this simply an act of kindness and generosity? Or was there an ulterior motive—by making friends with the shepherds they might be given sheep as a reward? (v. 8)

The time for sheep-shearing came round, when the sheep would be rounded up and brought to the farm. It was a festival time. Since sheep were sheared in the spring it could have been the feast of Unleavened Bread or even Passover, though, if so, we might have expected it to be mentioned by name. Clearly David now hoped to claim some reward and to be given some sheep to celebrate the feast with his men.

Wholly in character, Nabal refused (v. 10). Not only did he refuse but he did so in an insulting way and without any recognition of the service the outlaws had rendered him. He saw them just as outlaws, disgruntled and runaway slaves, and he couldn't see beyond the stereotype to what they were really like. How often is it the case that we treat people according to their dress, their colour, their nationality or their social class instead of looking for the real person and their true character? David's response was predictable. His anger was so great that he determined to destroy Nabal and his farm.

A PRAYER

Save us, Lord, from meanness of spirit which prevents us from treating people as we should. Help us to see beyond the stereotypes to what people really are, and respond to their need.

The FOOL'S WIFE

'Meanwhile, back at the ranch…'! One of the young shepherds told Abigail what had happened (v. 14) and she quickly set about putting things right. She was under no illusion about the danger that threatened, but it was no use talking to her husband. The shepherd had been right in saying that no one could speak to him about the affair. How she could assemble such an expedition without Nabal knowing anything about it is surprising. Perhaps he had shut himself away somewhere in a bad temper.

The meeting

The narrator draws a vivid picture of the two parties going to meet each other. Abigail set off with a large present (v. 18). David's men had not asked for a specific amount of supplies. They asked only for what he could give them. What Abigail could offer would not have gone far among six hundred men. Still, it was a generous present. She called it, literally, a 'blessing' in verse 27. A 'blessing' is usually something quite tangible, like this. Hidden from view by the hill, the servants went on ahead.

In the other direction came David and his men, intent on revenge for the sharp refusal of hospitality. We can almost hear him grumbling away to his men as they rode, and his threats were frightening, backed up by an oath. The Hebrew says that no one who 'urinates against a wall' will be spared (v. 22). The English translations need to find a euphemism!

As soon as she saw David and his men Abigail acted quickly. In its usual vivid way the Hebrew says she 'fell on her face before David's nose'. But it wasn't an accident! It was an act of deep respect. From the speech that follows, she appears to have known who David was and what he was destined to become.

A wife's plea

So throughout she used formal, courtly language, calling herself 'your maidservant' and calling David 'my lord'. She approached him with genuine humility. First she took upon herself responsibility for her husband's behaviour and begged David 'not to set his heart (or mind) on Nabal', that is, to take no notice of him. She hadn't much of an opinion of her husband. In fact, she calls him a 'son of Belial', a scoundrel, a term we have met before applied to the sons of Eli (2:12). Names were often thought to reflect character as, for instance, when Naomi, meaning 'pleasant', changed her name to Mara, meaning 'bitter', following the death of her husband and her sons (Ruth 1:20); or later when Jesus renamed Simon as Peter, the rock (Matthew 16:18). Nabal is the Hebrew word for 'fool' and Abigail makes great play on this. But *nabal* meant something different from what we mean by 'fool'. It refers to someone who is not only intellectually deficient, but morally deficient as well. We have no English word which corresponds exactly to this.

Verse 3 of this chapter says she was clever as well as beautiful and she showed this now by appealing to David's self-interest (v. 26). If he had killed Nabal and his family he would have started a blood feud and consequently any remaining relatives of Nabal would have been obliged to avenge his death by killing some of David's family. He wouldn't want that to happen, would he? The speech attributed to her then goes on to use language which later became familar when speaking about David's dynasty (see 2 Samuel 7:13 and Psalm 89:19–37). The phrase 'bound in the bundle of life' is a striking one. The verb 'to bind' means to store up something for safety. The word 'bundle' comes from the same verb and sometimes means a pouch or purse for storing precious things. REB's 'will wrap your life up and put it with his own treasure' is a rather free translation but it conveys the right idea. On the contrary, his enemies' lives were like stones thrown from a sling, like the stones David had slung at Goliath. Finally Abigail referred to his coming kingship, though she avoided using the term 'king' and preferred 'prince' or 'ruler'.

David's reply is predictable, thanking God for the good sense which prevented him from carrying out his threat. So he sent her home in peace (v. 35).

A PRAYER

Give us, Lord, the wisdom to defuse awkward situations and the strength of will to carry out your orders.

The OUTLAW GETS *the* GIRL

So far this has been an interesting story but the reason for its inclusion in the book has not been clear. Now it becomes clear.

A fortunate death

Nabal seems to have recovered from any bad temper he may have been in. Maybe he was pleased with himself for getting rid of the outlaws so quickly. Now he gave a right royal feast (v. 36). The wine flowed freely and he got well and truly drunk. It was no use Abigail trying to tell him that it was she who had made sure the outlaws didn't return to take their revenge. That had to wait until the morning after, when he had sobered up. When she did tell him he collapsed as a result of the shock on top of the heavy drinking. We may wonder how he could live for ten days with a dead heart (v. 37). It can be expressed like this because here the word 'heart' doesn't refer to the organ of the body. It really means his mind and his will. In Old Testament usage the heart is that part of a person which receives and stores information—the mind—and then prompts action on the basis of what it has received—the will. So what died in Nabal was the capacity to think and act. He had a heart attack or a stroke which left him in a coma and from which he died ten days later.

To have said that the Lord 'took' him would have been quite natural, for all events were seen ultimately to be due to God. 'The Lord gave, the Lord has taken away' (Job 1:21). But here it says the Lord 'struck' him, which means that Nabal's death was a punishment from God for his behaviour (v. 38). With this we may feel a little uneasy, especially for what does not seem to us to have been a particularly serious offence. Our view of God as love seems to contradict such ideas. The people of the Old Testament believed strongly in the love of God, but they also held firmly to the belief that God was just. It is not always easy to keep a balance between justice and love but both belong to God.

David's response

David's response when he heard the news expresses very clearly this notion of the justice of God. Later in his life he would have to learn about and depend upon the love of God and his readiness to forgive even more serious crimes than this (2 Samuel 12). He had a liking for beautiful women and the haste with which he pursued Abigail is almost indecent. Almost before her husband was buried he sent and 'spoke to Abigail with a view to taking her as his wife' (v. 39).

Her acceptance is just as quick, but we cannot be sure that this was because she was attracted to him or loved him. It may simply have been because it would be unusual for a woman to refuse. Or she may have recalled what happened to her husband for refusing David's request. She was clever as well as beautiful! She accepted with what seems like exaggerated humility. You can't get much lower than offering to wash servants' feet. Again we must remember that she believed David was destined to become ruler over Israel (v. 41).

David, of course, was already married, but that was no obstacle to taking another wife. After all, his son would have seven hundred! Moreover, Michal, whom he had left with her father, had been given to someone else in David's absence. So the situation was complicated. Abigail joined him in his hideout and remained with him and his men.

Of his second wife, Ahinoam, we know nothing more than we are told here (v. 43). This Jezreel from which she came was not the plain in central Palestine. It was a city in the same hill-country of Judah, captured by Joshua along with Maon, Carmel and Ziph (Joshua 15:55). Behind this brief statement there is almost certainly another story which is not told to us. Perhaps, but only perhaps, it was a similar one to this. We shall never know. The two women remained with David. Ahinoam eventually bore his first child and Abigail his second (2 Samuel 3:2).

A PRAYER

*Help us, Lord, to remember your justice as well as your love
and to rejoice in both.*

The KING SPARED AGAIN

If some of this chapter sounds familiar it is not surprising, for it repeats many of the things that were said in chapters 23 and 24. The Ziphites had already given Saul this information in 23:19 and he had acted upon it. He had taken his three thousand picked troops against David in 24:2 for the same purpose. It is possible, of course, that these things happened twice on separate occasions, but we must reckon with the possibility that, at one time, many stories about David's flight from Saul were in circulation and that some of them took similar forms. When the writer of Samuel and Kings came to set down his account of this period he simply used the stories as he had heard them. We must, however, credit him with sufficient intelligence and story-writing skill to be able to put them together into a continuous story which was consistent and credible to him and his readers. Our task is to read them from that point of view, as they now stand.

The expedition sets out

Saul's attitude to David had now changed again. The truce which had been called at the end of chapter 24 was now being broken again. There is no indication of the cause of that change, unless it was the renewed claim by the Ziphites that they knew where David was hiding (v. 1). Earlier they had been sent back to make sure of their facts. Perhaps they were unaware that Saul had acted on their information at once and so they now returned with confirmation of it. Therefore Saul set out again with his army. This time he had with him the commander of his army, Abner, who had introduced David to Saul after the defeat of Goliath (17:57) and who had sat at table with Saul and Jonathan when David went missing (20:25). He pitched camp in the area where David was said to be (v. 3). Again news travelled fast! David learned of his arrival and sent out his scouts to discover the disposition of Saul and his men. Saul should have been safe within the circle of troops.

Another opportunity

Who were these people with David? One was called Ahimelech (v. 6), like the priest at Nob whom Saul had put to death. This one is called a Hittite. It can be a misleading term. Earlier there had been a great Hittite empire based on Asia Minor, but that is not the ethnic group meant here. These Hittites were a part of the original Canaanite population of the area in southern Judah. They are often listed alongside others such as the Perizzites, the Hivites and the Jebusites. Ahimelech must have joined David either at Adullam or later. According to 1 Chronicles 2:16, Zeruiah was David's sister and in that case Joab and Abishai were his nephews. We shall hear a lot more about Joab later on.

Discipline cannot have been very good in Saul's army. If he and Abner had set guards they must have fallen asleep (v. 7). Without undue difficulty David and Abishai got through the lines and reached Saul himself so that they were able to steal his spear, presumably the one he had thrown at David and Jonathan, and his water jar. As in chapter 24, it would have been easy to kill him, as Abishai intended. He'd make sure he killed him first time (v. 8)! For the same reasons as before, David refused. Either God would strike Saul as he had struck Nabal, or he would die a natural death, or he would be killed in battle, as he eventually was. It was for God to decide. The familiar questions may be asked again. Did David regard Saul as legitimate king until his death from whatever cause? Or was he safeguarding his own position among the people who did regard Saul as the anointed king and over whom he himself would one day have to rule?

Now at the end of the passage we learn how it was that David and Abishai could get through the lines of troops. The Lord had made them all sleep so heavily (v. 12)! For the writer, God really was on David's side and would see to it that he became king as he had been anointed to be, so long ago.

A QUESTION

Can we always distinguish between God's will, our own desires and mere concidence? How?

MORE FOOLS

What a wonderful story this is! David made the commander-in-chief of Saul's army look a complete idiot in front of his own men. One of the differences between this story and the one in chapter 24 is that this time Abner was with Saul. The king should therefore have been perfectly safe. Since David had got close to Saul before, Abner, knowing that David and his men were in the area, should have made absolutely sure that it couldn't happen again. Instead security had broken down and Abner was largely to blame. David picked him out therefore for ridicule. Even when David called to him the penny did not drop. He didn't even recognize David's voice, though Saul did. Nor was he aware that anything had happened in the night. David's question was a rhetorical one: 'You're a man, aren't you? You're supposed to be the best in Israel.' You can hear the sarcasm in David's voice. Then he got serious and started to tell Abner what had happened. For such careless incompetence he ought to be put to death.

David's defence

Saul, as we have seen, did recognize David's voice (v. 17). As before, he addressed David as his son, whether sincerely or not we cannot yet say. Presumably he had missed his spear and water jar by now and David had drawn attention to their absence. His questioning of Saul's motive for seeking his life goes further than before. He not only draws attention to the fact that he had spared Saul's life and so could not be accused of treachery. Could it be that the Lord was encouraging Saul in his quest? If so, David would be quite prepared to make reparation to God. But it could be humans who were encouraging Saul. Who does David have in mind? Was it opponents at court? Or was it perhaps the people of Ziph who had betrayed his whereabouts? Anyway, the consequences were that David now had to live as an outlaw. The 'inheritance of the Lord' is often the promised land. As an outlaw, David could not claim his rightful share in it. Moreover, since he had no place in the Lord's land he could be compelled to acknowledge the gods of other lands, since foreigners were expected to worship the gods of the land where they settled. His plea was that he should not be killed outside the land where the Lord was to be found.

The question of where the Lord could be met and worshipped became quite an important issue. In the days of the patriarchs and of Moses, the Lord had travelled with his people wherever they went. As they settled in the promised land the Lord became 'settled' with them and his presence was more static. For those responsible for the book of Deuteronomy, the presence was further limited. The only place where the Lord could be worshipped was at the central sanctuary and this became identified with Jerusalem and the temple there. When the exiles were carried into Babylon they wondered, 'How can we sing the Lord's song in a strange land?' (Psalm 137:4). David's speech here reflects that view. It needed Ezekiel, among others, to show that the Lord related not to any particular place but to people wherever they were.

Sorry again

Saul didn't answer David's deeper questions. He limited himself to a promise not to harm David because David had spared him (v. 21). Though he calls himself a fool, he doesn't use the word *nabal*, which implied moral deficiency, but a fairly rare word which suggests lack of intelligence or sense. His confession, however, was simply that he had erred or made a mistake. There is no mention of the Lord and no admission of sin against him. Nor is there any oath to support the promise not to interfere again. It is altogether less fulsome than was the case in chapter 24.

Perhaps David was aware of his half-heartedness, for, although he allowed Saul to recover his spear, he did not ask him for safety. Rather he prayed that the Lord would keep him safe because, rightly, he had refused to harm the Lord's anointed (v. 24).

Still, Saul's blessing of David made no mention of the Lord. He did, however, realize that David would have great success.

A PRAYER

Lord, help us to be generous in offering forgiveness and wise enough to know when confessions are genuine.

A DOUBLE LIFE

To continue to live in caves in the Negeb was no longer a realistic option for David and his men. Sooner or later Saul would find them and that would be an end of David. But the alternatives were very limited. In fact the only way was to get out of Israelite territory altogether and that really meant going to live among the Philistines.

The defecter

It cannot have been an easy decision. David had spent some time quite recently fighting against the Philistines. He had defeated their champion in single combat (ch. 17) and then gone on to kill 'thousands' (18:7). It must surely have gone against the grain to seek protection from them now. Nor was he likely to be welcomed by them without a great deal of suspicion. On the other hand, if he could find shelter there he would be safe from Saul because Saul would not dare to seek him there. So the decision was taken. He 'went over' (v. 2). Probably this is meant literally; he went over the generally accepted border between Israel and Philistia. There were no Customs to go through and no official frontiers such as we now have between countries, but the territories would be roughly defined. 'Went over' also suggests defection to the Philistines, Israel's sworn enemy. His reception could not be guaranteed, but it seems to have been cordial enough. It was a sizeable company of people he brought with him—six hundred men and their families. They wouldn't be easily absorbed into the population of Gath.

The site of Gath is not known for certain. It was probably the Philistine city nearest to Judah. Each city had its own king. In spite of any difficulties, David and his company were allowed to stay there for some time and David was safe.

A town of his own

Perhaps conscious of the strain he was putting on Gath, but also perhaps with an eye to gaining a degree of independence, David asked to be allowed to move from Gath to one of the dependent towns. The appeal is couched in appropriate court language (v. 5). Achish, apparently convinced of David's loyalty by now, gave him the town of

Ziklag. Again, the exact location is not known but it must have been fairly near Gath. One possible location is about fifteen miles south-south-east of Gath and west of the area where David had previously been hiding. What the existing population thought of this influx of foreigners we are not told. Perhaps the town was sparsely populated. Anyway, David was made governor of the town, responsible to the overlord, Achish of Gath. His occupation of Ziklag meant that eventually it became a town belonging to Judah and it remained so down to the writer's own day in the sixth century BC (v. 6).

We have not been told how long David spent in the Negeb fleeing from Saul but we are now informed that he lived in Ziklag for a year and four months, until he became king of Judah at Hebron.

David had already helped various peoples who lived in this general area. He had defended Keilah from the Philistines (23:1–6); he had protected Nabal's shepherds (25:2–13), building up goodwill for himself. Now he had another opportunity. The people he raided all bordered on Judah in the south (v. 8). The Amalekites had already proved themselves a nuisance and had been defeated by Saul in this same area (ch. 15). They, along with the others, remained a constant threat to those who lived in Judah. David's raids upon them were therefore meant to protect the Judeans, hoping, no doubt, that it would stand him in good stead later. Of course he could not report this to Achish. Instead he claimed to have raided Judah itself and those people who lived within its borders (v. 10). It was a dangerous game and in order to safeguard himself it was necessary to make sure no one was left alive to tell the tale. What is recorded here is just a sample of his activity during this period of over a year. His double game worked. David was not averse to telling lies or behaving badly to further his own cause—or was it God's cause? Such behaviour raises a serious ethical question for us. In wartime we may feel it perfectly right to deceive the enemy for the good of the cause in which we believe. Was David's case any different? However, the question remains.

A QUESTION *to* PONDER

Do the ends always justify the means?

DANGER AHEAD

It was almost inevitable. The Philistines and Israel were almost certain to be at war again soon. The Philistines still had the idea that they should occupy the whole land, while Israelites believed the land was theirs, given to them by God as a possession for ever.

Preparations for war

None of the battles so far had been decisive enough to settle the issue. Both sides could claim victory in battle but the war was not over. Now another Philistine attack was being prepared and this time David was on the wrong side (v. 1). Achish, his overlord, first reminded David where his loyalties now lay. David's reply was scarcely wholehearted in its support. It was enough to persuade Achish of his loyalty, but it avoided an outright commitment to the Philistine cause: 'You will know what I can do' is at best ambiguous (v. 2). Achish took it as a positive reply and gave David's men a special place as his bodyguard. This might be seen as an honour, but was there still a hint of suspicion? As the royal bodyguard, David's men would be close to the king where they could be watched closely. It was a dangerous situation for David for he could find himself fighting against Israel and that wouldn't do his cause much good in the long run. However, the writer keeps us in suspense while he tells us something about Saul's preparation.

Advice needed

First he reminds us that Samuel was dead (v. 3). Although we've been told this before, it now has special significance. In spite of all the differences between them Saul could have turned to Samuel for advice if he'd been alive. Now he could no longer do that.

The two armies were drawn up in the usual way, facing each other in the northern part of Ephraimite territory, some forty miles from Ziklag as the crow flies. The Philistine army would be made up of soldiers from the five cities and it would appear that in these initial stages Achish's contingent had not yet reached them. Even so, it was a strong enough force to give Saul serious thought. He had once before gone into battle without waiting for Samuel to offer sacrifice

(13:8). What he would have given now for some advice from Samuel! He still had the usual methods for determining God's will. Dreams were often thought to contain messages, but not this time. We've described the use of Urim and Thummim before, the sacred lot operated by a priest. We are not sure who Saul's priest was. He had put to death Ahimelech and those with him at Nob. Abiathar had escaped and gone with David taking the ephod. There must have been some other at court, for Saul used the sacred lot, but it gave him no definitive answer (v. 6). Samuel had functioned as a prophet as well as a priest, but was no longer available. Those Saul had met earlier (10:10ff; 19:20ff) were presumably still around. In neither of their earlier appearances did they give any advice and they were not able to do so now.

An alternative would have been to consult a medium or a wizard, though this was forbidden (Exodus 22:18; Deuteronomy 18:10–11). In any case Saul himself had made as sure as possible that none were left in the land (v. 3). He was therefore on his own and he had to face the terrifying question of whether or not to engage the formidable Philistine force in battle. In despair he did the unthinkable. He decided to see if a medium could be found who could put him in touch with the dead Samuel (see v. 11). His servants found one at Endor, not far from the battlefield, and reported to Saul.

In spite of all his faults, Saul deserves some sympathy. He cuts a lonely, sad, confused and dejected figure, lacking any useful assistance in his task. Through his own folly he had cut himself off from all who could help him, and even from the Lord himself.

A **PRAYER**

Lord, there are times when we cut ourselves off from others and even from you. Then, in a crisis, we realize our need of help. Do not turn away from us, but, for Jesus' sake, come to our aid.

The KING & *the* WITCH

This story is unique in the Old Testament. Nowhere else is there an instance in which the dead are consulted about life on earth. It warns any who may still be tempted to try it that it is not only wrong; it is useless.

A story of the supernatural

As with all such stories, we need to use our imaginations. All is dark and three men, roughly dressed, call at the woman's house in secret. The leader has to be careful how he broaches the subject of their visit, so he whispers that he wants her to consult a 'ghost' for him, a figure from the past. Equally cautiously, she reminds him that the king has removed all mediums from the land. (We have heard nothing of this earlier.) So she implies she isn't one. It sounds like a trap and she isn't going to be caught in it. To persuade her, the visitor swears by the Lord that she will not be punished. Not knowing who it is, she takes him to mean that the whole thing will be kept strictly secret. Reassured by the strength of the oath, she agrees. But who does he want to consult? 'Samuel.' So she goes into a trance and sees Samuel. As soon as she does so, the penny drops. 'You're Saul!' she shrieks, now in a panic. Saul manages to calm her and asks what she sees. She looks again and says… What does she say? The word she uses is the common word for God or a god (v. 13). Whatever she actually meant, the use of that word was disturbing indeed. 'What does he look like?' asks Saul and she describes a figure which he recognizes as Samuel, whereupon he throws himself on the ground.

The ghost of Samuel is not best pleased to be disturbed. It should not happen (v. 15). 'There are extenuating circumstances,' says Saul, and goes on to describe the dilemma he's in. He's had no satisfactory advice. But why ask a prophet, if God has turned away? There's nothing a prophet can do about it, dead or alive. In any case, he already knew the answer because Samuel had already told him when he was alive (15:28). There's nothing more to be said than was said then. So the whole exercise was a waste of time for everyone.

Saul, however, is reduced to a shivering wreck and falls on the floor in terror. The woman tries to help him, offering him food, which he refuses. Eventually they get him up off the floor on to a bed and persuade him to have something to eat. She's very good to him, killing the fatted calf, kept for special occasions. On this occasion it is not for rejoicing, but to tempt him to eat. Next day, when darkness falls again, he and his servants go back to the camp, no wiser, except that the outcome of the battle which Saul must now fight is assured, as it always has been if only he'd listened.

The dead

The story needs to be read against the background of Israelite belief about the dead. Among Israel's neighbours the dead were thought to have an influence on the living. By contrast, in Israel, the dead were thought to go to Sheol. This was a place of pitch darkness (Job 10:21) and there was no return from it (Job 7:10; Psalm 49:15). Although they continued to exist, the 'shades' were unable to praise God (Psalms 6:5; 88:12); they were motionless (Psalm 31:18) and they did not know what was going on on earth (Job 14:21). This existence could hardly be called life, for the spirit or breath which gave life (Genesis 2:7) was removed (Psalm 104:29). In this state they were to be allowed to remain undisturbed (1 Samuel 28:15).

Consequently, consultation of the dead, called necromancy, was strictly forbidden in the laws (Leviticus 19:31; 20:6, Deuteronomy 18:11) and those who practised it were to be put to death (Leviticus 20:27). The prophets also forbade it (Isaiah 8:19). In Leviticus 19:31 it is one of a group of laws which are followed by the affirmation 'I am the Lord', as though the practice of necromancy was, in some way, denial of the Lord. The fact that the prohibition had to be repeated again and again means it was a practice which died hard.

The laws as we now have them were codified and committed to writing later than the time of Saul, but it is clear that even in his day the same prohibition was known and he knew he was wrong to try to call up Samuel to help him. So he went in disguise, all to no avail.

A REFLECTION

If God won't help us, who can?

LUCKY *for* DAVID

At the beginning of the last chapter a Philistine force was drawn up against Saul and the Israelites near the hill of Gilboa. This was probably an advance unit. Now the Philistines mustered their main force at Aphek. There are several different places called Aphek. This one was situated in the valley of Sharon, some forty miles south-west of Gilboa. It lay in the northern fringes of Philistine territory and was a good place for the armies from the various cities to assemble. From there they could then march into Israel. So division upon division came there.

Suspicions aroused

Among the last to arrive was the army of Achish, king of Gath, which included David and his men. The sight of Hebrews, distinguishable by their looks and their armour, surprised the other Philistine commanders (v. 3). They were even more surprised and suspicious when Achish told them who they were. Achish himself, totally unaware of the game that David had been playing in the Negeb (27:8–12), regarded him as trustworthy enough. The others were not prepared to take the risk. They knew of David's reputation against other Philistine forces and realized that it would be possible for him to upset all their plans by turning against them at the critical moment. It would be a way of getting back into Saul's favour. Whether David ever entertained such an idea we cannot know, but it certainly was not impossible.

Unless he had some such idea in mind he was in a very awkward situation. He could scarcely refuse to go with Achish, for to have done so would have been to jeopardize his position in the area close to Judah and to risk being killed by Achish as a traitor. On the other hand, if he went to fight on the Philistine side against the Israelites, that would jeopardize his chances of becoming king on Saul's death, as his anointing by Samuel promised. Or was he perhaps just going along with events, hoping, like Mr Micawber in Dickens' *David Copperfield*, that something would turn up? All we can do is to bear in mind the various possible attitudes he may have taken.

Help rejected

The commanders ordered Achish to send David and his men back to Ziklag and he had no option but to obey (v. 4). Assuring him of his confidence in him, Achish asked him to go quietly without making a fuss, which could have been awkward for both of them (v. 7).

David's response must have been made with his fingers crossed. He doesn't actually tell a lie, but his questions give the quite wrong impression that he had done nothing disloyal, in spite of what we have heard about his exploits in the Negeb. To call Achish 'my lord the king' and to refer to Israelites as enemies (v. 8), while strictly accurate, sounds all wrong on the lips of one who is destined to become king of Israel.

What does all this say about the character of David? The writer presents him as a very human figure with the strengths and weaknesses of our human life. Then he leaves us to draw our own conclusions. We may envisage David as a clever, scheming individual, intent on achieving his goal of becoming king of Israel. Or we may think of him as one of those lucky people who always seem to come well out of awkward scrapes. Or we may see all his affairs as in the hand of God who has chosen him for kingship and who takes him step by step along the road which leads there. Perhaps for the writer, as for us, it was unnecessary to keep all these three things apart. People whom God calls must use every effort to become what they are called to be. They must take advantage of any fortunate opportunity that comes along. They must be grateful to God that, through thick and thin, through human success and failure, he is able to accomplish his purpose.

A PRAYER

Help us, Lord, as we seek to fulfil your purpose for our lives. Use our best efforts, and our failures, as we try to do your will. Make us into the people you want us to be.

MORE DANGER AHEAD

David's troubles were by no means over. The road to the kingship was full of obstacles which had to be overcome in one way or another.

A cowardly attack

It took David three days to get home again from Aphek and a dreadful situation greeted him. Taking advantage of the absence of the Philistine armies in the area, some Amalekites attacked various settlements in the Negeb, including southern Judah and also the town of Ziklag (v. 1). When David and his men went off to war it had been left virtually unprotected and so the Amalekites had little difficulty in overcoming any remaining resistance. The destruction of the town by fire was bad enough, but, worse still, they carried off women and children, no doubt to be used or sold as slaves.

When David and his men returned they were devastated. We have seen pictures of people in that part of the world mourning, weeping and wailing, covering their faces and prostrating themselves and so perhaps we can imagine what it looked and sounded like. David was not immune. He had lost his two wives.

Events then followed what is a fairly common pattern. When they could weep no more the mourning turned to anger, and then the anger demanded that they should find someone to blame. And who should it be but David? David was held responsible for the tragedy because he was in charge of the town. Even the men who had followed him so faithfully for so many months now turned against him and threatened to stone him to death. Their anger is understandable. They had been on the march for a week, all for nothing, and they had arrived home tired and looking forward to being with their families and friends again, only to find that they were not there to welcome them. It looked bad for David and desperate times call for desperate measures.

The pursuit is on

There was only one to whom David could turn, not exactly as a last resort, but certainly in a time of extreme danger and sorrow. He 'strengthened himself in the Lord' (v. 6). In 4:9 the same word is translated 'take courage'. Only the Lord could now give him courage to face the challenge of the future. He couldn't pull himself up by his own bootstraps, but only by turning to God.

Using the priestly ephod carried or worn by Abiathar, he sought guidance from the Lord as to whether he should pursue the Amalekites. He didn't just hurry off on his own accord; he made sure that it was what God wanted him to do. He received confirmation that he was to go after the Amalekites and retrieve the women and children they had taken. Surprisingly, the men who had wanted to stone him were now ready once again to follow him. The thought of recovering what they had lost overcame their anger with him (v. 9).

After twenty miles or so, some were too exhausted to go any further and so they were left behind with some of the equipment. The remaining four hundred pressed on.

The abandoned Egyptian

They were in wide open country and it would be difficult to follow the tracks the Amalekites had left. Then, as luck would have it, some of David's men came across a solitary young man, almost at the end of his tether. He was an Egyptian (v. 11), probably a slave who had been taken by an Amalekite in a previous raid on an Egyptian caravan. When he had eaten, he came round sufficiently to tell them they were heading in the right direction. He had been with his master on the raiding party. David's attitude was quite gentle. He didn't order him, but asked him politely where the rest where. Needing assurances that he would not be killed or sent back into slavery, he agreed to take them to the Amalekite camp (v. 15). We hear no more of him.

Totally unaware, the Amalekites were having a party to celebrate. From dawn till dusk David attacked them. Four hundred Amalekites escaped on camels—it must have been quite a sight! David was able to recover everything that had been taken from Ziklag, including his own two wives, and a great deal of other spoil. It saved the day as far as David was concerned, for instead of wanting to stone him they now celebrated his achievement with, 'This is David's spoil' (v. 20).

A PRAYER

Save us, Lord, from the temptation to blame others too readily.

EQUAL PAY

The men who had been left behind, looking after the equipment, had no doubt been watching anxiously for David's return. There was no need to ask about the outcome of the expedition, for they would see approaching not only their fellow soldiers, but their wives and children and all the animals and other things taken as spoil. It must have been a welcome sight. Eagerly they went to meet them (v. 21).

Fair's fair

It was David, however, who was concerned about them. He 'saluted' them is not really an adequate translation. He wanted to know how they had been getting on. Before they could reply, those with David answered by making their own demands. They had always been a bunch of malcontents, people in debt, runaway slaves, outcasts (22:1–2). But they had now been with David for some time and had become more disciplined. Even so, a short time before this they were still prepared to stone David when things went wrong (30:6). It is not surprising, therefore, that we read of rogues and scoundrels among them (v. 22).

Before we condemn them too harshly, however, we should think again about their demands. All they wanted was 'danger money'. After all, they had done nearly all the work. They'd gone the extra distance which the two hundred couldn't face. They'd been in a battle lasting a whole day or more. We have not been told how many were killed in the fighting, nor of the wounded now returning. It is scarcely credible that there had been no casualties in such a battle, even though the Amalekites were taken unawares. Surely such people were entitled to extra reward. They were quite happy for the others to have their own wives and children, of course, but as far as the material taken as spoil was concerned they justifiably felt that they should have more than those who had waited in safety. That was only fair, wasn't it? Pay should depend on the amount of work done and on the risk involved in it. In our modern society it would be hard to argue against that principle.

David would have none of it. 'You shall not…' (v. 23) is exactly the same form of speech as is used in the ten commandments. It is a strong prohibition: 'You must not...' Why? Because the victory and the spoil were due not to their own skill and bravery; they were a gift from the Lord. When David had asked whether they should go after the Amalekites, the Lord had said 'yes'. This was the Lord's will and the victory was due to him. He had kept them safe; he had given them the spoil. It was not earned, it was a gift, and a gift should be shared, irrespective of what was deserved. Those who had remained with the supplies had done their job. They had all shared in the same enterprise.

It would not be right to elevate this into a principle binding on modern society. It applies specifically to those enterprises which are undertaken in response to God's demand. We are reminded of the story in the gospel of the employer who paid the same wages to all, no matter how long or short a time they had been working (Matthew 20:1–16). Here also the idea is that any reward from God for work done at his bidding is divided equally. It is little wonder that the early Christians had all things in common (Acts 2:44). They were all engaged in a common enterprise—the spread of the Good News—and all were to share equally in any rewards.

For the writer of 1 Samuel it was obviously an important matter. The incident marked the beginning of a principle which applied throughout the whole period of the monarchy in Israel and Judah (v. 25). It was not always followed and the prophets had to reassert it by calling upon the rich to share with the poor and threatening retribution if they did not. Among the people of God, God's gifts must be shared equally.

Wider distribution

The spoil must have been an enormous amount! Part was shared among David's group and part was given to no less than twelve settlements in the area in which David had roamed. This was not only a reward; it would also be a 'sweetener' to prepare the way for David later.

A REFLECTION

How far do God's people today share God's gifts equally?
What would it mean for us and our churches if we did?

TRAGEDY STRIKES

So, after a few interruptions, the writer now comes to the battle of Gilboa itself. It is a major battle between the combined forces of the Philistines and the Israelites. Yet in one sentence he says all he is going to say about it. We might have expected some description of the fighting. Who took the initiative? How fierce was the fighting? Did the Philistines have much superior armour? Were there more of them? How many perished in the first action? Or did the Israelites run away without a fight? All we are told is that 'the Philistines fought' and 'the men of Israel fled' (v. 1). Obviously it is not the battle itself which interests the writer and prompts him to write; it is the consequence of it which is the point of the story.

Royal deaths

We are now approaching the first great climax in this story of Israel. Ever since chapter 16, events have been moving steadily towards this moment, for Saul's death will now make it possible for David to become king. Not only was Saul wounded in the battle, but three of his sons were killed outright, including Jonathan. Since Saul was the first king of Israel there was no tradition about the succession. On the basis of what happened elsewhere, the eldest son would be expected to succeed. In what order Saul's sons were born we do not know. Only Jonathan has been mentioned and Saul regarded him as the natural successor (20:31). Now he was dead too (v. 2).

The picture of Saul is pitiful. With his three sons dead, he was still pursued by the enemy. Their archers came within range and shot him. Though he did not die at once, flight was now impossible and the end couldn't be far away. The swordsmen would soon come and finish him off. Before doing so they would taunt him and make fun of him, humiliating him more than he could bear. So he sought an 'assisted suicide'. To kill the king, even at his command, was something his armour bearer was unwilling to do. In certain circumstances killing was allowed and legitimate. The death penalty for crime was not forbidden by the sixth commandment, nor was revenge taken in a blood feud. But what the young man was asked to do could be regarded as murder, a breach of the commandment. It could even begin a blood feud. More than all this, Saul was the king, anointed by the Lord, and even David had felt unable to take his life when he had the opportunity. So the armour bearer refused (v. 4).

This left Saul with no alternative. Since in Israel it was believed that only God could give and take away life, suicide was not an option, although in fact there was no law which specifically forbade it. This, however, was an extreme situation. Death by his own hand was preferable to death by a Philistine. So he 'fell on his sword'. Either for fear or from sympathy, his armour bearer followed suit.

Those people who lived in towns in the Jezreel valley and in the Jordan valley nearby became refugees, as the Philistines occupied their lands (v. 7). Strategically, the Galilean area was now effectively cut off from the central Ephraimite area and from Judah, and the main trade routes through Israel were in Philistine hands.

Nevertheless, the road to kingship was now opening up for David and it is this, rather than the political and economic situation, which will be the focus of the story for some time.

A **PRAYER**

Bless, O Lord, those whose lives have become unbearable, through pain and weakness. Be merciful to them and give them courage to face whatever lies ahead.

56

A Last Act of Kindness

The day after the battle and the flight, the Philistines visited the field again to collect the spoils, the armour and anything else of value left by the Israelites. They came across the bodies of Saul and his sons (v. 8).

A final indignity

The treatment of dead bodies is still important. Different peoples have different ways of dealing with them properly. Burial, or some form of cremation, is the most common. In Israel, only when the body was safely buried could the dead person be at rest in Sheol. This feeling, that somehow a person is not at rest until the body has been properly disposed of, still persists to this day. For Saul and his sons to be treated in the way the Philistines treated them was not only a disgrace; also it allowed them no rest. Beth-shan would be one of the towns evacuated by the Israelites. It was situated towards the eastern end of the valley of Jezreel. There the headless bodies were nailed to the wall of the city for everyone to see, as trophies for the Philistines or as examples to any remaining Israelites left in the area (v. 12).

So comprehensive was the victory that the people back home must be told about it so that appropriate celebrations could take place. Saul's armour was taken as a trophy and placed in the temple of Ashtarte (v. 10). There would be several of these in the Philistine cities. We are not told in which one the armour was hung, but probably it was in the temple at Ashkelon which seems to have been the most important shrine of this goddess.

A final kindness

Jabesh-gilead was about ten miles south-east of Beth-shan across the Jordan. It would be interesting to know how the people there learned that the bodies were hung on the walls of the city. In whatever way they received the news, they acted upon it. Through the hours of darkness they made their way to Beth-shan and secretly removed the bodies from the wall. They took them home with them and disposed of them more appropriately, completing the period of mourning by fasting (v. 13).

Why did they go to all this trouble? To find the answer we have to go back a few chapters to chapter 11. There we were told that Saul had rescued them from the Ammonites and it was as a result of this that he was proclaimed king. Such an act was not forgotten and they retained a soft spot for Saul. If they couldn't repay him in his lifetime they could do so after his death.

The first king

It is worthwhile to pause here and consider the character and life of Saul. Generally speaking, he comes out of the story badly on account of his madness, his jealousy and his pursuit of David. However, there are certain things which should be remembered in mitigation. He was the first king in Israel and was pioneering the idea of monarchy among a people not used to it, some of whom were opposed to it on religious grounds. Even with a fair wind behind him it would have been a difficult task. Externally Israel was faced with serious threats from her powerful neighbours, the Philistines, who had access to weapons which Israel did not possess, iron ones instead of bronze. They also aimed to dispossess Israel and take over the whole land. Saul had to handle this situation, which was far more serious than anything faced by the Judges previously.

He might have expected some help from Samuel and initially he did receive it. He had been anointed king by him, albeit somewhat reluctantly. Later on it is difficult to avoid the conclusion that Samuel was obstructive. It was his delay in coming to make the sacrifice before the battle with the Philistines which caused Saul to do it himself (ch. 13) although it was not something a king was allowed to do. While Saul was still alive and active, Samuel anointed another as king. Even though he wasn't to take up the office until Saul's death, David's presence and his popularity made life very difficult.

It was a task which would have tested anyone and it is hardly surprising that, in time, Saul began to crack under the strain. His mind was affected and his jealousy only made matters worse. Certainly he made mistakes. When all is said and done, it is not easy to play second fiddle as Jonathan was prepared to do. If we are looking for a model we would do better to look to John the Baptist, who was prepared (according to John 3:30) to decrease while his cousin and successor increased.

A PRAYER

Keep us humble, Lord, and obedient to your will.

BAD NEWS TRAVELS FAST

The second book of Samuel records events during the reign of David, but before that reign can begin there remain a few obstacles to be overcome.

News from the front

When David had been sent home by the Philistine commanders he had proceeded to recover his wives and others who had been carried off by the marauding Amalekites during his absence. He brought them back to Ziklag, his own base. There he waited for news of the battle between the Philistines and the Israelites under Saul and Jonathan. It was brought by a messenger whose very appearance in mourning told the news. Nevertheless, David needed to hear it from his lips. The messenger, as though reluctant to tell David, withheld the news of Saul and Jonathan until the end of his report (v. 4).

Could the news be trusted? To make sure, David asked how the messenger came to know it. His reply to some extent contradicts what we were told in 1 Samuel 31:4. There Saul fell on his sword and died. Here he was found leaning on his spear and, at his own request, was killed by the messenger who happened upon the scene. He was an Amalekite and so perhaps was less aware of what he was doing than the armour bearer of Saul in the earlier account. It is just possible to reconcile the two accounts by assuming that the suicide attempt was only partially successful and that the messenger found him dying, but not dead, and finished him off. The messenger's motives, however, are suspect because he had brought with him the royal insignia to David (v. 10). Apparently he knew enough about court affairs to realize that David was to succeed Saul. He thought this action would stand him in good stead with the future king.

Court mourning

Instead of being pleased with the news and with the crown and armlet, David and his followers went into mourning. We can be sure that David was genuinely distraught at the death of his friend, Jonathan. But what about Saul? His death meant that the threat which had hung over David for a long time while he had been pursued in the Negeb was now removed. He could have been forgiven for being delighted at the news of Saul's death. However, his mourning is consistent with his attitude throughout the previous events. Twice he had refused to kill Saul when the opportunity arose, on the ground that he was the Lord's anointed (1 Samuel 24 and 26). If we were to be cynical we could say that it was good policy to mourn the king's death if he was to have any chance of succeeding him. It would not be surprising if his feelings and motives were mixed at this time. Few of us can claim that our motives are always completely unselfish.

The messenger's fate

David's reaction to the messenger himself is somewhat extreme. Instead of welcoming him and thanking him for bringing the crown and the armlet, he had him put to death. This wasn't because he was an Amalekite, the traditional enemy. He was the son of a 'resident alien', a word which is sometimes translated 'stranger' (v. 13). These were people who, for one reason or another, had settled in Israel. They had no property and therefore no rights, but along with widows and orphans, who were in a similar position, they were protected by law (Exodus 22:21; 23:9; Deuteronomy 24:17) because Israel had been in that situation in Egypt.

David's accusation was that the man had done what he himself had consistently refused to do; he had killed the Lord's anointed (v. 16). For this he deserved to die. At the same time the execution would show everyone that David could not by any means be regarded as disloyal to the king of Israel or in any way subversive.

Neither David nor the executioners could be held responsible for the man's death. It was a judicial killing and he had brought it upon himself by his rash, or his calculated, act.

A REFLECTION

It is always easy to discover ulterior motives behind other people's actions, but how often are our own motives mixed?
Only Jesus was completely selfless.

The MIGHTY FALLEN

This is one of the most moving poems in the whole of the Old Testament. We sometimes quote 'How are the mighty fallen' to celebrate the fact that some upstart has got his come-uppance. In both Hannah's song (1 Samuel 2) and the Magnificat (Luke 1:46ff) the downfall of the mighty is celebrated with satisfaction and even joy. This is not the mood of this song. This is a genuine lamentation for the death in battle of two great men.

It is described as a lamentation and often poems of this kind have a special kind of metre which consists of three accented syllables in the first line and two in the second of each pair. A good example of this in found in Amos 5:1:

> *Fállen no móre to ríse*
> *is máiden Ísrael,*
> *forsáken ón her lánd*
> *with nóne to ráise her up.*

Hebrew poetry, however, is flexible. It does not usually have rhyme and the metre is not rigidly fixed. Here the lament metre illustrated above is not used. Nevertheless, this has to be read as poetry and we read poetry with a different expectation from that which we bring to prose. We do not expect precise information. The poet may use exaggeration as well as pictures and metaphors to produce the response which he requires and it is a response of feeling rather than of intellect. This poem admirably meets these requirements.

It is not clear why the song should be called 'The Bow' (v. 18). The mention of Jonathan's bow in verse 22 is hardly sufficient reason. It is possible that the three Hebrew letters which make up the word for 'bow' should be understood as an acronym or abbreviation for 'the lament for this pair' (so REB). The poem was regarded as sufficiently important to be written down and taught to future generations of Judeans. The book of Jashar is mentioned only here and in Joshua 10:13, where it is said that a victory song was recorded in it. Other than this we know nothing of it.

The sorrow

Saul and Jonathan are described as the 'glory' of Israel (v. 19). The word is not the same as that used of the Ark in 1 Samuel 4:21. It is a word which really means 'beauty' or 'decoration'. They are like a garland which beautifies Israel (see Isaiah 28:5 where the Lord is so described). Now they lie dead on Mount Gilboa. There is no mention of the fact that, in Saul's case, his death was due to suicide or assisted suicide. Of course, the Philistines would know about the victory of their armies and would rejoice in it, but the poet looks upon the possibility of such rejoicing with extreme distaste.

He longs to see Mount Gilboa remain infertile as a permanent memorial of what happened there. He sees lying there, and exposed to the elements, the weapons of the Israelite army as well as those of Saul and Jonathan. The warriors' shields were 'defiled' (NRSV), that is, they became 'tarnished' (REB) or 'disgusting' (remember this is poetry) because the leather from which they were made was dry and cracked. Saul's shield, too, would crack and disintegrate for lack of oil.

The obituary

The second half of the poem praises first Saul and then Jonathan. With proper poetic exaggeration the poet describes Saul's achievements on behalf of the womenfolk of Israel. Is there any significance in the fact that he makes no mention of any victories that Saul achieved? There is no mention either of the quality of his rule. The only reference is to the wealth he generated for the women at court (v. 24). Perhaps, however, we should not make too much of these omissions. The lament for Jonathan is much more personal to David, as we might expect. His loss was a more serious blow. We have already discussed the relationship between them. Here again some may be tempted to think of a homosexual relationship since Jonathan's love 'surpassed that of women'. We should beware of reading into the poem what is not there. David certainly knew the love of women. He had received it from Michal, though they were now no longer together. Abigail and Ahinoam were still with him and he had just rescued them from the Amalekites. We must leave room here for hyperbole.

A PRAYER

Lord, make us generous in our praise of others and help us to give it while they are still alive.

KING *in* HEBRON

Saul's death began to open up the way for David to claim the king-ship for which he had been anointed by Samuel. In the first instance this was limited to Judah. Judah does not seem to have been fully integrated into Saul's kingdom, but rather to have retained a fair degree of independence. Moreover, David had, for some time, culti-vated a friendship with the Judeans. By his raids on neighbouring tribes he had protected them (1 Samuel 27:8–12) and had shared some of the spoils with them (1 Samuel 30:26–31).

The coronation at Hebron

David needed to be sure that the time was right for him to make the move and so he 'inquired of the Lord', doubtless using the ephod which was in the possession of the priest (v. 1). Hebron was one of the main towns in Judah. Abraham had built an altar there (Genesis 13:18), Sarah and Abraham were both buried there (Genesis 23:19 and 25:9–10). At the time of the occupation its king was defeated and killed by Joshua (Joshua 10:23) and it was allocated to Caleb, a Judean tribe. Altogether it was an appropriate place to choose as capital. David and his company simply settled there and in the sur-rounding towns. We are told virtually nothing about the circum-stances of his becoming king. It is almost taken for granted that the Judeans would make him king (v. 4). For seven and a half years his kingship was limited to this southern land where he had been born and where he had recently been so active.

Rewards for loyalty

Jabesh-gilead was further north on the eastern side of the Jordan. We have learned that it was the relief of the town which resulted in Saul being crowned king (1 Samuel 11) and that they sought to repay him by removing his body from the walls of Beth-shan, and burned it in their own city, burying the bones (1 Samuel 31:13). David now expressed his thanks to them for this act of loyalty, but there was more to it than that. By promising to reward them he was already hinting strongly that he soon would be in a position to do so. His word to them in verses 5–7 is a thinly veiled invitation to make him king, as the people of Judah had done.

A rival

It was not to be just yet. There was a further act to be played out in this drama of David's rise to power. Though Jonathan had been killed alongside Saul, there was another son, called Ishbaal. There could be no tradition of hereditary succession since Saul was the first king in Israel, though perhaps the people were sufficiently aware of what happened elsewhere. Ishbaal's succession cannot have taken place immediately since he reigned for only two of the seven and a half years David was king in Hebron. We have no information about the five year gap. With the Philistines in control, following their victory on Mount Gilboa, there was little the people could do but submit to their rule, especially on the west side of the Jordan. Eventually Saul's commander, Abner, decided to revive Israelite spirits by taking Ishbaal over the Jordan and making him king there (v. 8). Ishbaal, a man of forty, seems to have been a tool in the affair. In other words it was an army rising using the royal prince. The claim to kingship was not just to the eastern region but to the whole of Israel.

The king's name is interesting. It contains the element Baal, the name of a Canaanite god, and means 'man of baal'. The word 'baal' also meant simply 'lord' (or even 'husband') and so the king's name need not have implied that Saul, who gave it to him, worshipped a Canaanite god. It was, though, an unfortunate choice. Later, when the rabbis came to read the text, they were unwilling to pronounce the name 'Baal' and substituted the word 'bosheth' which meant 'shame' or 'disgrace'. This eventually replaced 'baal' in the written text, as well as in the reading of it. So some English translations retain the name as Ishbosheth (so REB).

There were now two rival kingdoms, Israel under Ishbaal and Judah under David. It was David's task to unite them and so he did, although some eighty years later, on the death of Solomon, they divided again.

A REFLECTION

Sometimes it takes longer than we may wish for God's purpose to be fulfilled. We have to learn to wait his time with faith and confidence.

NORTH v. SOUTH: FIRST ROUND

The site of the first battle between Israel and Judah was the pool of Gibeon, a cavity some eighty feet deep, with a spiral staircase leading down to the water table below. It was situated some fifty miles south-west of Mahanaim and thirty miles north of Hebron. It was in the territory occupied by the tribe of Benjamin, Saul's own tribe. Verse 8 suggests that it was Benjaminites whom Abner had taken along with Ishbaal into Transjordania and so the battle was fought on their own ground.

Twelve-a-side

At Abner's suggestion (v. 14), the battle was to be decided not by one single combat, as in the case of David and Goliath, but by single combat between representative teams, twelve men from each side. The result was bizarre. Pictures in Egypt show victors holding their victims by the hair with one hand and clubbing them with the other. Something similar happened here except that they used swords. They struck simultaneously so that all twenty-four were killed. The text says that they 'fell', which may simply mean that they died, but since they were on the edge of the pool it may mean that they fell in!

Since this was inconclusive, a proper battle had to be fought. David's men, under the command of Joab, were victorious (v. 17). Their losses were nineteen men in all, while Ishbaal's men, under Abner, lost three hundred and sixty. So it was a substantial victory and Abner's men had to retreat in haste.

Bad blood

As Abner's men fled, one of Joab's brothers, Azahel, a class athlete, chased after him and was catching up with him. Abner fancied his chances against him if it came to a fight but was reluctant to open a blood feud between himself and Joab (v. 22). In a way this was a civil war and therefore different from a war with another country, where the pursuit and killing of an opposing commander would have been acceptable and desirable. Asahel paid no attention to Abner's request nor to the reason for it. He was not content to take a common soldier instead; it was Abner he was after. The result was gruesome. Abner struck him with the butt end of his spear, not the sharp end, but it must have been a hefty blow because the spear passed right through his body (v. 23). Abner's fears were realized. It did open up a blood feud between him and Joab. It had now become Joab's duty to avenge his brother's death. Feuds are always easier to begin than to end.

The truce

Joab and his remaining brother continued their pursuit and would have done so right through the night. Normally fighting took place only in daylight hours and so, as night began to fall, Abner gathered his men together on a hill. Again he proposed a truce (v. 26). After all, the two sides belonged to the same people. He could see that if hostilities were prolonged it would have disastrous results for both sides. So Joab agreed, the two sides parted and each marched through the night back to their headquarters, reaching Hebron by first light and Mahanaim by noon the following day.

Throughout it was Abner who showed a reluctance to get involved in a civil war. It was he who proposed the representative combat; it was he who sought to dissuade Asahel from forcing a showdown. Now it was he who sought to stop the fighting. Of course, this may have been because he recognized the superior strength of David's men. But this is not the reason given here. It was that he recognized the blood ties between the people of Judah and the rest of Israel. As we have seen already, Judah was never fully a part of Saul's kingdom, but it is certain that there was a kinship between them. They all worshipped the same God, the Lord. Samuel, from the north, had anointed a Judean king to succeed Saul and this would lead to a united kingdom. This ambiguous relationship between Israel and Judah is important for an understanding not only of this pre-Davidic period but also of the post-Solomonic period.

A PRAYER

Help us, Lord, not to pay back evil for evil, but to remember that vengeance belongs to you.

The TWO COURTS

The conflict between Saul's house and David continued for a long time, though we are not told for how long exactly. Knowing what we do of David's anointing, the outcome is not in doubt and the writer here points the direction in which things will go. The balance of power tilts towards David (v. 1).

Family matters

He breaks off the story of the conflict to tell us about David's family matters. These few verses, 2–5, may not seem to have any great importance at the moment, but their significance will become clear later on when questions arise as to who will succeed David. The mothers of his two eldest children, Ahinoam and Abigail, we have already met. He had married them while in the Negeb, fleeing from Saul. Of the remaining wives we know nothing more than is written here. His sons, Amnon, Absalom and Adonijah, will all feature prominently later.

A split in the party

As far as the monarchy based at Mahanaim was concerned, Abner was the power behind the throne. It was at his instigation that Ishbaal had crossed the Jordan and set himself up as king of Israel. It was important to Abner to maintain and, if possible, to strengthen his power base in the kingdom. He therefore had sexual intercourse with one of the late king's concubines (v. 7). This was not just an instance of a courtier being physically attracted to a member of the king's intimate court. Concubines were regarded as possessions owned by the king. On his death they would pass, along with all his other possessions, to his successor. To take a concubine was therefore to lay claim to royal authority and was seen as an act of rebellion against the king. Whether Abner intended to carry out a coup and become king is not clear, but he was certainly claiming a position of even greater authority than he now possessed.

Ishbaal clearly misunderstood what was going on and regarded it as a sign of an intended coup. He therefore challenged Abner about it. True or not, such an accusation angered Abner. Did Ishbaal think of him as low enough to go over to the Judeans against whom he had been fighting? Since the king owed his present position to Abner who had been entirely loyal to him, did he now begrudge him the extra power that the possession of Saul's concubine would give him? (vv. 8–10).

The readiness with which Abner now threatened to go over to David's side (v. 12) makes us wonder if Ishbaal's fears were justified. The threat is accompanied by the most solemn oath and the die is cast. Abner now apparently recognized that Ishbaal's was a lost cause. He is said to be aware of the Lord's promise to David. In defiance of that promise, he had supported Ishbaal as long as he was in charge of affairs. Now that he was challenged about his intentions and not allowed the free hand that he expected, he was ready to withdraw his support and go over to the side which was winning and which was destined to succeed.

Ishbaal himself was now helpless. Instead of having Abner put to death, as he had every right to do, he accepted his rebuke with fear. Without Abner his own position was fatally weak.

First love restored

Abner lost no time in sending to David and seeking an agreement with him, promising him his support and also that he would persuade all Israel to defect with him. David agreed to this on one condition: that he would bring back Saul's daughter, Michal (v. 13). She had been given by Saul to David, she had helped him to escape, but then she had been given instead to Paltiel when David had been forced to flee from court. Now he wanted her back. Perhaps he loved her, but without doubt he wanted her because she was Saul's daughter and so any son he might have by her would be Saul's grandson. So the houses of Saul and David would be united and this would please the Israelites of the north. The picture of poor Paltiel following and weeping is pathetic, but he was sent back home by Abner (v. 16). The cause was more important than the individual.

A PRAYER

Save us, Lord, from putting our own schemes before your will.
Help us always to seek first the kingdom.

62

SWEET REVENGE

Abner's first task was to win the support of the people of Israel for
David. It would appear that many had already been keen to have
David as king. Abner's appeal to the elders was not on the grounds
that it was God's will. It was directed rather to their self-interest.
David was well known for his victories over the Philistines and so the
thought of him becoming king was attractive to those living in the
area controlled by them (v. 18). This is what Abner offered them. The
'elders' would be representatives from the various towns in that part
of the land occupied by the tribes of Ephraim on the west of the
Jordan and of Manasseh to the east. In addition to these, he made a
special point of enlisting the support of the Benjaminites (v. 19). They
lived to the south of Ephraim, bordering on the north of Judah itself.
Moreover, the royal house of Saul were Benjaminites and so it was
important to have their support, even if they were not directly influenced by the Philistines. Armed with their promise, Abner returned
to David.

He then sought permission to go and complete the defection of all
the Israelites to David. They would make a treaty with him and
become his subjects so that his kingdom would be all that he wanted
(v. 21). Little now stood in the way of David becoming king over all
Israel and Judah. Only the very limited presence of Ishbaal remained.
David therefore sent Abner on his way with an assurance of his safety.

Bad blood

While all this was happening Joab was absent with the army, skir-
mishing among neighbouring tribes (v. 22). When he returned with
the spoils, Abner had gone, but Joab was told what had happened.
Now it must be remembered that Abner had reluctantly had to kill
Joab's brother, Asahel, who had pursued him after the battle of
Gibeon (2:18–23). He had not wanted to start a blood feud but had
had little alternative. Consequently Joab was now out to take
revenge. He accused Abner of spying and treachery, quite falsely, as
it happened, though he had no means of knowing he was sincere. In
any case the need to avenge his brother's blood would have been
sufficient.

Sweet revenge

Unknown to David, Joab sent men after Abner and they brought him back to Hebron. The brief account leaves open so many questions. Did Abner know why he was being taken back? Did he go willingly? Did he think David had recalled him? Did Joab's men give that impression? They took him to Joab and not to David, so one would have thought that would have made him suspicious, especially when Joab took him into a quiet place for a private conversation. Did he trust Joab or think he had forgotten? Did he perhaps think he could take care of himself? Or did he rely upon the protection which he expected from David in exchange for the help he had given him? We can only ask these questions; there is no way in which we can answer them. All we know is that Joab stabbed Abner to death and so gained his revenge (v. 27).

Abner's death left David in a precarious position with regard to the Israelites whose support Abner had pledged to him. They would hardly be likely to trust him to deal fairly with them if they believed he had killed their commander. So when he heard of it, David at once did two things. First, he publicly disclaimed all responsibility for Abner's death (v. 28). That in itself would hardly have been sufficient, but he also laid the blame squarely on Joab by cursing him and his family. He did not use the oath formula 'May God do so to me...'. But he clearly prayed that there would always be in Joab's family those afflicted with running sores and skin diseases, sons unfit for anything but spinning wool, and that they would be killed either in fighting or by hunger (v. 29). It was a terrible curse.

How far this reflected genuine regret and anger over Abner's death and how much it was meant to impress the Israelites, it is hard to say. Joab remained as David's commander throughout his reign, though he appointed others besides. The relationship between them was probably never quite the same again.

A PRAYER

Help us, Lord, to forgive as we have been forgiven and so to heal relationships, not impair them.

ANOTHER FUNERAL

We are not told how David became aware of Abner's death or of who was responsible for it. Such an event could hardly be kept secret, however, and David knew that Joab was the culprit. He therefore called on Joab personally to mourn his death, along with the men who had been engaged in the plot with him. If Joab did as he was told he must have been extremely hypocritical, though the writer doesn't mention him again. What David called for were the usual signs of mourning, the 'rending of garments' and the wearing of sackcloth (v. 31). The cortège was led by the king himself. As with the death of Saul, now again David found it necessary to make a public show of his mourning.

The lament

Naturally, the lament is not as emotionally charged as that sung over Saul and Jonathan. All the same, it needed to be sufficient to demonstrate his sadness and to show to all that he had no part in what had happened.

He described Abner's death as a 'fool's death' and asked whether this was the proper end for such a man. We already had a fool's death in 1 Samuel 25:36–38. There, however, it was what may be called a natural death, albeit brought about by the news he was given. It was the death of a man who was a fool by name and by nature. It could be argued that Abner was something of a fool. Remembering that this is a term which implies some immorality, it is clear that Abner had been guilty of going against what he knew to be the will of God. He had lacked that 'fear of the Lord', that reverence and respect for God which leads to wisdom (Proverbs 1:7). He was foolish also in the more usual sense. Anyone with a grain of common sense would have avoided giving Joab the private opportunity to avenge his brother. There is a sense, therefore, in which Abner's death may be regarded as a fool's death. What David lamented was that this had happened to him.

Also the lament makes it clear that his death was not a judicial killing, but a murder by someone of evil intent. He had not been bound or chained because of any wrongdoing. He had come to David and had been treated not as an enemy but as a friend. He was a free man, going about David's business. His death was like a death at the hands of a criminal, and everyone would know whom David meant (v. 37).

The mourning

After the burial David continued the mourning by fasting for the rest of the day. Again this is done almost ostentatiously against the advice and the urging of his courtiers. Verse 36 hints quite clearly at the purpose of it. We cannot say it was insincere, but we are bound to say that the show he made of it was meant to impress people and please them. This included not only his immediate friends and fellow Judeans, but, significantly, the Israelites as well, the people of Ephraim, Manasseh and Benjamin. To them he made it abundantly clear that he had had no hand in Abner's death. It was not a judicial killing; it was a murder in revenge.

As though to make this even more clear, he praised Abner for his ability as the commander of Saul's and Ishbaal's army, even calling him a 'prince', though the term may not mean anything more than 'commander of the troops' (v. 38).

Then David claimed to be powerless in the face of the violence of Joab and his remaining brother. In doing so, in expressing his own vulnerability, he nevertheless reminded them that he was the anointed king.

Finally, he called on the Lord to take vengeance on Joab. It was a general request for evil to befall the wicked, but there could be no mistaking whom he meant.

We have met these mixed motives in David before and we shall do so again. In one sense we can put it down to his humanity. He is presented not as a saint but as a man controlled by human thoughts and ambitions. Yet, at the same time, he was aware that his ambitions coincided with God's will for him, that he should become king of a united Israel.

A PRAYER

Grant us, Lord, the gift of 'purity of heart', the true sincerity which will enable us to see God.

TREACHERY REWARDED

There was now only one obstacle in the way of David becoming king of a united Israel and Judah. Ishbaal, king of Israel, was still alive and so long as he remained so David's hands were tied. This chapter tells how this last obstacle was overcome.

Panic at Mahanaim

The news of Abner's defection and subsequent death caused great consternation in the court of Ishbaal. It was Abner who had been in charge of affairs, with Ishbaal little more than a figurehead. Not only Ishbaal but his people also were dismayed. The writer draws attention to two captains whose forebears were from Beeroth (v. 2). This was some forty miles south-west of Beersheba and so very far outside Benjaminite territory. For some reason now no longer known, its inhabitants had fled to Gittaim, a town in Benjamin whose location is also unknown. There they lived as resident aliens, people who were allowed to settle there but had no land rights. The point being made is that these two were not native Benjaminites, but settlers living there. This is perhaps intended to account for their subsequent actions.

The lame grandson

Before going on to say what they did, the narrator breaks off to tell, in verse 4, of Saul's grandson. The verse seems quite irrelevant to the story, but the writer must have had some reason for including it here. It may be intended to inform us that the only legitimate successor to Ishbaal was Jonathan's son, Mephibosheth. As with Ishbaal, the 'bosheth' hides an original 'baal' and in the book of Chronicles he is called Meribaal. The accident following the news of Abner's death had left him crippled and therefore not fit to become king in succession to Ishbaal. We shall hear more of this man later.

The assassination

In NRSV the assassination is described twice, in verses 6 and 7, and the order of events is somewhat odd. The Greek translation, which is followed by REB, is very different and makes better sense. The two men escaped the notice of the female doorkeeper who had dozed off in the midday heat while sifting wheat. They then killed Ishbaal. Which reading is original hardly matters. The fact remains that Baanah and Rechab murdered Ishbaal, cut off his head and took it overnight to David as proof of what they had done (v. 8).

The reward

Clearly they expected to be praised and thanked for their help to David. They had removed the last obstacle. Knowing what we do of David, his reaction comes as no surprise. Consistently he had refused any violent action against Saul and his family. He was prepared to bide his time. As far as he was concerned the anointing of Saul as king remained valid, even when he himself had been anointed and when the spirit which had enabled the king to rule properly had been transferred to him. He also knew that any act of violence would alienate the people of Israel from him. It was important that they should come of their own volition to make him king. He therefore dealt with the two captains in the same way as he had dealt with the messenger who, in the same spirit, had brought him Saul's armour and armlet (v. 12). The head of Ishbaal was given a proper burial alongside his general, Abner.

In spite of David's angry reaction, the fact remained that the two traitors were right in their judgment. The last obstacle had been removed. It had been a long and tortuous journey since David was first anointed king by Samuel in Bethlehem. Throughout it all, David had kept his hands clean as far as Israel was concerned. We can see the purpose of God being worked out, often through what appear to be strokes of good fortune. This, at any rate, is how the writer intends us to view David.

A PRAYER

Lord, give us the patience to wait and the faith to believe in your purpose for us and for the world.

KING *at* LAST

The long journey is now over. Everything that stood in the way of David becoming king of Israel as well as of Judah has been removed.

Israel united

'All the tribes' approached David (v. 1). Although they had been a kingdom under Saul, the tribes of the North still retained their sense of identity. We have mentioned Ephraim, Manasseh and Benjamin several times already. They were the tribes which had settled in the centre of Canaan and they were dominant. The tribes further north, in Galilee, have played little part in events so far, yet they also were part of Saul's kingdom. The same is true of the tribes on the east of the Jordan, Reuben and Gad. All of these now made up Israel and followed the lead given by the central tribes. The transition from a group of tribes to a nation state began under Saul, but local loyalties die hard. The Scots and the Welsh retain their identity even now within the United Kingdom and seek to reaffirm it.

Judah had stood outside that kingdom and indeed had been a separate state for seven and a half years under David. Prior to that, various cities each had their own king who ruled over the city itself and the surrounding area (see Joshua 10). They too had now been united under David, though certain Canaanite kings still retained some local power. Jerusalem, for example, was still in Canaanite hands.

For all the difference between Israel and Judah, it was recognized that their peoples had a common ethnic origin. 'Bone and flesh' represents what we today should call 'flesh and blood'. Tradition held them all to be sons of Jacob. It is now widely held that Judah had settled in Canaan independently of Ephraim, Manasseh and Benjamin, not having been involved in the Exodus from Egypt along with the others. Nevertheless, they all came from a similar background and they all officially recognized the Lord as their sole God. There was therefore a great deal in common between them and it made sense to come together in unity.

The links between the two, Israel and Judah, were already strong. David, a Judean from Bethlehem, had been accepted at the court of

Saul, the Benjaminite. He had risen to important rank, in spite of his youth, as leader of Saul's army and had won for Saul many battles against the Philistines. With the Philistines now in control of part of their land and threatening the rest, it made sense to Israel to accept David as their king.

Shepherd and ruler

In their approach to him they avoided the term 'king', whether intentionally or not (v. 2). We have seen that there was some reluctance in Israel to go down the monarchical road and it may be that they preferred the less specific terms 'shepherd' and 'ruler'. In the Old Testament, 'shepherd' is often used of kings as well as of other political leaders. Ezekiel 34 is the clearest example of this. The prophet called the rulers of Judah at that time 'bad shepherds' and went on to say that the Lord was their good shepherd, the good King. When Jesus referred to himself as the 'good shepherd' in John 10 the Jews understood this as a claim to kingship. So here, David the shepherd boy has become David the shepherd king.

They also used the term 'ruler' or 'prince' which had been used of Saul when he was anointed by Samuel in 1 Samuel 9:16. That also was to save Israel from the Philistines. This term also becomes widely used for kings.

David, it is said, 'made a covenant with them' (v. 3). We have already met this word 'covenant' in passages where it simply means a solemn agreement, a pact or treaty (1 Samuel 18:3; 2 Samuel 3:12). The terms of the agreement are not specified but they certainly included David being crowned king.

It may come as something of a surprise to be told that David was only thirty years old. So much has happened, so many decisions made, so many victories won, so much maturity shown, such strong leadership given. Since he reigned seven and a half years at Hebron, he was only twenty-three when he became king of Judah. The forty years of his reign may be a round figure. Since he is usually thought to have died in about 922BC all the events we have been describing must have happened between 1000 and 950BC.

A REFLECTION

How often does God choose young people to do his work.
Jesus, too, was only about thirty.

A New Capital

At the end of the last section, in the summary of David's reign, verse 5 says that he ruled in Jerusalem. This is in anticipation of what now follows, which is a brief description of the capture of Jerusalem. It is so brief that it is difficult for us to see precisely how it was accomplished.

Why change?

Before we read the account of the capture of the city we need to ask why David bothered. He had his capital already at Hebron and might have remained there. Hebron, however, was a Judean city and the Israelites would perhaps not have looked favourably on it. In any case it was too far south to be serviceable for a united kingdom. Saul had had his court at Ramah, which was certainly more central but may not have been acceptable to the Judeans. It was more practical and politic to choose a site which belonged to no tribe, but was still in Canaanite hands. Jerusalem was held by Jebusites, who were a Canaanite people, and most probably had its own king.

Why Jerusalem?

There were other reasons also for choosing this particular city. Whether David was aware of it or not, Jerusalem already had a place in tradition. According to Genesis 14 Abraham had once met the priest-king of the city, called Melchi-zedek, and had paid him tithes. Later, when Joshua entered the promised land, Jerusalem's king, Adoni-zedek, was one of the five who opposed him unsuccessfully. Both Jewish and Muslim tradition identify Jerusalem as the hill Moriah where Abraham was prepared to sacrifice Isaac (Genesis 22).

Even more important from David's point of view was the fact that it was easily defended. It was built on one of the hills in the hill-country of Judea. To the east was the Kidron valley, which was deeper in those days than it is now. To the south was the Valley of Hinnom. At this time the city was built on the south-eastern slope and not on top of the hill. There was a city wall well down the slope, but not at the very bottom. This made it difficult for an attacker to breach the wall. The water supply was from a spring, Gihon, outside the wall, but there was a vertical shaft leading down to it from inside in case of a seige. All this made it an excellent site for a capital.

The capture of the city

This also made Jerusalem very difficult for David to attack and capture. The Hebrew text indicates that the Jebusite ruler warned David of the difficulty. NRSV suggests that he claimed that even the blind and lame would be able to defend it against David. It is possible, however, that he meant that he and his people would defend the city, down to the very last man, even the blind and the lame (see REB).

Precisely how the attack was carried out is not wholly clear. Our English translations suggest that David asked someone to climb up the water shaft, from the spring into the city, to attack the 'blind and the lame' in view of the boast of the Jebusite king. Since 1 Chronicles 11:6 says that Joab was the first to enter the city, it is sometimes assumed that he volunteered. The Hebrew text makes no mention of climbing; it simply says that he attacked the blind and the lame 'by' or 'in' the water shaft. We cannot even be certain that the word means water shaft for it occurs only here and in Psalm 42:7, where it does seem to mean waterfall.

The important fact is that David captured the city and he did so with his own personal troops and not with men from the tribal armies. Consequently no one tribe could claim that the city belonged to them, not even Judah in whose territory it actually lay. It was a neutral city; it became David's city.

We are not sure where the Millo was, but David built and fortified the city (v. 9). King Hiram of Tyre apparently recognized David's strength and sent him timber and workmen to build him a house—it is not called a palace—at the top of the hill overlooking the city (v. 11). The gift was presumably a token of peace. The kingdom of Israel under King David was now firmly established.

A REFLECTION

What difference would it have made if David had never captured Jerusalem and made it his capital? Can you imagine either Judaism or Christianity without it?

The OLD ENEMY DEFEATED

David already had several wives and childen born to him at Hebron. The writer now lists those born after the court moved to Jerusalem. It is a summary list covering many years. Only one of the children mentioned will be of great significance later, but the point of the passage is to indicate that David succeeded in establishing a powerful monarchy. The wives and concubines displayed the wealth and grandeur of his court. Polygamy does not seem to have been the usual practice among ordinary folk outside the royal court, but it was common enough among royalty of that time. Often these marriages were part of political agreements with foreign nations. David was becoming a typical eastern monarch in this respect.

War: Round One

One of the factors leading to David's kingship over Israel was his reputation as a conqueror of the Philistines. After the battle at Mount Gilboa they were in control of territory which Israel regarded as its own. Once David's rule was established, therefore, the removal of the Philistines was a priority. They, on the other hand, took advantage of the new situation to try to extend their influence from the outset. Their attack came from their traditional home in the area of the five cities which they occupied on the south-west coastal plain. To meet this attack, David went down to the 'stronghold' (v. 17), the cave of Adullam which had been his base during the period when he was an outlaw. It is described as the 'stronghold' in 1 Samuel 22:4, 5 and 24:22. He was, of course, very familiar with this part of the country. The valley of Rephaim was somewhere to the south of Jerusalem. Its name means 'giants' and the term was used to denote certain early inhabitants of the land of Canaan (Genesis 15:20, Joshua 17:15). Perhaps there was a tradition that they once lived here. It was an appropriate place to meet the Philistine army. David was careful to observe the preconditions for a battle. He 'inquired of the Lord' (v. 19), probably using the priestly ephod. Given an assurance of victory, his army engaged with the enemy and defeated them. He took no credit for this himself but gave all the credit to the Lord. As often is the case, the name of the place was to reflect what happened there.

'Perazim' is very close to the Hebrew word for 'break through' or 'burst forth', which is what they had done. The use of 'Baal' with this suggests that probably the place already had this name. It is doubtful whether David would have used the name himself. Idols, representatives of the Philistine gods, were carried into battle and were now captured by David (v. 21). It was a reversal of what happened in 1 Samuel 4 when Israel carried the Ark into battle and it was captured by the Philistines.

Round Two

The Philistines were not yet finished and they prepared for another attack. Again, unlike Saul, David followed the right procedure by enquiring of the Lord. This time he was warned against a direct confrontation and was told to go round and attack from the rear. This meant going through a wood. The trees are called 'balsam trees' in NRSV. The Hebrew word occurs only here and in the parallel passages in 1 Chronicles 14:14 and in Psalm 84:7 where the reading is doubtful. REB calls them 'aspens', trees whose leaves tremble with the slightest movement of air. When they heard this happen, they would know that the Lord was passing through to lead his people into battle. Attention is drawn to David's complete obedience (v. 25), and the Philistines fled before him as far as Gezer which is just to the north of the five cities. There would be one more attack on the Philistines, mentioned briefly in 8:1, but their power over Israel was now virtually at an end and they were confined to their cities in the south-west.

We may not feel very comfortable with the idea that God gives such detailed instructions for fighting battles. In Israel there was a strong tradition of the 'war of the Lord', sometimes called the 'holy war'. Israel were the instruments by which he waged this war. So it was less a matter of God helping his people and more a case of Israel helping God to carry out his will. The aim of this 'war' was the establishment of his kingdom. This doesn't remove our difficulties with the idea and Christians will think of the way in which his Kingdom was to be established in the future, through the sacrifice of God's son and the sacrificial service of his people.

A PRAYER

May your name be hallowed, your Kingdom come
and your will be done.

A RISKY MOVE

The bringing of the Ark into Jerusalem was a big occasion and called for huge and careful celebrations.

Why bother?

There were several reasons why it was a good idea. David wanted not only a political but also a religious centre which would provide a focus for all the various tribes within his newly united kingdom. In Jerusalem no such focal point existed. Until now it had been a Canaanite city associated with the worship of Baal under the title El Elyon, God Most High (Genesis 14:18, 20). The fact that this also became a title for the Lord (Psalm 46:4), along with other considerations, suggests that David may well have decided to use some of the existing *forms* of the worship there, but changed their *meaning* because they were now used to worship the Lord.

However, David needed something distinctively associated with the Lord, and what better than the Ark? The tribes that had been familiar with the Ark in days gone by were those that had settled in central Canaan and become the leading part of Saul's Israel. It had rested for some time at Shiloh which was in Ephraim (1 Samuel 1–4), and it was now at Kiriath-jearim (1 Samuel 7:2). Since Jerusalem was in Judah it would do no harm at all to the cause of unity to have this Israelite sign of the Lord's presence there.

The abortive attempt

The story of the transfer of the Ark to Jerusalem is, in one sense, a continuation of the story of the Ark which came to a full stop in 1 Samuel 7:2 with the Ark lodged at Kiriath-jearim. The Baale-judah of verse 2 refers to the same place. The occasion called for participation from all parts of the new kingdom. Therefore, David did not use his personal troops, but called for troops from all Israel to join in the procession, a distance of about ten miles. At this stage the Ark was still just a wooden box, but later it was embellished and had a cherub at each end.

Seeing that it represented the presence of the Lord, it was a holy object and had to be treated wih care. David may have recalled what happened to the Philistines when it was there and what happened to the people of Beth-shemesh when they treated it wrongly (see on 1 Samuel 5:19–21). As the Philistines had done, they made a new cart to carry it. The two sons of Abinadab, in whose house it had rested for many years without mishap, were chosen to guide it, Ahio going in front and Uzzah alongside (v. 3). The dancing was probably more than a celebration; it was more likely a religious dance in honour of the Lord who was on his way to Jerusalem.

Disaster!

All went well for a while, though the roads were rough and unmade. Just how far they had gone when it happened, we do not know. The oxen pulling the cart stumbled. Uzzah did what was natural, what anyone would have done. He put out a hand to stop the Ark from falling off. What happened next disturbs us greatly. We might have understood it if it had said that Uzzah, realizing he had touched a holy object, had a heart attack and died. That is not what it says. It says quite clearly, 'God struck him.' We may alleviate the sharpness of this by saying that, since all that happened was regarded as due to the Lord, therefore Uzzah's death is attributed to the Lord and not to 'natural causes'. This hardly removes the sense of injustice we feel. Did David feel the same? Certainly he was angry, whether with God for his harshness, or whether because his plans had been frustrated. At any rate he decided to abandon the project and left the Ark at the house of a man from Gath, a Philistine city. Unlike Uzzah, he and his family, who probably avoided touching the Ark like the plague, prospered.

It is useless to try to explain away this incident. All we can do is to understand it from the Old Testament point of view. 'Holiness' was always dangerous (Isaiah 6 and Ezekiel 1). The difference between God and humanity must always be maintained and there was need for reverence and awe in God's presence. The coming of Jesus puts a new perspective on it, but doesn't lessen the need for awe before God.

A PRAYER

Holy God, we thank you that we may draw near to you through Jesus. Help us never to take this privilege for granted, but to approach you in wonder and awe.

A DISILLUSIONED WIFE

The fact that Obed-edom had flourished while the Ark had been lodged with him encouraged David to have another try to bring it into Jerusalem.

Success at last

This time David took great care with the Ark, moving it only six paces, and then, when all seemed well, making a sacrifice to the Lord (v. 13). Once more he took up his dance. Now we are told that he was wearing a linen ephod which, as we have seen, was a priestly garment. It appears also to have been short and David wore nothing under it.

So the mission was accomplished. David had prepared a place for the Ark in the city and it was duly placed in the tent he had erected. There followed a great religious celebration. Two kinds of sacrifice were offered: whole-offerings, in which the whole animal was burnt on the altar as an offering in homage to God; and peace- or shared-offerings in which some parts were retained and eaten by the worshipper and his friends and family as a sign of their common allegiance to God (see 1 Samuel 2).

Next David pronounced a blessing on the people, assuring them of the presence and help of God (v. 18). This was followed by the 'bun-fight', except that it was probably the eating of the shared-offering in which all those in Jerusalem shared and by which they were bound into a community.

Sometimes in the Old Testament, when it is said that a person offered a sacrifice it means that a priest offered it on that person's behalf, and this may be the case here. But the fact that David is said to have made the sacrifice, coupled with his wearing of the ephod and the blessing of the people, which was also a priestly privilege (Numbers 6:22–27), may well suggest that David took this priestly role upon himself.

An angry wife

David's wife, Michal, Saul's daughter, was looking on as the procession entered the city. What she saw turned her against David. Verse 20 suggests it was the shortness of the ephod and the lack of other cloth-ing which upset her. Although in an ideal world nakedness would be normal and natural, in the real world it was now a matter of shame, and coverings were needed to avoid this (Genesis 3). Self-exposure, therefore, was frowned upon. David's abandoned dancing had exposed him in the sight of everyone, even the servant-girls, snigger-ing behind the curtains! Michal's sarcasm is biting. Honour? He had demeaned himself like one of the 'empty ones', shallow, empty-headed people. REB's 'clowns' is not far from the mark (v. 20).

David's reply was that it was all done 'before the Lord', in front of the Ark on which the invisible Lord was seated. That excused his extravagant behaviour. But can foolish, even degrading behaviour be excused on the grounds that it is offered to God? To say yes would be to leave the door open for all kinds of irregular behaviour in the course of worship. David, however, is unrepentant. He is willing to become even more contemptible—a strong word which sometimes means 'to curse'—and be humiliated in his own eyes. But those servant-girls mentioned by Michal would hold him in honour. So her sarcastic remark would actually turn out to be true.

We may wonder if it was only David's uninhibited dancing that upset Michal. It is emphasized here that she was the daughter of Saul and she may well have recalled how the kingdom was taken out of her father's hands because he acted as a priest in Samuel's prolonged absence (1 Samuel 13:8–14). Now David was assuming priestly func-tions and getting away with it. We may share Michal's puzzlement at this. What was the difference? Was it, perhaps, that David's priestly action was one of thanksgiving whereas Saul's was to seek God's help?

Finally we are told that Michal never had a child. It does not say she was made incapable of bearing children. More likely she refused David from now on and so never bore him a child who could succeed him. He had hoped for a son by her who would then have a good claim to the throne as both the son of David and the grandson of Saul, so cementing the unity of the kingdom. This was why he had insisted on her rejoining him in 3:14. This option was now closed off.

A QUESTION

Is it ever possible to excuse unacceptable behaviour so long as it is done in honour of God?

A DIVINE PROMISE

This is an extremely important chapter because upon the events described here there came to rest all those Messianic hopes which Jews have cherished over the centuries and which Christians believe have been fulfilled in Jesus Christ. Much of the language in which the chapter is written reflects the style of the author himself. It is similar in many respects to that of Deuteronomy. We need to remember that he was writing at a time when the Davidic dynasty had come to an end and when Judah no longer had a king of any sort.

The kingdom at rest

David's rule over a united Israel was now firmly established. He had been accepted as king by all the people; he had acquired a new capital, Jerusalem; he had built for himself a house of cedar from Lebanon, supplied by the king of Tyre; he had made Jerusalem a religious centre by moving the Ark there. He was under no pressure from enemies from within or without. What more needed to be done?

In a discussion with his prophet, Nathan, he thoughtfully drew attention to what seemed an anomaly. He had a rather splendid house, while the Ark was housed in a tent (v. 2). Nathan's advice was that he should follow his own instincts. We are left to guess, for the moment, what these were. It quickly becomes clear that he had been toying with the idea of building a temple, a laudable thing to do, surely.

However, prompted by the Lord, Nathan had second thoughts overnight and was told to report his change of mind to David. The grounds for this are given. First, the question expects the answer 'no', but there is also emphasis on the word 'you', as NRSV brings out well (v. 5). It rules out the building of a temple by David but leaves it open for another to do so. Further, it seems to cast doubt on the need for a temple at all. While the Israelites had been on the move in the wilderness, it had been necessary for God to move with them and so the Ark had been portable. The idea of a permanent home was out of the question. Notice how the Judges are called 'shepherds', a term which had already been applied to David in 5:2 (see note on that passage). The situation had now changed. The people were settled and the Ark had made its last journey. But the answer to the question, 'Shall I build a temple?' is still, 'No'. The time is not yet ripe.

A mirror image

Instead of David building a house for the Lord, the Lord would build a house for David (v. 11)! The play on the word 'house' is clear. It was as clear in Hebrew as it is in English. The word may mean either a building to live in or a family, and in the case of a royal family, a dynasty, as in the house of Windsor.

God's word to David, given through Nathan, begins by reminding him of the ways in which God had brought him to this present position. Any promises for the future need to be based on divine activity in the past. Unless confidence is given in this way it is difficult to trust promises for the future. From shepherd of sheep to shepherd of Israel, that was the remarkable story of David, and we have followed its course. Now come the promises. First, a 'great name' (v. 9), that is, fame which extends beyond Israel. David will be on a par with other famous rulers. Though Israel was a small kingdom compared with Egypt or Assyria, David would have an honoured place alongside their rulers. Second, Israel would now become a well-established nation with its own land. The promises made to Abraham and the other patriarchs, and to Moses, had come true and would remain so, with Israel secure from all enemies (v. 10). Third, there would be a dynasty based on David which would last for ever (v. 16). This does not necessarily mean it will never end; it means it will not end in the foreseeable future. In fact the kingdom split into two on the death of David's son, Solomon, but in Judah (apart from one brief seven-year interlude) there remained on the throne a descendant of David right down to the last king, Jehoiakin, who died in exile in Babylon.

The privilege of building a temple would be left to Solomon. His descendants would sometimes be disobedient to God and would need to be punished but the monarchy would remain in the hands of David's descendants. This was in contrast to what happened to Saul, whose disobedience resulted in the kingship being taken away from him.

A PRAYER

Faithful God, whose past mercies fill and enrich our memories, may our confidence in the future of your Kingdom never waver.

The KING'S RESPONSE

In this prayer David simply accepts the promise in humility and with gratitude. The actual language used is similar in many respects to that of the book of Deuteronomy (cf. Deuteronomy 4:7; 5:6; 7:17ff) and, as we have mentioned earlier, writers often composed speeches which they placed on the lips of their characters. This is almost certainly the case here. But although the actual language may be that of the writer, we may assume that the content of the prayer tells how David responded to God's promise.

Covenant

The promise to David and his response to it are frequently described as a 'covenant'. We have already met covenants or agreements between human people, for instance, David and Jonathan in 1 Samuel 18:1–5. The idea that God had made a covenant with Israel had become a central element in Israel's self-understanding by the seventh century BC. In the Old Testament there are three other covenants made by God with people. In Genesis 9:11 the covenant consisted of a promise to all humankind never again to destroy the world by flood. The sign was a rainbow. In Genesis 17:4 the covenant with Abraham promised a long and numerous race of people descended from him. The sign this time was circumcision. In Exodus 24, God made a covenant on Mount Sinai with the people he had brought out of Egypt. The promise was that he would be with his people, but the emphasis is less on God's promise and more on Israel's pledge of obedience, which was essential before the covenant could be sealed. Moreover, it was not made with Moses as an individual, but with the whole people who must make a communal response. The seal of this was the blood of sacrificed oxen. Its terms, which are set out in advance in Exodus 19:4–6, are sometimes summed up in the formula, 'I will be your God and you shall be my people.' This formula may be reflected in verse 14 of our present chapter. But this 'covenant' with David is more like that with Abraham. It is made with an individual and concerns his descendants. It requires nothing from the human side, other than the acceptance of the promise. It is not between God and people but between God and his king, Father and son.

In actual fact the word 'covenant' is not found at all in this passage and it may be safer to use the word 'promise'. Having said that, it is clearly referred to in Psalm 89:28 and there it is called a covenant.

Although no requirements are laid on David as conditions, the acceptance of the promise implied a willingness to obey God, and punishment was threatened for any descendant who was disobedient. Nevertheless, the promise of a dynasty would stand firm.

Humble acceptance

So there is no sacrifice or sign or seal mentioned, but only a simple acknowledgment in prayer and a humble acceptance of the promise. David 'went in', presumably into the tent where the Ark was housed, and 'sat' before the Lord (v. 18). In certain contexts the verb 'to sit' means 'to sit enthroned' and it may be that here we are meant to see the human, enthroned king in the presence of the heavenly King enthroned on the Ark.

The prayer begins with David recalling his humble beginnings, and recognizes that God is so great that to raise a shepherd boy to the rank of shepherd king was easily accomplished. There is a strange phrase in verse 19: 'May this be instruction for the people.' It is probable that this was a note written later in the margin—'This is a lesson for humankind'—which was then copied into the text. It was already there when the Chronicler used this as a source and so he tried to make sense of it by writing something which seems to mean 'You regard me as of high rank' (1 Chronicles 17:17).

God's greatness is seen not only in what he had done for David, but in what he had done for Israel. David saw that the promise of a lasting dynasty would not only make his reputation great but, more importantly, would enhance the Lord's reputation, his 'name', throughout the world until all recognized him as God (v. 26).

It is in this spirit that David took on board the promise of God and trusted him for its fulfilment. Even when the dynasty came to an end, the hope lived on that God would send a new David or a son of David to save his people.

A REFLECTION

Are these hopes fulfilled in Jesus, 'great David's greater son'?
What hopes still remain for Christian people?

A GOAL REACHED

In this chapter we reach what is almost the highest point in David's achievements. His empire is secured.

Foreign affairs

David brought all the neighbouring nations under his control. The Philistines are dismissed in a single verse (v. 1). These powerful people who had troubled Israel for so long were now finally subdued. Moab lay to the east of the Dead Sea. Zobah was way up in the north beyond Damascus. Troops from there went to help their neighbour but they too were defeated. Hamath, further north still, avoided war by making a substantial contribution to David's treasury. Back in the south, Edom became subject to him. This left only Ammon and Phoenicia outside David's control. Ammon will be dealt with in the following chapters. Phoenicia's king of Tyre had already supported David by sending timber and workmen to build his house.

This looks like a large kingdom, but we need to keep our perspective. A glance at a map will show that it was quite small compared with nations like Assyria and Egypt. Nevertheless, it was a considerable achievement. The chapter speaks of David's 'name' being made great (v. 13). He had a great reputation, at least within this limited area. Yet the success was put down to the Lord so that the Lord's name was also great.

The promise of chapter 7 was fulfilled.

Home affairs

The final four verses of the chapter have some interesting and important things to say about David's rule. First we are told that he administered 'justice and equity'. These are two important Old Testament words. The second is often translated 'righteousness'. They feature prominently in the picture of the ideal ruler, the new son of Jesse, in Isaiah 11. Righteousness is the fulfilment of obligations incurred by a relationship. Israel is God's chosen people and God's righteousness is seen as he fulfils his obligations to his people, by caring for them. His people are righteous when they respond as they ought in worship and obedience and when they fulfil their obligations to one another as God's people. These obligations may be set down as laws but behind the laws is the fundamental requirement truly to be God's people and to behave as they ought. 'Justice' describes the whole system where this can operate and where wrongs can be righted. Such was David's kingdom.

Of the personnel surrounding David, we have already heard of Joab and of Abiathar, the father of Ahimelech. But there are two new figures who will feature prominently in the story later on. Joab was in charge of the army but Benaiah was in charge of the Cherethites and Pelethites (v. 18). We know nothing of the latter, but the former were mentioned in 1 Samuel 30:14 as a people living in the Negeb and now part of David's kingdom. Together they formed his personal bodyguard under Benaiah.

Where did Zadok come from, who now became a priest alongside Ahimelech (v. 17)? We do not know, but there are suggestions, which are very feasible, that he was the Jebusite priest-king of Jerusalem before David captured it. David did not destroy the Canaanite inhabitants but allowed them to continue to live there. We have already seen how the title of Baal, 'Most High', was transferred to the Lord in Jerusalem. We should also recall that the earlier priest-kings who are known to us were called Melchi-zedek, king of righteousness, and Adoni-zedek, lord of righteousness. It is entirely possible that the priest-king in David's day was called ?-zedek, but after David's capture the ? was dropped, leaving Zadok. We then must assume that he changed his allegiance from Baal to the Lord and so became priest. The link between the name of the priest and the fact that David ruled in righteousness, and the fact that Jerusalem ideally should be the 'city of righteousness' in Isaiah 1:26, is unmistakable.

Jehoshaphat was possibly the one who wrote the annals or kept a record of state affairs. Seraiah was a secretary of state and perhaps an adviser to the king. We hear little or nothing of these people. The other remarkable thing is that David's sons are also designated priests. Did the royal house also have a priestly role? The subsequent narrative makes no mention of them acting as priests.

A REFLECTION

Does it make any difference if we think of righteousness as doing what we ought for our fellows, rather than as obeying laws?

A KINDLY ACT

If the closing verses of chapter 8 look like a concluding summary it is not surprising, for in chapter 9 a new part of the story begins. It is generally thought that 2 Samuel 9 to 1 Kings 2 was a separate writing already completed, which was then incorporated into the overall narrative (see Introduction, p. 18). There are differences of style and content between these chapters and those we have read so far. One of the differences is that whereas the Lord has played a prominent role in events so far, he is mentioned much less frequently in these chapters and mainly at critical moments in the story. This whole section has become known as the 'succession narrative' because it deals with the claims of several of David's sons to follow him as king until finally Solomon does so.

We saw that chapter 8 was a kind of high-water mark in David's career. These following chapters show a gradual decline in his fortunes, not so much in foreign as in domestic affairs.

Who was responsible for this narrative before it became part of 2 Samuel, we cannot say for sure. There are grounds for thinking it may have originated among the 'wise men', often counsellors at court responsible for teaching life-skills to young men. Proverbs is an example of their work. They tended to see events working out in a natural way, but believed that behind this natural course of events there is the Lord, even though his direct involvement is not always obvious.

If the information is historically reliable then we have to say that the author or authors were wise men intimately associated with the royal court.

An act of devotion

This writer is obviously well aware of the close friendship that existed between David and Jonathan, since he begins his story with this act of kindness to Jonathan's son. There may have been a lingering wish to recognize the validity of Saul's kingship by bringing one of his descendants to the court. The emphasis, however, is on the relationship with Jonathan, described earlier as a 'covenant'. Though Jonathan was now dead, the need to retain a link with his family remained. The 'kindness' (v. 3) which David showed is rather more than that. The word is often translated 'steadfast love'. Our nearest equivalent is perhaps 'devotion'. It is often used for the love and loyalty within a given relationship, such as that between David and Jonathan. In verse 3 David calls it the 'devotion of God', by which he means that he must show to Saul's descendant and Jonathan's son the same kind of devotion as God showed to his chosen people. This 'devotion' is not just something that may be felt. It needs to find expression in activity. The verb that is consistently used with it is the verb 'to do'. David wanted to 'do devotion', to express it practically. It is always easier to feel love and loyalty than to do them. Real love always needs to be expressed in action.

David seemed to be unaware of the existence of Mephibosheth. We heard a little about him in 2 Samuel 4:4. We heard about the death of his father and grandfather when he was five years old. His nurse picked him up and fled, but in her haste she dropped him and this damaged his feet. He was now brought to David's attention and, in spite of his lameness, he was taken into David's household. Still we have no mention of Jonathan's wife, or of Mephibosheth's, for he was now grown up and already had a son. When he was introduced to David he showed his humility and allegiance (v. 6). The meeting is described in 'courtly' language.

Twice, attention is drawn to his lameness (vv. 3 and 13) as though this might have been a good reason for David to have ignored him, the physical deformity being regarded as a defilement. Instead David welcomed him into his court in Jerusalem, made sure he inherited Saul's property and allowed him his own servants. It could have been a dangerous move to give one of Saul's descendants such a position. We shall see later that it did have its risks, though any danger was quickly averted.

A PRAYER

Help us, Lord, always to be faithful in our loving
and to express our love in deeds.

An INSULT

There was apparently a treaty between the Ammonites and David. We do not know how this came into being but it explains why David did not include Ammon in his conquests at the end of chapter 8. The death of a king often caused complications and could give rise to pretenders seeking to take the throne. The name of this king appears, at first sight, to be Nahash, but this is hardly likely since Nahash was the king of the Ammonites who had gouged out the eyes of Israelites at the end of 1 Samuel 10 and who had beseiged Jabesh-gilead in chapter 11, when he was defeated by Saul. It is possible that this is another Nahash but it is more likely that the phrase 'son of Nahash' really means 'grandson of Nahash', just as 'son of your master' in the Hebrew of 9:9 means 'grandson of your master'. The treaty would then have been made with the unnamed son of Nahash and father of Hanun.

Condolences rejected

There is another parallel with chapter 9. Just as David 'did devotion' with Saul's grandson, so now he 'did devotion' with Nahash's grandson (v. 2). The 'dealt loyally' of NRSV represents exactly the same phrase as its 'showed kindness' in the previous chapter. David is presented to us, then, as a king who is anxious to fulfil all his obligations, both those internal, to Israel, and those external, to his neighbour, whatever the risks may be. To the Ammonites he expressed his devotion, demanded by the treaty, by sending a delegation to offer his condolences to the new king, Hanun. It would be a sign that he wished the treaty to remain in force. Precisely how it was done we are not told. It was possibly something more than a verbal message; perhaps they shared in the court's mourning in some way.

The enmity between Israel and Ammon went back a long way (see Judges 11) and now it surfaced again among the nobility of Ammon. David's best intentions were regarded with deep suspicion (v. 3). Perhaps they knew something about David's earlier dubious activities and were determined not to be taken in by him. On this occasion, however, his deeds were genuine. Nevertheless, the nobles persuaded Hanun that it was a trick, that the delegation were really spies sent to discover the weak points in the defence of the capital city, Rabbah.

Hanun's reaction was not to kill them but to humiliate them and send them back, throwing David's kindness back in his face (v. 4). To shave off just half of their beards was to disgrace them. So it was also to cut off their tunics at the waist, leaving them exposed. We saw how Michal regarded it as disgraceful when David's ephod was so short as to expose him (ch. 6).

It is not clear how David learned of the plight of his servants, for they couldn't return home in that condition. He could, of course, have sent them new tunics, but there was nothing he could do about their beards! Only time could repair that damage and so they stayed at Jericho on the eastern frontier until their beards had grown again. Only then dared they return to Jerusalem. It was a deep insult to David and to all Israel, and the Ammonites must have known that it would be seen as a challenge to Israel to take revenge.

This motif—a kindly act, well-meant but misunderstood, the insulting reaction leading to a conflict—is well enough known in fiction and in film. This is not to suggest that the present story is fictional; it is simply to draw attention to the fact that the storyteller's art can be seen in this present narrative. This writer is very skilful indeed at portraying character and developing plot.

For REFLECTION

It is not all that unusual for our best intentions to be misunderstood. The question is: how do we react to this? Do we respond in anger? In vindictiveness? How did Jesus respond?

INSULTS AVENGED

The Ammonites knew full well what they had done. The challenge had been thrown down by their insulting behaviour and could not be refused. It was therefore essential to make whatever preparations they could for the war which would surely follow.

Allies needed

Aware of the reputation and the power of David, they recognized that they would need help and so they began to look round for allies. The Arameans under Hadadezer had been defeated by David. He had taken away their gold shields and their bronze to Jerusalem (8:3-8). So it would not take much to persuade them to join in a war against Israel in order to regain their independence. Other city kings in the area were ready to go along with them and so they formed an alliance of considerable strength. The numbers given may seem large but we have suggested before that one thousand may well refer to a military unit rather than to an actual number. Even so, the numbers are impressive.

The attack

David's first move is described with a minimum of detail in verse 7. He sent Joab with all the fighting men, probably the regular army. From what follows, we gather that he sent them to attack the Ammonite capital, Rabbah. As they approached, the Ammonites made a sortie out of the city and took up positions in front of the gateway. The Aramean allies, however, were not with them. They were out in the open country round about. So, when Joab encamped outside the city, facing the Ammonites, he found himself caught in a pincer movement. Trapped between the Ammonites and the Arameans, all he could do was to divide his forces and fight in both directions. He left his brother Abishai in charge of one part of the army to face the Ammonites, while he himself led the remainder in the opposite direction against the Arameans. The two brothers made an arrangement that each would be able to call on the other if things got too hot to handle. With a patriotic rallying cry and an expression of dependence on the Lord, he attacked the Arameans, who quickly withdrew and fled. When the Ammonites fighting against Abishai saw that the Arameans were being defeated, they panicked and retreated into the city for safety within its walls (v. 14).

A ceasefire

For the moment, fighting stopped and Joab returned to Jerusalem. The Arameans, though, were not finished yet. Hadadezer, their king, called up reinforcements from beyond the river Euphrates. Under his commander, Shobach, they marched southward again into Ammonite territory somewhere between the Jordan and the capital Rabbah. The precise location of Helam is not known, but it must have been somewhere in this region. For the third time in this chapter David received information which allowed him to deal with the situation (see verses 5, 7 and now 17). We can only assume he had an excellent secret service and spy network!

War resumed

This time David led out his army himself to do battle with the Arameans. His army is described as 'all Israel' and perhaps this means that whereas Joab had used the regular army, David now called out the militia from the various tribes as well. They engaged with the Arameans who were again defeated and fled. Typically we are told of the large losses on the Aramean side, but nothing of the losses among the Israelites (v. 18). War-time propaganda has obviously not changed much!

The vassal kings who had joined Hadadezer's coalition had now had enough and so they sued for peace with Israel and became subject once again. This still left the Ammonites to be dealt with, but with no allies left to help them. No doubt it was too late in the year to take action against them at once. In ancient times there was a 'close season' for warfare throughout the winter when no fighting took place. It was probably impossible to maintain supplies for an army out in the field during the winter months. The logistics would have made it out of the question. But, come spring, the new season could begin.

A PRAYER

Give us the courage, Lord, to fight for what is right, not with the weapons of warfare but with the 'whole armour of God'.

A TEMPTATION TOO FAR

In the spring the attack on the Ammonites was resumed. This time David did not lead the army in person but entrusted the war to Joab. He quickly made his way through Ammon to the capital, Rabbah, which he besieged.

Meanwhile...

The narrator breaks off the story of the siege of Rabbah to tell us about David in Jerusalem. The story he tells would have had the tabloid editors ready with their cheque books in no time. It is a disgraceful episode in David's life and the writer makes no attempt to tone it down or to make excuses for him. We are bound to wonder who was the 'whistle blower'. It is hardly likely that David himself would have revealed all the details. Bathsheba might have done, for she could hardly conceal what took place for very long. Nathan the prophet clearly learned about it in general terms, if not in detail. No doubt there was plenty of gossip in court circles. So the truth came out and the narrator knows how to tell a good story and make the most of it.

If we are to picture what happened, we have to remember that David's house was situated at the top of the steep hill while the rest of the city was built on the hillside below. He therefore overlooked the city and could see the rooftops and courtyards of the other houses. One evening before it got dark he got up from his 'siesta' and took a stroll on the flat roof of the palace, as he probably had done countless times (v. 2). We can imagine him looking over the city with a great deal of satisfaction and pride. On this occasion, however, something special caught his eye. In one of the houses below was a woman taking a bath. He watched long enough to realize how beautiful she was and his lust got the better of him. He made enquiries about her and was told she was a married woman. That ought to have been sufficient to warn him off. Her husband was a Hittite. We met a Hittite earlier who had joined David's men at the cave of Adullam (1 Samuel 26:6). Uriah was presumably another who had joined him there and was now one of David's personal troops. At the moment he was with Joab besieging Rabbah. This only made David's adultery the more reprehensible. Instead of forgetting all about her, he sent for her to come to the palace (v. 4). There he had intercourse with her and then let her go back home. We are not told anything about Bathsheba's thoughts about all this. Was she a willing partner? Or did she feel compelled to obey the king out of fear?

The bath she had been taking was not an ordinary bath, but a ritual one. She had just had her monthly period and this was a purificatory washing. It wasn't that there was anything morally wrong which needed to be cleansed. The point is that blood symbolized life (Leviticus 17:11) and belonged to God. It was important to deal with it carefully. So after menstruation, bathing was required to deal with it. The law in Leviticus 15:19ff says a woman is unclean for seven days afterwards. So intercourse at this time was risky.

So it turned out. The result was worse than David could have hoped for. In a few weeks' time he learned the worst. Bathsheba sent word that she was pregnant (v. 5) and since her husband was away at the war the father could only be David. He had broken the eighth commandment and, to make matters worse, the husband was one of his trusted soldiers who had contributed to his success. Now the adultery could no longer be hidden.

The cover-up

Some quick thinking was needed to avoid public disgrace. The plan was to get Uriah home from the war (v. 6). The assumption was that, after being away so long, he would want intercourse with his beautiful wife. They would then be able to claim that the baby was her husband's. The trouble was that Uriah was much more self-controlled than his king. Soldiers on duty were forbidden to have sexual intercourse and, although home from the front, Uriah regarded himself as still on duty. He therefore refused to go home but slept with the palace guards. Even when David made him drunk he still refused. Now more desperate measures were needed.

A PRAYER

When we are tempted, Lord, make us strong.

A SPIRAL *of* DECEIT

The attempted cover-up having failed, Uriah was sent back to the front, carrying his own death warrant. How lucky for David—how unlucky for Uriah—that he was too honourable a man to open it and read the contents. Uncertainty as to why he had been sent back to Jerusalem might have tempted him, but he resisted the temptation.

The fatal message

The message was clear enough. Uriah was to be set up by Joab (v. 15). Put in the most perilous position, he was to be left there alone so that the Ammonites would kill him. This was nothing less than murder made to look like the fortunes of war. How low would David stoop? This is what happens when once a person steps on the slippery slope of deceit.

The commission

Joab did as he was told. Although there had been a falling out between Joab and David over Joab's murder of Abner (2 Samuel 3:26), Joab remained the loyal soldier who obeyed orders from David. The story does not say that he called off the other soldiers to leave Uriah exposed in quite the way David had suggested. Rather he set him among some of the best troops who would bear the brunt of the fighting (v. 16). The Ammonites, as expected, tried to break out of the city and raise the siege. After some initial success they were driven back into the city. Joab's men approached the gateway, but archers on the walls shot at them and killed some. Among those who died was, as planned, Uriah.

The tactics were wrong, of course, and Joab knew it. He should have known better than to take his men within range of the archers, but it was a deliberate mistake. There was apparently a well-known example of such wrong tactics—perhaps it was in the training manual! In Abimelech's case it was not arrows fired by archers, but a millstone dropped by a woman which did the damage (Judges 9:50ff). David would be likely to quote this when he heard of the loss of some of his men. So any criticism by David was to be met with the news, 'Uriah is dead too' (v. 21).

News, good or bad?

The messenger took the news to David. As the story is told he didn't give David a chance to show his anger and criticize the tactics. He hurried on to tell him of Uriah's death. Did he guess that this was the important part of the message?

Certainly it had the desired effect. Instead of sending back an angry message, David told Joab not to worry. Deaths do happen in war. He showed no concern that some of his men had died because of the strategy he had imposed. Indirectly he was guilty of murdering others besides Uriah, but shrugged it off as of no account. His object had been attained. Bathsheba was now a war widow. That was all that mattered.

The messenger was to encourage Joab, not to criticize him (v. 25). He was to get on with completing the attack on Ammon.

The widow

What Bathsheba made of all this we shall never know. Did she go willingly to David in the first place or was she afraid to disobey the king's summons? Did she ever know how Uriah met his death? Did she know that he had been home to see David and hadn't called to see her? Did she guess that his death was somehow linked to her pregnancy by David? Of course, she mourned Uriah and that may have been quite sincere, but it would be expected of her anyway and she could hardly do otherwise. As soon as the period of mourning was over, as soon as decency would allow, David sent for her again and once more she went, whether willingly or reluctantly.

David, we know, already had several wives. Bathsheba was added to them and so she bore his child, conceived by adultery, but born within marriage.

No wonder that the writer ends by saying that what David had done displeased the Lord (v. 27).

A REFLECTION

Cover-ups lead us further and further into wrongdoing. It takes courage to confess to wrongdoing but it is the only way to break the chain of evil.

The REBUKE

How do you get a person in David's condition to recognize and then to admit that they have done wrong? The direct accusation will probably get nowhere. It will only harden attitudes and make them dig their heels in harder. A more subtle approach is needed.

A tale with a moral

There was a lot that was good about David. In 2 Samuel 8:15 we were told that he ruled, administering justice and equity to all his people. There was a genuine desire to see that people did what they ought to do in respect of each other. The Lord in his wisdom therefore took a rather oblique approach to David's misbehaviour. Nathan was already a trusted prophet for whom David had much respect and so the Lord used him to confront David with his sin. He appealed to David's sense of fair play by telling him a story which would make him see the difference between right and wrong. It was courageous of Nathan to be ready to show David where he had gone wrong.

The story is a very simple one, but it was presented to David as though it were a case requiring his judgment. Two men lived in the same city. The rich man needed food to entertain a visitor and instead of killing one of his own sheep, which he would never have missed, he took the only lamb belonging to the poor man, a lamb which the poor man treasured and which was all he had. The wrong was so obvious that David was immediately angry. The rich man deserved to die and he must be made to restore what he had taken from the poor man fourfold (vv. 5–6).

Like a hammer blow, Nathan's reply comes: 'You are the man!' David has condemned himself! Imagine David's reaction. He was probably stunned and, for just a moment, needed to ask himself how he had been as wicked as the rich man. But it would not take him long to see the point of the story and how it applied to him. In case there was any misunderstanding Nathan spelled it out for him (v. 9).

He began by telling David that this was not simply his own opinion; it was the word of the Lord. That gave it a seriousness that had to be reckoned with. The condemnation of his sin is not from Nathan but from God. God began by pointing out to David how all his present riches had come from him. All that had once belonged to Saul—his kingship, his dynasty, his wives, his kingdom—had been given now to David. If David hadn't been satisfied with that and had asked for more, he would have given it. God's generosity was overwhelming and yet David had to take what was treasured by someone else. When we want something so badly, it is easy to forget what we have already been given. God then accused him of both adultery and murder. God knew that Uriah's death was not due to the chances of battle; it was contrived. It may have been by the sword of the Ammonites that he had died, but it was David who had killed him.

The punishment

If David recognized that the rich man should be punished, he could not complain when God now set out his punishment. It was twofold. First there would be trouble within his own family from now on (v. 11) and this would be no secret affair, as David's act had been; it would be out in the open for all Israel to see. The remaining chapters of 2 Samuel will show how this punishment is carried out.

Second, David should really have lost his life (v. 13). Both adultery and murder were punishable by death and that would have been a just punishment. However, David now confessed his sin. It was the simplest statement of confession but apparently it was genuine. There was no need for a long and detailed confession of all he had done wrong, or for sacrifice. All that was needed was this genuine acknowledgment and the understanding that what he had done was not just a wrong against Uriah. It was a sin against God. The later prophets also condemned the exploitation of the poor by the rich, but this was not just a social evil. Israel was God's people and therefore sin against a fellow Israelite was a sin against God himself. 'Inasmuch...' said Jesus (Matthew 25:31ff).

However, although David himself would be spared, the child whom Bathsheba would bear to him would not live long.

A REMINDER

If we confess our sins he is faithful and will forgive...

1 John 1:9

REMORSE

The writer makes no bones about it. The Lord struck the child.

Divine anger

It sounds incredibly harsh to us and points to a God who is far less than the loving Father revealed to us by Jesus. Why should the child suffer? It wasn't his fault. He didn't ask to be born. To punish David by making his child ill offends our sense of decency. It is child abuse by God himself. To speak or think in this way is to impose our modern concern for children on a writer whose values were very different and whose view of God was only partial. First, we should see that all events were regarded as due to God's activity and therefore, if the child was ill that was, somehow, part of God's plan. Second, the attitude to children was less sentimental than our own. Not that people were negligent or unconcerned about children. David cared deeply, as we shall see. But children simply had their place in the scheme of things. Third, God's promise to David must be kept and therefore he himself could not be killed at this stage. The one destined to be his heir was not yet born. So the greatest punishment was to take away that which David loved most, Bathsheba's son. If the child was taken ill then it would raise the question: why? In all the circumstances, those concerned could only put it down to God's judgment on David.

A father's concern

David's confession when confronted by Nathan's parable and told its meaning was brief and terse. The genuineness and sincerity of that confession is shown by his attitude to the child's illness. Although he had been told that the child would die, he still dared to hope that God would change his mind and spare him. He therefore went to great lengths on behalf of the child. He prayed, he fasted, he undertook night vigils (v. 16). This went on for a whole week, in spite of the urging of the elders, the older and so the wiser men, whose views should be listened to carefully.

The death

By the seventh day the servants saw that the child had died, but David was too distraught to see it. Such had been the intensity of his emotions that they dared not tell him for fear of what he might do to himself when he learned of it. It was only their hushed conversation that eventually opened David's eyes. He realized the child was dead and they confirmed it.

What would he do now? The normal thing would have been a period of mourning. Ever unpredictable, David harmed neither himself nor his servants, nor even engaged in any mourning rites. The change in verse 20 is quite dramatic and remarkable. To the astonishment of his servants, he discarded all signs of mourning and had his first meal for a week.

It would be easy to see this in a negative light and to say that David was willing to do all in his power so long as there was a chance for the boy, but as soon as it became obvious that this was not so, all concern disappeared. The writer does not put this negative 'spin' on it. Instead he shows David's realism, his readiness to accept what God had decreed and then get on with his life.

We should be careful how we interpret David's final remark (v. 23). It does not express the hope commonly held today that we shall meet our loved ones again in heaven. It is simply an acknowledgment that there was no way back from the dead and that all, at death, went to Sheol. This was the belief for most of the Old Testament period. It was only in the latest part of the period that any belief in resurrection was clearly expressed. It is a view which needs modification in the light of the New Testament and the resurrection of Jesus. Similarly, the view that God carries out his judgment upon people by killing their children needs to be revised in the light of the teaching of Jesus about children. It remains true that human sin has its effects upon other people, but we cannot hold God responsible.

We should remember, too, that confession and forgiveness do not always remove the consequences of sin. These may have to be lived with.

A PRAYER

Help us, Lord, to live with the consequences of our sins and,
having received forgiveness, to get on with our lives.

ALL'S WELL *that* ENDS WELL

The aftermath

Whatever David's feelings were about the boy who died, Bathsheba was sad. We do not learn of any previous chidren whom she may have had by Uriah and perhaps this son by David was her first child. To lose him soon after his birth must have been distressing, though the writer says little about it. She needed consolation and David gave it to her. It reads as though the consolation took the form of further sexual intercourse, as a result of which she again became pregnant (v. 24). When the son was born, David called him Solomon. The name comes from the same Hebrew root as *shalom*, meaning peace or well-being. But another form of the root means 'to be whole or complete'. In yet other forms it means 'to make good, to compensate, to requite'. Perhaps it was this latter meaning that David had in mind when he chose the name of his son. Solomon made good the loss of Bathsheba's earlier child.

There then occurs one of those statements about the Lord which seem to have special significance for the whole story. We are told that the Lord loved Solomon (v. 24). Not only David and Bathsheba, but also the Lord loved him. Because of this divine love his future is assured and, amid all the chances and changes of the following chapters, he will emerge as king in succession to David. Through his prophet the Lord gave him a different name, which means 'Beloved of the Lord'. He is now a marked man. It is rather odd that this name didn't stick. Nowhere else is he called Jedidiah.

It is worth spending a moment, at this point, to think about the portrayal of David in this whole episode. When the writer was putting his material together to write the story of David and his reign, David already had a reputation as the greatest king of the united Israel. So much so that when people looked forward to a time in the future when the fortunes of the people would be restored by God, they thought in terms of a kingdom ruled by an ideal king, a new David. Yet, for all that, the narrator does not make the real David anything other than the man he was, a man with a mixture of good and bad, honestly portrayed. Such honesty is typical of scripture. In the New

Testament also, Peter and Paul, for instance, have their failings and yet are used by God in remarkable ways. This should be an encouragement to us all, though we should never forget that David was humble enough to confess his sins and to acknowledge his dependence on God. By contrast, the book of Chronicles, which is out to show David in the very best light, omits this story altogether.

Victory at last

The unfortunate incident over, the narrator can now return to the story of the war which formed the background to it. The Ammonites were finally defeated and their capital taken. Although verse 26 says that Joab captured the 'royal city', the following verses indicate that it was accomplished only in stages. REB has therefore assumed that there is an error in the text and that this, too, should refer to the pool and not to the city itself. However, it is perhaps better to regard verse 26 as a summary statement, with the following verses describing the manner in which it was captured. First, Joab captured the 'city of waters'. Again it is difficult to know what this means. The Hebrew word for 'city' is not much different from that for 'spring' and maybe we should read that he captured the 'spring of water', that is, the water supply to the city.

To have captured the city itself in the absence of King David would have invited people to call it Joab's city. Joab believed it would be better if David himself led the army in the final assault so that Rabbah would rightly belong to the king of Israel (v. 28). Here is another example of Joab's loyalty to David.

So David took the advice and captured the city in person. Once more there is some uncertainty about whose crown he took. The Hebrew text says it was the 'crown of their king' (*malcam*). The Greek translation, which NRSV and REB have both followed, reads 'the crown of Milcom', Milcom being the god of Ammon (1 Kings 11:5, 33). Whichever is correct, it signified the transfer of the sovereignty of Ammon to David.

A REFLECTION

Think of a few people whom you know, who have been used by God is spite of their faults.

RAPE *within the* FAMILY

David's family troubles now begin. From all that happened at court, our narrator chooses to tell us only of those things which showed how the threat of 12:11 was carried out.

A lovesick son

The first thing that went wrong concerned Amnon, the eldest of the sons born to him while he was still king at Hebron, who was probably regarded as the eventual successor to David (2 Samuel 3:2–5). Amnon's mother was one of the wives who had been with David during the last days in the wilderness before he became king of Judah. He had a half-brother, Absalom, whose mother was the daughter of the king of Geshur, an area to the east of the Sea of Galilee. How David came to marry her we are not told. All the family lived in Jerusalem where the sons had their own houses near David's.

Tamar, Absalom's sister, was a beautiful girl and Amnon, her half-brother, fell in love with her. In one way he would have been pleased to see her almost every day, but the sight of her also brought him face to face with a great temptation. We are given a picture of a lovesick young man who can see no way of expressing his love. Whether or not the laws of incest as set out in Leviticus 18:6ff were in force at this time, it is fairly certain that similar laws would have applied. Sexual activity with a half-sister was forbidden. So there was nothing Amnon could do but live in misery (v. 2).

He had a cousin with whom he was friendly. Jonadab is described as a very 'wise' man, but it was what we might call worldly-wisdom. He knew how to get what he wanted. Amnon's lovesickness was noticeable every morning when they met. By addressing his friend as 'son of the king', Jonadab may have been making it clear that, as the heir to the throne, he had nothing to be miserable about. In any case, as a prince with all the privileges of royalty, he ought not to be depressed, but we all know that even people in privileged positions may feel depression for various reasons. When he learned what was wrong, Jonadab came up, as usual, with an idea to get Amnon what he wanted. As often with tempters, he put only half an idea into Amnon's head, explaining how he could get Tamar into his house and no more than that. The rest will take care of itself. So, on his advice, Amnon feigned illness and asked that Tamar should attend him (v. 6). David is perfectly innocent in all this. He seems to have been completely taken in by Amnon's pretence.

To have her in his presence and to watch her preparing his meals only made his desire for her grow stronger, until the temptation became too much to bear. He cleared everyone out of the house so that he could be alone with her and then invited her to bring his food into the bedroom. When she did so, he asked her to get into bed with him (v. 11). Being a virgin and a virtuous girl, she refused, not apparently because she hated him, but because it would have been wrong. Both of them would be disgraced by such behaviour. Instead she suggested that Amnon should ask David for her hand in marriage. She seemed fairly sure that David would allow this; perhaps she was unaware of any laws of incest. But Amnon could not wait. Already he was in such a state that to wait for even another moment would have been impossible, let alone wait for permission to marry. His sexual urges got the better of him. From his 'sick bed' he caught hold of her, overpowered her and raped her (v. 14).

In some ways it is a case of like father, like son. David's lust for a beautiful woman had led him to adultery and murder. His son's had led him to rape and, as we shall see, to further wrongs in consequence.

A REFLECTION

'Though the bird may fly over your head, let it not make its nest in your hair.' Think about this Danish proverb in relation to temptation and the way we deal with it.

The AFTERMATH

In David's case his lust turned into love; in Amnon's case his lust turned into burning hatred. Psychologically, such a reaction is not uncommon. The guilt experienced leads to self-loathing and then the loathing is transferred to the person who unconsciously caused it. Amnon's hatred was more intense than the lust it replaced.

A wronged woman

As Tamar lay alongside him he dismissed her peremptorily with a 'Get up and go'. No pity, no remorse, no concern for the young woman, just a burning hatred and a desire to put that which had caused his fall out of sight. But Tamar was not to be dismissed so easily. Ignoring for the moment the fact that they were related, there was a law which said that if a man violated a woman he should then take her as his wife (Exodus 22:16f) or, if her father did not approve, he should pay the bride price. Just as David's sin had led him on to murder, so now Amnon's led him to the further wrong of sending away the woman he had wronged without any proper recompense. It will eventually lead to further disaster.

Amnon had tricked her into his bedroom; now he called his servant to put her out (v. 17). He couldn't use her name and couldn't even bear to call her a girl or woman. The Hebrew simply says 'Take *this* away from me.' The door was to be locked in case she tried to return. Tamar herself performed all the signs of mourning, not for the loss of a loved one, but for the loss of her virginity. Especially appropriate was the tearing of the robe, for it was a special one worn by princesses who were virgins.

Brotherly love

Absalom, her full brother, guessed what had happened when he saw her, and sought to comfort her. He presumably knew that she had been sent to Amnon and possibly was aware of Amnon's feelings towards her. His words were hardly likely to bring much comfort to a rape victim. It is hard to see what difference it would make that Amnon was her brother. In fact it was likely to make matters worse. It certainly doesn't seem to have done much for Tamar. In fact, as we

shall see, Absalom's apparent lack of concern only masked his determination to avenge the wrong done to her. David, too, was angry but
was unwilling to punish his eldest son (v. 21). The reason given is that
he loved him, though we may suspect that he was reminded of his
own misconduct and could hardly punish his son for a similar offence.

Revenge is sweet

From then on, the two brothers were not on speaking terms and
Absalom's anger grew and grew. It took two whole years before it came
to the point of action. The royals apparently kept sheep on the hills
outside Jerusalem. The text says it was near Ephraim but almost certainly this is a miscopying, the familiar word 'Ephraim' being copied
for the less common 'Ephron'. Ephron was a hill just a few miles
north-west of the capital. Whether the sheep were kept for commer-
cial purposes or were meant to be used by the royal family, it is hard
to say. In any case, sheep-shearing in the spring was a time for festivi-
ties. Absalom invited his brothers to join in the fun. He also invited
his father to attend and pressed him quite hard (v. 25), but whether
he really wanted him there is very doubtful. It would appear that
Amnon was reluctant to go along. After all, they were not best friends.
However, Absalom asked his father to persuade his brother to go.
David was puzzled as to why he should be so keen to have this brother
present when they were not on speaking terms. He knew there was
bad feeling between them but does not seem to have suspected anything as serious as what actually happened. So Amnon joined the rest.
The party began and it was no mean party. The plan is fairly obvious
to us as we read the story now, though those present would not have
been aware of what was going on. The order to the servants was clear
enough. When everyone had had too much to drink Absalom would
order his servants to kill Amnon. They seem to have been hesitant to
kill the heir to the throne and needed reassurance from Absalom, but
perhaps they thought there was a hint that he would become king if
anything happened to Amnon and they wanted to be on the right side.

Once again the original wrong had led to murder, only this time it
was the wrongdoer himself who was murdered.

A REFLECTION

*'Love your enemies' (Matthew 5:44). How difficult it is to
remember that 'vengeance belongs to the Lord' (Romans 12:19).*

The FAVOURITE FLEES

Before the brothers had reached home David had already heard a rumour that all his sons were dead. Again, as often in the past, David seems to receive news in unexpected and unexplained ways. Were there other shepherds in the area who heard the noise and reported to David—wrongly, as it happened? But, then, how did they reach home before the brothers? Anyway, the rumour caused great consternation and the whole court went into mourning (v. 31).

The rumour scotched

Jonadab also seems to have had some prior information which contradicts David's; or was he just guessing? The cousin, the 'wise' one who had set the ball rolling in the first place with his advice to Amnon, realized that only Amnon was dead. Doubtless he knew of the breach that had occurred between the two brothers, and had an idea that Absalom would eventually take revenge on Amnon for the rape of his sister. So he consoled David by assuring him that the news was not quite as bad as he thought. Only one son was dead and not all of them, as was at first feared.

The murderer escapes

Three times the storyteller tells us that 'Absalom fled' (vv. 34, 37 and 38). The first time it is an interjection between Jonadab's report to the king and the confirmation of it. There is nothing leading up to it or following from it. It is an important piece of information which needs to be passed on at this point, though it will be taken up again later. It is vital to his story. Meanwhile, when the brothers returned, Jonadab simply said to the king, 'I told you so.' He had been very confident about his knowledge. He might even have heard whispers about what was planned.

It didn't put an end to the mourning, but now it was for only one son and not for all of them. Nevertheless, it must have been a great blow to David, who loved Amnon, and anticipated that he would succeed him.

The second 'Absalom fled' is slightly different from the first. There is much greater emphasis on Absalom. 'As for Absalom, he fled.' It seems to contrast his flight with the mourning of the court. He fled back to his mother's family. Talmai was his grandfather on his mother's side (2 Samuel 3:3). The last phrase in verse 37 simply reads, 'He mourned his son' in the Hebrew, leaving us to guess to whom the pronouns refer. The subject is clearly David. 'His son' is indefinite. Which son is meant? On the face of it, it would be Amnon because we have already heard about David's mourning for him. But, coming where it does, in the midst of the account of Absalom's flight, it may refer to Absalom. Not only did David lose Amnon whom he loved; he also lost Absalom and we learn later how much he loved him. The whole episode resulted in the loss of his two favourite sons, both of whom would have had some claim to the throne in due course.

So again in verse 38, 'Absalom fled'. This time we are told that he remained away for three years. Gradually, for David the sorrow over the death of Amnon was replaced by affection for Absalom and a yearning for his return to court (v. 39).

So the first part of the story of the succession ends with the chief claimant dead and another in exile. David's family affairs are truly in a mess, as was threatened. How will the succession work out now?

A REFLECTION

God moves in a mysterious way
his wonders to perform...
Deep in unfathomable mines
of never-failing skill
he treasures up his bright designs,
and works his sov'reign will.

William Cowper, 1731–1800

The PERSUADER

Once again David is compelled to make a judgment about others which has repercussions for himself. In chapter 12 it was Nathan, his prophet, who told the story; here it is a wise woman from Tekoa, acting on the instructions of Joab.

The loyal soldier

Joab recognized how much David missed his son and longed to have him back. It was not easy, though, for David to invite home one who had killed his brother and heir to the throne. Amnon's blood should be avenged. This was the reason he had run away. To take him back would be to fail in these duties and would put a question mark over David's 'just and fair' rule (8:15). On the other hand, Joab could see how it would benefit the nation if David were happy and not constantly thinking about Absalom. He therefore decided on a plan to persuade David that it would be all right to call his son back home.

The woman of Tekoa

We know nothing more about this woman than is told us here. It is fairly clear that she was not just a woman living in Tekoa who happened to be wise. She was a person known for her wisdom to whom people could go for advice, and one who could instruct people on matters of conduct. Tekoa was some nine miles south of Jerusalem. From there the land sloped down to the Dead Sea. It was the town from which Amos was later to come.

The woman, therefore, was sufficiently skilful in speech to be able to carry out Joab's plan. We are told that Joab put the words into her mouth (v. 3), but what she told David was not a careful recital of what Joab had said. He had told her what he wanted, but the actual address to the king was doubtless her own. Unlike Nathan's parable this was not a story about 'someone I know'; it was a made-up story about herself and her family. Her address is couched throughout in court language. She refers to David as 'my lord' and to herself as 'your servant'.

The parallel between her story and the events surrounding Amnon and Absalom is clear to us, but an unsuspecting David saw it as nothing other than genuine. The two sons had fallen out, one had killed the other and the rest of the family meant to avenge the death even though the murderer was heir to the estate. Should her 'remaining ember' be put to death, then her deceased husband would lose both name and descendant and these were the only way by which a man could be thought to live on after death (v. 7).

The woman was nothing if not persistent. When David postponed judgment she pressed him further. She was prepared to take full responsibility for wanting to save her son and to absolve the king. David promised her royal protection but she pressed him still further. The 'avenger of blood' is the *go'el*, the 'redeemer', the next of kin who must fulfil the obligations that fall to him. Finally David gave her the answer she sought. The king made a most solemn promise that her son would be protected by his decree (v. 11).

Now she could show how David had really made a judgment about his own family. Everyone must die in the end, but God would find a way to spare Absalom from blood revenge if he were allowed to return, and David would not be blamed. This is the most likely meaning of a difficult verse 14.

She then reverted to her own assumed case. Feeling threatened, she had appealed to the king and did so now with a large amount of flattery. He was like an angel, a messenger of God. 'Good and evil' may refer to right and wrong in law, but often a phrase such as this, where two extremes are juxtaposed, really means 'everything'. This meaning is confirmed by the similar words in verse 20.

The Penny Drops

She was right, of course, about the king's wisdom and, at last, he saw through her story and guessed that Joab was behind it. There was no denying it. It was Joab's idea, a way of 'breaking out of the circle of events', probably the ongoing call for blood revenge.

A PRAYER

We thank you, Lord, that you do not always treat us as we deserve, but reach out to us in love and forgiveness.

A REUNION

The woman was apparently sent away with a promise that David would recall Absalom to Jerusalem, for the next we hear, David is speaking to Joab.

The son's return

David's words to Joab were, literally, 'I have done this thing' (v. 21). In giving his promise to the woman he had already set the wheels in motion leading to Absalom's return. So he now confirmed it to Joab and sent him off to Geshur to bring Absalom back. This was as yet only a halfway house. Absalom was to return to his own house or family, but was not allowed into David's presence. Not much, therefore, had been gained. Absalom was no better off in Jerusalem than he was in Geshur and, as far as David was concerned, he might as well have stayed where he was.

The handsome prince

Our writer now breaks off his story to tell us a bit more about Absalom (v. 25). In doing so he is preparing us for what comes later. We shall know why people respond to him so readily. He was the most handsome man you could possibly imagine, perfect from head to toe. He had his hair cut only once a year, but when he did the cuttings weighed about five pounds, so long and thick did it grow. We recall that long hair was a sign of strength in Samson, as well as of beauty (Judges 16:17), though in his case he grew it in fulfilment of a vow.

There is no mention of Absalom's wife and we do not know whether the children were born at Jerusalem or Geshur (v. 27). Nor are we told the names of his three sons, but only of his daughter, who was given the same name as his raped sister, perhaps named after her. Like her father, she was beautiful. What a splendid person he was!

Reconciliation

Two years passed and Absalom still hadn't seen his father. He was now getting impatient. He wanted to be back in court. There is no hint yet that this was anything more than a natural wish but, as we shall see later, there may have been more to it than that and the writer, with his description, has prepared us for it. Since Joab had fetched him back from Geshur it seemed natural to ask him to make further overtures to the king for his full reinstatement. However, there is a touch of arrogance in the way he sent messengers to tell him to come and see him. Was it beneath his dignity to go and find Joab, who lived near enough, and ask him to put in another good word with his father? Joab, old enough to be his father, was not prepared to be treated like this by the young prince and refused to go and see him. Twice he refused. Absalom, with a mixture of anger and disdain, ordered his servants to set Joab's barley-field on fire. That brought him. The confrontation was not as 'fiery' as we might have expected (v. 31). When Joab asked why he had been summoned, he was told that Absalom's return to Jerusalem had so far been pointless and he would have been better off staying in Geshur. So Joab must go and ask for him to be allowed back in court. Again the arrogance is there. There is no sorrow for what he has done; he does not feel guilty for killing his brother, as he had every right to avenge his sister's rape. But if the blood revenge still remained active, then let David bring it to an end by killing him. He must have known that David would not do this, since otherwise he would never have let him come home.

Any anger Joab may have felt seems to have been dispelled quickly and he agreed. So Absalom was allowed into his father's presence and welcomed with a kiss.

It is worth noticing how skilfully this writer draws his characters. He does not describe their moral strengths and weaknesses, but in the way he tells their story he lets us see what kind of people they are. This is the mark of a good writer.

A PRAYER

Save us, Lord, from pride and arrogance. Give us grace to admit our faults and to receive forgiveness and strength from you.

An ATTEMPTED COUP

The hints given in the previous chapter are now proved correct. What he wanted was not just a place in the royal court. His ambition was to become king.

Currying favour

First he acquired the equivalent of a royal Daimler, a chariot with horses and a full escort. You would have thought that this might have aroused David's suspicions for he must have known about it. Absalom couldn't do this in secret, nor did he want to. It was to add to his prestige. But David loved Absalom and seems to have been incapable of seeing any wrong in him. In certain respects David was ruled by his heart rather than by his head, expecially in family matters.

Whether David was aware of the next move we cannot say; probably not. Absalom made a point of watching out for people visiting Jerusalem seeking redress for wrongs done to them (v. 2). By getting on the road early, he intercepted them and when he had ascertained where they were from he informed them that there was no one to hear their case, however good that case may be. Then he added the punch-line. If only he were judge he would see to it that their case was heard and justice done. The word 'judge' is somewhat ambiguous, perhaps intentionally so. It often has the force of to 'rule' and by using it Absalom planted a seed in their minds. The whole excuse was false, of course. If only they had persisted and gone into Jerusalem they would have found that there were procedures in place for their cases to be heard, as we saw with the wise woman in the previous chapter who had no difficulty in presenting her alleged case to David. But what Absalom did and said showed David up in a negative light and himself in a positive one. The petitioners had no reason to suspect that his words were anything but true. They would return to their homes disgruntled and prepare to share their disenchantment with their neighbours. With no media and no spin-doctors to help him criticize the government, Absalom found a way of his own.

Then, also like present-day politicians, he was not averse to 'pressing the flesh' or 'baby kissing'. As prince, the people would naturally show him respect, but he responded in a much more positive way than usual. Along with his good looks, this put him in favour with the people. So he 'stole their hearts' (v. 6). The 'heart' is much more than their feelings or even their affections, though it includes these; he also stole their minds so that they would be ready to follow him when the right moment came.

The rising

The process took a little time. The Hebrew text says forty years, but this can hardly be right. The copyist has written the more familiar phrase for the less familiar four years. Still, Absalom was patient. This was not something to be hurried. When the time came he made an excuse for visiting Hebron, where David had first begun to be king over Judah. There was no way a rising could begin in Jerusalem where David's personal troops under the faithful Joab were in charge. Why he should have vowed to worship God in Hebron while he was in Geshur in the north, no one seems to have questioned. After all, it was an important town where the patriarchs were buried. At any rate he was allowed to go there and at once he sent messengers to the various tribes to call out their tribal soldiers in support, since he had now been proclaimed king.

We are bound to wonder whether there were not also some genuine reasons for people's discontent with David. Was there perhaps a feeling of unease at the concentration of power in the capital where the king was supported by his personal troops and where the Lord was probably being worshipped in new ways, with the king playing a very prominent part? Were the old tribal identities being submerged under this central government? The tribes certainly feature prominently in this chapter as Absalom's supporters. It may also be that the common purpose which had drawn people together to fight off their enemies was being lost in the subsequent time of peace. Were these feelings, common enough in the present day, also there in David's time? For whatever reason, the rebel forces grew, enhanced by the wise counsellor, Ahithophel—it was probably he, rather than Absalom, who was offering sacrifices when he was summoned.

A PRAYER

Help us, Lord, to be wise as serpents as well as harmless as doves.

A STRATEGIC WITHDRAWAL

This time David's information service let him down. By the time he heard what was going on, it was too late. Absalom's forces had reached such numbers that the personal troops, however disciplined and well-trained, were no match for them.

The flight

Only one course remained and that was to withdraw from Jerusalem, at least for the time being, and there was no time to lose (v. 10). If they had stayed in Jerusalem Absalom would have come to attack it and cause untold destruction in the capital. We may imagine David's feelings as he decided to abandon the city, *his* city, but it was better to do that than to see it devastated by siege and warfare. If that was his decision, all his attendants and soldiers were ready to follow him. This is the first we have heard of David's harem. We know that he had several wives but apparently he had followed the practice of other kings in having concubines also in his court. The procession went down the city streets towards the spring of Gihon and on the very outskirts of the city David stopped to let his people pass by, all his officials and his bodyguard. The city itself was not evacuated but the people left there would be mainly ordinary householders.

Among those who marched past were six hundred Gittites under their leader, Ittai. These were not part of the regular troops. The only Gittite we have heard of previously has been Obed-edom, into whose house the Ark was taken after the first abortive attempt to take it into Jerusalem (ch. 6). Gath, their original home, was a Philistine city. These people had arrived recently in Jerusalem from Gath for reasons unknown to us. Had they heard of Absalom's coup in Hebron and come to help David because they were uneasy about the new king's attitude to them? We can only speculate. At all events, in spite of their recent arrival they were ready to go with David.

The picture of David standing at the outskirts of Jerusalem, watching his troops cross the Kidron valley and climb the Mount of Olives, is a poignant one. It was a complete reversal of his fortunes, the very opposite of his capture of the city some years previously. To make matters worse he was in flight from his own son, the one he loved and had restored to his court. That threat of trouble in his own household, spoken at the time of his misconduct with Bathsheba (2 Samuel 12:11), must now have haunted him.

The Ark

Worse was to come; the reverse was to be even more complete. His two priests, Abiathar, who belonged to the old Shilonite family, and Zadok, who had appeared only when Jerusalem was captured, followed the procession, the Levites carrying the Ark (v. 24). Presumably they thought that David would want this symbol of the Lord's presence with him if he was going to be in exile and if he was likely to be engaged in battle. It was about to leave the city by the route along which it had been brought in. But the thought of the Ark leaving the city was too much for David. Instead he sent it back to its place, along with the two priests and their sons. No longer does he seem to have believed that the presence of the Ark would be a guarantee of victory as had once been believed (1 Samuel 4).

Indeed there was no attempt to coerce God, either by taking the Ark or by anything else. David was resigned to his fate but his fate was in the hands of God (v. 26). It was for God to decide whether he would still look on him with favour or whether he would withdraw his help. This didn't mean, however, that he would capitulate to Absalom without making any effort. As we shall see, he took steps to see that he regained his throne. He prayed to God but kept his powder dry. Still, the ultimate outcome was in the hands of God.

The return of the priests with the Ark meant that he had friends in the capital to keep him informed about events there. Already he had an eye on the future.

A REFLECTION

When misfortune comes our way, do we just give in to it? Or do we take all steps to alleviate it, still remembering that our lives are in the hands of God?

DOWN *but* NOT OUT

If the incident with Bathsheba marked the moral low mark in David's career, this and the following chapter mark the low point in his political fortunes. When his entourage had passed him, David followed them over the Kidron brook and up the Mount of Olives from which he would be able to see clearly his own city and his own house within it. No wonder he wept. All he had lived and fought for he was now leaving behind. So it was a sad procession which marched to the shrine at the top of the Mount.

A counsellor to be feared

In 1 Chronicles 27:33 two people are specially mentioned as part of David's inner circle. First is Ahithophel, who is described as a counsellor or adviser to the king. To his dismay David, on reaching the summit of the Mount of Olives, discovered that this man had gone over to Absalom. This was a great blow because Ahithophel's advice could always be relied upon and so it was important to have him on your side. Now that he was with Absalom there was nothing left for David to do except pray that somehow God would ensure that on this occasion Ahithophel got it wrong so that he would look foolish instead of wise (v. 31). How often have we prayed that God would frustrate the plans of those who devise evil!

The secret agent

The second person mentioned in 1 Chronicles 27:33 is Hushai the Archite (v. 32). This is the name of the clan to which he belonged and not the name of the place from which he came. The Archites are said to have settled not far from Bethel at a place called Ataroth (Joshua 16:2). He is also described as the king's friend, as he is in verse 37 of this present chapter. It appears that this described some kind of office rather than just a social friendship, but what his functions would be is not altogether clear. In 1 Kings 4:5 there is a list of 'high officials' at Solomon's court. Among them is someone called Zabud who is said to be a priest and king's friend. Hushai, then, was a close associate of the king within his inner cabinet and he, too, gave advice as it was needed. Unlike Ahithophel, Hushai remained faithful to David and met him there on top of the Mount of Olives. He intended to go with David, but David had other plans for him. It is not easy to see why he would have been a burden to David, but it is easy to see how he could be an even greater help to the king by not going with him. If he went back to Jerusalem and deserted to Absalom as Ahithophel had done, he would be able to act as David's agent in court. However reliable was the advice given by the king's counsellor, that of the king's friend would have to be taken just as seriously. He could also keep his ears open and discover what Absalom was planning to do.

The two priests and their sons were also part of the scheme (v. 35). They would be Hushai's contacts to whom he would pass any information he received. The sons were apparently young and agile enough then to carry the information to David in his place of exile. So David put in place a neat network to make sure he had all the necessary information. He might be willing to submit to the Lord's will but he was not going to do so lying down and without making a fight of it. He had lost nothing of that old cunning and skill in dealing with awkward situations which he had shown in the wilderness before he became king.

So Hushai was back in Jerusalem just in time to be there as Absalom was entering the city (v. 37). He was not, therefore, suspected of any deceit but was able to welcome the new king and take his place in his court.

A REFLECTION

The acceptance of God's will in advance does not mean that we have to suspend our own faculties. It demands that we use our gifts and trust him for the outcome.

The BANDWAGON ROLLS

Often when a coup takes place there is a period of general unrest and confusion. It was no different in David's case. Here are two incidents which show how fickle people can be.

The lame pretender

Mephibosheth had been treated with the utmost kindness by David (ch. 9). David had sought him out in order to repay his debt to Jonathan, Mephibosheth's father, and had taken him into the court, giving him all the property which had belonged to Saul. Gratitude for such kindness lasted only as long as David's fortunes remained good. As soon as things began to go wrong for David, Mephibosheth saw an opportunity to take advantage (v. 3). It is true that as the remaining member of Saul's family he had some claim to the throne, but how he thought he could take it when Absalom was already in control, only he knew. His was a lost cause from the start. His servant, Ziba, had more sense and more loyalty. He met David just after he and his people had left the top of the Mount of Olives, bringing with him supplies to help them on their way. The donkeys were quite heavily laden, but even so, what he brought would not go very far among all those who followed David. It was the thought that counted! Just as David had given all Saul's possessions to Mephibosheth, so now he promised them to Ziba instead. Of course that would have to wait until he had been restored.

Curses galore

The second incident concerns this man called Shimei (v. 5). Little is known about him. He was a descendant of Gera, and in Genesis 46:21 one of Benjamin's sons was called Gera. We shall meet him again in chapter 19, where we learn that he was a Benjaminite and he lived in Bahurim. If this Gera was actually Shimei's father then he had the same name as one of his ancestors, but it may be that 'son of' here really means a descendant of this son of Benjamin who lived a century or two earlier. He was perhaps a man of some standing. Later he was put to death by Solomon for disobeying a curfew which the king had laid upon him (1 Kings 2:36–46). Obviously he was another unreliable fellow. When David reached his home in Bahurim just to the east of Jerusalem, he came out and began to curse David. It seems to have been an individual protest unsupported by others. It is a protest which sends David on his way out of Jerusalem with curses ringing in his ears. The style of the protest hasn't altered much today! His claims, however, are not true. At least, they are only partially true. That David was a murderer cannot be denied, but Shimei was not referring to the death of Uriah. It is clear that he was accusing David of shedding the blood of Saul's house. This, as we saw, David would never do. He took great pains not to harm either Saul or his son, Ishbaal, and he had gone out of his way to do good to Mephibosheth, Saul's grandson. There was no way he could have incurred blood guilt which needed to be avenged (v. 8).

Abishai, Joab's brother, was all for catching Shimei and cutting off his head. Zeruiah's sons were a bit like that! (see 2:21 and 3:27). David quickly dissociated himself from such an idea. We have seen before how David, although he was taking the trouble to try to win his throne back, was uncertain whether Absalom's coup was the will of God. He seems to have been uncertain, too, of Shimei's standing. Was he a prophet who was declaring God's word of condemnation to him? If he was, then there was no point in putting him to death. That would not change things. If he was not, then it didn't matter much what he said. Underneath this uncertainty on the part of David, there was a feeling that he must accept the insults heaped upon him, and that in the end he would be vindicated by God (v. 12). So Shimei was allowed to go on cursing and throwing stones, a practice common then as now.

The Hebrew text does not say where they eventually reached. The ancient Greek translation says it was the Jordan and this is very likely correct. The safest place for the time being was across the Jordan. No wonder they were tired, mentally and emotionally as well as physically, and needed a rest.

A REFLECTION

How fickle is human loyalty compared with the steadfast love of God.

FRIENDSHIP QUESTIONED

This passage picks up again the story of Absalom from the moment he entered Jerusalem with his chief adviser, Ahithophel.

Whose friend?

On David's instructions Hushai was there to meet him with a greeting which affirmed his kingship. 'Long live the king' was the regular formula by which a king was popularly recognized (cf. 1 Kings 1:25, 39). By it he expressed his loyalty to Absalom. Needless to say, Absalom was suspicious and showed it by making much of Hushai's title. The two words for 'friend' which are used here (vv. 16–17) are virtually identical, though the first is rather more specialized as a title. Such difference as there is would be well expressed in English by the use of a capital letter for one and not for the other (see REB). If Hushai is David's Friend (see 15:37), then David must be his friend. Such friendship demands loyalty (steadfast love or devotion). Why then was Hushai going back on his friendship? Why was he not showing devotion to David by going with him? His reply began with an emphatic 'No'. He was the King's Friend, not David's friend. Now Absalom was the legitimate king, chosen by both God and the people, the two things which validated kingship in these early days. Loyalty was to the king. When David was king he had served as the King's Friend. Now that David's son had succeeded him, Hushai would be the same for him. In other words, loyalty was to the king as king and not to the king as friend.

All this, of course, was false. He still was David's friend as well as the King's Friend and all his protestations of loyalty to Absalom were lies in order to gain his confidence and become David's secret agent in Absalom's court. Certainly the Lord had not chosen Absalom, but to say he had was to flatter him and to attribute to him a status which he didn't really have.

Whose advice?

It was not to Hushai that Absalom turned for advice but to Ahithophel. Here we learn just how respected he was and how much his advice was valued. David had relied on it when he was effectively king. Now Absalom, having taken on the kingship, did the same (v. 20). There were, of course, other people whose function it was to give guidance in times of uncertainty. Nathan the prophet had advised David on the question of building a temple. The word of the Lord had come to him to forbid it. Before going into battle it was customary to consult the ephod, the garment in which the priest kept Urim and Thummim, the sacred lot. Through this, the word of the Lord was given to the person seeking help. Ahithophel was neither prophet nor priest. He was simply the political adviser. Yet the advice he gave was every bit as reliable as that received through prophet or priest (v. 23). Though the term is not used of Ahithophel, he was probably one of the wise men who dispensed wisdom, gave counsel and taught life-skills in the royal court. So the counsel of the wise was as reliable as the word of the Lord mediated through prophet or priest.

Consequently it was to Ahithophel that Absalom now turned for advice as to how he could advance further his claim to the throne of Israel. An acknowledged way of doing so was to use the concubines of the departed king. Abner had done just this with Saul's concubine, so claiming precedence over Ishbaal (3:6ff). Now David had left ten concubines in Jerusalem to look after the palace (15:16). So Ahithophel's advice was that Absalom should use these openly (v. 21). Not only would this offend David; it would show to all and sundry that Absalom was now king for certain, so encouraging their support. Therefore a tent was erected on the palace roof in full view of the people of Jerusalem and there Absalom took his father's concubines and used them as his own.

So the writer presents us with these two rivals in Absalom's court: his genuine supporter, Ahithophel, highly respected for his advice, and the King's Friend, Hushai, David's undercover agent whose task was to influence affairs of state in a way favourable to David.

A QUESTION for THOUGHT

How far and in what circumstances is it legitimate to use lies and deceit in the furtherance of right or in the service of God?

CONFLICTING ADVICE

The question now was what to do about David. Absalom had got himself established in Jerusalem and, by and large, the people seem to have accepted him as their king. But while David was still at large he could never feel safe. He still had his loyal bodyguard with him and that was a force to be reckoned with. How was Absalom to get rid of this threat?

The wise man's advice

Ahithophel's advice was to muster twelve divisions and pursue David at once (v. 1). The idea was to catch him and his people while they were tired with the journey and depressed about having to flee. With morale at a low ebb it should be easy to isolate David from his people. They would then quickly give in, and once David was on his own he could be killed, without fighting and killing the rest of them. They would then return to Jerusalem to live under Absalom. Notice how both Ahithophel and later Hushai deliver their advice using picture language to drive home their point. David's people would return 'as a bride comes home to her husband'. It was customary for the bride-groom to fetch his bride from her family home and take her to his own, where she would go willingly and joyfully. In actual fact, this simile is not found in the Hebrew which means, literally 'like the return of the whole'. This doesn't make much sense and so most translators and commentators follow the Greek translation as both NRSV and REB have done. Ahithophel's advice made good sense to both the king and his court.

The friend's advice

Why Absalom wanted further advice is not clear, seeing that Ahitho-phel was so well respected, but he did. He sought confirmation of it from Hushai. So presumably Hushai had convinced Absalom of his loyalty and that his advice was worth hearing. Hushai acknowledged that Ahithophel was usually right, but on this occasion he declared that he was wrong.

Hushai's arguments were also convincing and true. Far from being tired and dispirited, David and his men would be furious, like a bear whose cubs had been taken away. Then also David was a wily and experienced commander of his bodyguard who were utterly loyal to him. Moreover, far from being able to isolate David so as to kill only him, they would not be able to find him because he would be securely hidden, already away from his men. When Absalom's men attacked, they would not be able to find him. They would suffer considerable losses and the rest of the army would then flee in fear. David's reputation as a warrior was so well known, even among Absalom's men, that once defeat was imminent the whole force would give way.

Hushai then proposed a different scheme (v. 11). Instead of sending a limited force Absalom should send a large army drawn from all over Israel and he himself should lead it. Such an army would surely win any battle. Not only would David be killed but also his bodyguard with him. Should they escape and become holed up in a city, then the city could be reduced and destroyed.

The picture language of Hushai is even more impressive than that of Ahithophel, even if we accept the Greek translation of the latter. A bear robbed of its cubs, a heart like a lion, a number like sand on the seashore, the dew falling on the ground, the city dragged into the valley with ropes—such figures of speech are typical of the writings of the wise men especially, as may be seen in the book of Proverbs.

In style, but also in content, Hushai's advice seemed better than Ahithophel's. At least Absalom thought so, as did members of his court (v. 14).

The hidden Lord

Behind all the scheming of these two men, there is another at work. They may be thought to be giving their advice on the basis of their own understanding of how things were, but, in fact, it was the Lord who was really at work. Just as the writer's comment at 12:24 that the Lord loved Solomon shows that he was involved in human affairs, so here again. Things are not haphazard; they are not controlled by some impersonal fate. It is the Lord himself who is in control. Again this perspective is typical of the wise men.

A REFLECTION

God moves in a mysterious way
his wonders to perform.

William Cowper, 1738–1800

The SCHEME WORKS

There was quite a network of David's supporters in Jerusalem. The two priests, Abiathar and Zadok, had been sent back along with their two sons, Jonathan and Ahimaaz (15:27). These latter seem to have been unable to enter the city itself. It looks as though they were under suspicion, though we are not told why. So Hushai told the priests, who told a servant-girl, who told Jonathan and Ahimaaz, who were to tell David.

The spies in danger

The servant-girl was caught giving the news to the two young men and it was reported to Absalom. What happened to the girl we do not know, but the boys were forced to hide. En-rogel, where they had been staying, was just outside Jerusalem itself and now they fled to Bahurim, a village not far from the capital, where Shimei had cursed David. However, there were also some of the residents who were faithful to David, and the young men found their way there. The woman of the house hid them in a well in the courtyard and camouflaged it so that it would look undisturbed. She then lied to their pursuers, who believed her and made off (v. 20).

The report to David

Jonathan and Ahimaaz advised David to get across the Jordan as quickly as possible. They appear to have been uncertain whether Absalom would follow Ahithophel's advice and pursue David quickly with the more limited forces, or Hushai's, which would mean a little delay until the larger forces could be gathered from the outlying areas. So, to be on the safe side, they urged David to cross the river and he did so (v. 22). The urgency was not really necessary, for Absalom, as we know, had decided to follow Hushai's recommendation. Ahithophel's reputation was now in ruins and his pride was so damaged that he went home to Giloh, his home town, and committed suicide. There is no critical comment about this, although life was held to belong to God and to be at his disposal to give or take away. The writer's interest in Ahithophel has now disappeared and it is enough to record his end (v. 23).

The retreat continues

Having crossed the Jordan, David next made his way northwards to Mahanaim, which lay another thirty miles away from the point of the crossing. This was the town where Ishbaal had set up his kingdom on the death of his father, Saul. The time it took for Absalom to gather his forces allowed David this leeway and he was able to put a fair distance between himself and Absalom, who followed him over the Jordan and camped in Gilead, south of David's position. We are not told exactly where (v. 26).

For this campaign Absalom needed a commander-in-chief. Joab, of course, was with David. Ahithophel had offered to lead the smaller force himself if his plan had been chosen, but Hushai's scheme needed Absalom himself to be in charge. Nevertheless, a commander was also needed and we are told that he appointed Amasa who was part Ishmaelite (v. 25). The Hebrew text says his father was an Israelite, not an Ishmaelite, but it would be quite unnecessary to say he was an Israelite. The need to give his nationality would only arise if he were a foreigner and 1 Chronicles 2:17 tells us that Amasa's father, Ishra (or Jether), was an Ishmaelite. On his mother's side he was a cousin of Joab; their mothers were sisters and, according to Chronicles, sisters of David. He was therefore a reasonable choice.

Meanwhile, at Mahanaim David was well cared for. Even those who had been his enemies now brought him supplies. Shoba was the brother of Hanun who had rejected David's condolences about his father's death, an act which led to the Ammonite war (ch. 10) and the capture of Rabbah, the capital city (12:26). Machir was the one in whose house Mephibosheth had lived after the death of his father Jonathan. This is the first we have heard of Barzillai, whose home was further north still. All these became friends of David and met the needs of his followers plentifully.

All this is due to the vaunted ambition of Absalom, the son whom David loved and had accepted back at court in spite of his murder of his brother. Now we find the two lined up ready to do battle against each other. The tragedy goes on.

A PRAYER

Forgive us, Lord, when we let our selfish ambition run away with us and hurt those who love us most.

CIVIL WAR

David's army seems a particularly large one until we remember again that a 'thousand' and a 'hundred' do not represent the precise number of men but are technical terms for military units. All the same, there were enough of them to be divided into three groups (v. 2). Of the three commanders, we are already very familiar with the brothers, Joab and Abishai. Ittai we met in 15:19 as a comparative newcomer who insisted on going along with David into temporary exile.

The king's presence refused

It was usual for a king to lead his army into battle as Absalom was doing on the other side. David's decision to do so was expressed in very strong terms: 'I will certainly go out, yes, I myself with you.' Yet we may wonder what role he was going to play, seeing that he had appointed a commander for each of his three divisions. Indeed, in view of what follows, we may suspect that his reason for wanting to be present was so that he could keep an eye open for Absalom so as to make sure he was kept safe.

However, the commanders were adamant that he should stay behind in Mahanaim so that he could provide assistance if necessary (v. 3). They were aware that the enemy would do their best to find David and kill him because that would then throw the whole army into disarray and ensure victory. Joab and the others were not prepared to risk that. Tactically it was better that the king should remain in the city and leave the fighting to them. Against such strong opposition David had little option but to acquiesce. So, as they left the city, he charged them to deal gently with Absalom if they met him, and he made sure that everyone heard him give this order so that no one could pretend that they had not heard it. Everyone would know of his concern for his son's safety.

We may regard this concern in two ways. On the one hand it shows David's love and loyalty to one of his children and his readiness, as a father, to forgive his rebellion. He could even overlook the fact that his son was out to be rid of him in order to fulfil his selfish ambition. On the other hand, we may see it as a weakness in David in that he was ready to put his own sentimental feelings for his family before the need of his nation for stability and prosperity. As often, in the character of David as drawn by this writer we find a mixture of motives which is true to our human experience.

The battle fought and won

The account of the battle is straightforward (v. 6) and the only question that arises is the whereabouts of the 'forest of Ephraim'. The area known as Ephraim with which we are familiar is much too far away. It is miles to the south on the west bank of the Jordan and the battle could not have been fought there. REB has altered the text to 'forest of Ephron'. In 13:23 it read Ephron for Ephraim quite rightly, but the mount of Ephron mentioned there is even further away, not far from Jerusalem. It is best to assume that there was a forest of Ephraim just to the south of Mahanaim. It is possible that it was so named following the defeat of the Ephraimites by Jephthah the Gileadite recorded in Judges 12:1–6.

Just what is meant by 'the forest ate more troops than the sword ate', which is a literal translation of verse 8, is hard to say. It could mean that many soldiers got lost in the forest and died there, or that they were attacked by lions or other wild beasts. But it may, more reasonably, anticipate what is now to follow. Absalom, the leader of the rebels, was caught and killed there and he was worth more than any number of soldiers. Just as David was worth ten thousand to his side (v. 3) so also was Absalom to his. Once he was killed, the rebellion would be over and victory complete. But this is to anticipate what is still to come.

A PRAYER

Lord, give me the courage to do what is right even if it means personal disappointment and sorrow. Help me to 'seek first the Kingdom of God' (Matthew 6:33).

A SAD END

It was by chance that one of David's men found Absalom in a most awkward and embarrassing situation. We recall that he had a wonderful head of hair which was one of the features which made him so attractive. He had it cut only once a year. How he must have wished he had had it cut just before this battle! Riding through the forest, his hair caught in the thickly entwined branches of an oak tree. It became so entangled that he could not free himself and his mule went on its way, leaving him hanging there helpless. It must have been with some amusement that the soldier reported this to Joab (v. 10). Joab was not amused, however, and chided the man for not killing Absalom there and then. He had gone to a great deal of trouble to get Absalom restored to the court in Jerusalem because David wanted it, but instead of being grateful Absalom had taken advantage of his new position to ingratiate himself with the people and, when the opportunity came, to try to oust his father. All this, along with Joab's undoubted loyalty to David, was sufficient for him to want Absalom removed altogether so that he could cause no more trouble. He would have given a generous present to the soldier if he had killed him as he hung in the tree, even though David had said they were to deal gently with him.

The man was not afraid to answer back. Like everyone else, he had heard David's instruction and meant to obey it. He does not seem to have had much confidence in Joab, for he did not believe that Joab would have stood by him when the king discovered that he had killed his son. Why he didn't immediately cut him down and take him captive, we do not know. Perhaps he just wanted to make sport of him first.

Joab went back to the spot with the man while they were talking. Joab's response to the man is not altogether clear. REB comes nearest to the proper meaning. He claimed that the man's accusation that he would not have supported him was a lie and to prove it he began to kill Absalom himself (v. 14). There is not a word of conversation between Joab and Absalom, no plea for mercy from the one and no word of condemnation from the other. It was no quick kill. First Joab stabbed him in the chest three times as he hung there helpless, and then his armour bearer finished him off. It was a cruel and gruesome act.

With Absalom out of the way the rest of the troops had already begun to run away, and when he was finally killed it marked the end of the rebellion. Joab's men were recalled from pursuing them as they made their way home again. Meanwhile, Absalom's body was unceremoniously dumped in a pit in the forest with nothing but a large heap of stones to mark the spot.

A monument to a pretender

The note about this monument in verses 18–19 raises a few questions. We can say for certain that at the time of the exile in Babylon, in the writer's own day, there existed in Jerusalem a monument to Absalom. Its location is uncertain. The King's Valley may refer to the foot of the southern slope of Jerusalem where later kings were buried. In Absalom's own day, only one king of Israel had died, Saul, and he was buried at Jabesh-gilead. However, in Genesis 14:17 we read of a valley of Shaveh which was known to the writer as the King's Valley. It was where Abraham met Melchizedek, king of Sion, and it may well have been the place where the pre-Israelite kings of Jerusalem had been buried. Perhaps later Israelite kings were buried in the same place.

It was not unusual for kings in the ancient Near East to set up monuments for themselves. Often they showed the authority of the king over the area around. The reason given for Absalom's monument is different. Since there was no belief in a meaningful life after death, people could be thought to go on living in their children or in their 'name'. Since Absalom had no children, according to verse 18, he erected this monument to perpetuate his name. What had happened to the three sons mentioned in 14:27 we do not know. We must then ask when Absalom erected it. The text says he did it when he was alive. Was he king for longer than we imagine between David's flight and the raising of an army to pursue him? Could it possibly have been before he became king while he was winning the people's affection? Or is the notice here simply the result of a tradition that had grown up about a monument in Jerusalem? In any case it is a sad end.

A REFLECTION

How do you wish to be remembered?

GOOD & BAD NEWS

Ahimaaz was the usual carrier of news, a good long-distance runner. Joab, however, was reluctant to let him take the news of the battle to David on this occasion, for he knew what David's reaction would be when he learned that Absalom was dead. Instead he entrusted the task to a foreigner. If David reacted violently it would be better for a foreigner to suffer than for the priest's son. Ahimaaz was not prepared to let someone else do his job without a protest. Eventually Joab's reluctance was overcome and he gave him permission to follow the Cushite (v. 23).

Watching and waiting

Mahanaim was a walled city with a double gate. The inner and outer gates would be set at an angle to make it difficult for intruders to enter. Between the two gates was a room with the usual flat roof. From this vantage point a watchman could see anyone approaching the city. It was from here that one of them saw a runner and reported it to David. If there had been a lot of men running back to the city, it would have meant that they were retreating before the enemy to seek sanctuary in the city, but since there was only one man it must mean that he was bringing news of the battle and it could only be good news. When a second runner appeared, it might have denoted the beginning of a retreat, but again he was alone and so must be another messenger. There was evidently something distinctive about the way Ahimaaz ran which made him recognizable as he drew nearer. David seems to have assumed that because Ahimaaz was a good man the news also must be good (v. 27). Perhaps he thought that if it had been bad, Joab would have entrusted it to someone else not so good.

The good news

'Shalom,' said Ahimaaz—all is well! The traditional greeting carried with it the implication that the news was good.

The rebels had been beaten and, typically, he attributed this success to the Lord. 'Blessed' here carries the meaning of 'thanks' (v. 28). It is all thanks to the Lord. David showed little interest in the outcome of the battle. He did not ask about the losses sustained or about the welfare of his generals. He was interested in only one thing. It was the concern that had been with him throughout. What about Absalom? Had they dealt gently with him? Where was he now? Was he all right? At this point Ahimaaz's courage failed him. He dared not tell the king what had happened. He did what many of us would do in these circumstances when we are bearers of bad news. He made out that he wasn't sure what had happened. It had all been rather hectic. Certainly there had been something going on to do with Absalom but he hadn't been able to see what it was (v. 29).

Now the bad news

So David waited for the second runner, who gave him almost exactly the same news. You can almost feel his impatience. Again, what about Absalom? In a roundabout way the Cushite told him that he was dead. It was something that couldn't be said openly; it needed to be wrapped up to soften the blow (v. 32). The wrapping about the king's enemies, the rebels, was good enough, but the pill inside was bitter indeed.

David's grief was inconsolable. The verb that is used means 'to shake, to quiver, to be agitated'. The picture of the king shaking with grief and sobbing, making his way into the room over the gate to be alone, calling his son's name, is indeed a moving one (v. 33). How much he must have loved Absalom in spite of everything! Years before, his son born to Bathsheba had died instead of him. Now he would willingly have died instead of his son. Then the Lord had said that he would raise up trouble within his family. Like a snowball, that trouble had got larger and larger, with the death of Amnon at the hands of Absalom and now the rebellion and death of Absalom himself. 'Father of peace' his son's name meant, but he was anything but the bringer of peace. He had brought nothing but disturbance and grief. And there was yet more to come.

A PRAYER

Lord, when our anxiety turns to grief, be near us
and sustain us by your grace.

A CHANGE *of* HEART

What should have been a time of rejoicing had been turned into a day of mourning. With the king grieving so deeply, the people who were with him were unable to celebrate their victory. Instead they crept about in silence, just as they would have done if they had run away from the battle. And all because of Absalom.

Pull yourself together

It would hardly be necessary to tell Joab. He must have been as aware of it as anyone and, as commander of the army, felt cheated of the victory celebrations. So he went to see David, to give him a piece of his mind. The time for sympathy had passed; what was needed was some straight talking and Joab was just the man to do it. Sometimes, even in the depths of grief, we need to be reminded of other people. Otherwise it may become merely selfish. This is what Joab did (v. 5). What about all the people who had saved his life and his kingdom? Didn't they deserve a thought? His obsessive grief had demonstrated to all and sundry that he thought more about the treacherous Absalom than he did about his faithful followers.

It is doubtful whether anyone other than Joab could have spoken to David in this way. The relationship between them is a very interesting one. Joab had served David faithfully from the very earliest days when he was holed up in the cave of Adullam. In that service he had been ruthless whereas David had been soft-hearted. This difference in temperament had resulted in some disagreements but the long-standing relationship had always been restored. Contrary to David's wishes and behind his back, he had killed Abner (3:27) when he had come over to David's side. Whether it was because he couldn't trust such a man to be loyal to David or whether he was afraid of losing his position, we cannot say. Perhaps there was a mixture of both. Ostensibly it was because there was a blood feud between them. David condemned this violence and uttered a curse against Joab and his family (3:29). Yet Joab was prepared, so it seems, to climb up the water shaft to capture Jerusalem, and was ready to help him get rid of Uriah, Bathsheba's husband (11:6–21). He couldn't bear to see David miserable over the absence of Absalom and, against his better judgment, took a great deal of trouble to get him back to Jerusalem and ultimately into David's presence. He had gone out of the capital with David when he was forced to leave, and now had led his army to victory. Now, with great cruelty he had killed Absalom against the express command of David. It was only on the strength of this long and close, if stormy, relationship that he was now able to take David to task. David, for his part, accepted the criticism and went out to meet the men who had fought for him.

Stirrings of restoration

We are not told the immediate consequences of David's appearance before his troops (v. 8). We are left to presume that they were thanked and things got back to normal. REB leaves a space in the text here. Instead, attention is directed to the Israelites back in their home towns. The feeling spread around that, now that Absalom was dead, they should invite David back. However, this desire does not seem to have spread as far as Judah. The differences between the Northern tribes and Judah had not been overcome completely, in spite of David's efforts, and now they come out into the open again. Oddly enough, this time it is Judah which lags behind. Earlier they had made David king there seven years before he was invited by the Northern tribes to become king of all Israel. Now it is Judah which needs to be reminded that it would be a good idea to invite him back (v. 11).

The appeal to Judah

One would have expected Zadok and Abiathar to have been among the first to welcome David back. Instead they needed nudging to do so. Perhaps it was Amasa, Absalom's general, who held them back and so David appealed to him as well. He made him the remarkable offer of the post of commander of the army instead of Joab. No doubt the death of Absalom still rankled in his mind. He addressed him as one to whom he was closely related and we saw earlier (17:25) that in Chronicles Amasa was related to David. They took the strong hint and brought him back to Jerusalem.

A REFLECTION

How do we respond to criticism from friends?

FORGIVENESS & REWARDS

David's return to his own land raised serious questions for those who had either opposed him or refused to support him. Ziba was not one of these. He had supplied David with provisions at the time he was leaving Jerusalem, and now he was here again to help David and his people back across the River Jordan. There was a ford in the river and Ziba, with his sons and servants, went back and forth over it, helping to transport the king's possessions (vv. 17–18).

The curser blessed

Shimei, it will be remembered, was the one who had cursed David as he was leaving Jerusalem. He was therefore in a dangerous position now that the king was returning (v. 16). So he took the initiative and approached David with an apology and a fulsome confession of his wrongdoing. All he could do was to appeal to the king for clemency. Abishai, who, along with his brother Joab, was renowned for his quick temper and his readiness to take vengeance, was all for putting Shimei to death. He had been ready to do the same when Shimei had cursed David and had had to be restrained by David (16:9, 11). With a similar reply David spared the man yet again. This was a day for rejoicing; he was king again. Why spoil it by taking revenge?

Lame excuses?

Mephibosheth also came to meet David, doubtless afraid of the reception he would get (v. 24). He was required to say why he had stayed in Jerusalem and had not gone with David. David already had one answer. Mephibosheth's servant Ziba had told him it was because he hoped to become king (16:3). Now Mephibosheth blamed Ziba and accused him of lying. According to him, he had asked Ziba to saddle a donkey for him since he was too lame to walk. Although he doesn't actually say so, we have to assume that Ziba failed to do so. Like the wise woman of Tekoa in 14:17, he compares the king to an angel of God. The point of comparison for her was that he was able to distinguish between right and wrong, and the same is probably meant here. David was wise enough to know whether Ziba had been telling the truth or whether Mephibosheth was doing so now. Perhaps, however, David was not so sure, for he was willing to restore half of the possessions he earlier transferred to Ziba. It is difficult also for us to decide. Certainly Mephibosheth was not a strong character, yet the text says that he had neglected himself, as a sign of mourning, all the time David had been away.

David's readiness to forgive both Shimei and Mephibosheth may be out of the kindness of his heart at a time when he was rejoicing in his restoration. We are bound to ask, however, whether there may not have been another motive. As when he was banished in the wilderness he was anxious not to antagonize the people of Israel, so here, too, he may have wished to keep them on his side by his generosity, especially to Mephibosheth, Saul's grandson.

Loyalty rewarded

The fourth person to be with him as he was about to cross the Jordan was the man who had helped him so much when he had retreated to Mahanaim. Barzillai had travelled south with him and was now ready to make the journey back home (v. 31). David offered him the chance to go with him to Jerusalem and to live in the court there. But at the age of eighty, Barzillai felt himself too old to be able to enjoy the delights of life in Jerusalem and so asked permission to return home to his family. He requested instead that Chimham should go with David. Just who Chimham was we are not told. Was he perhaps one of Barzillai's sons? Or was he just a trusted servant? It doesn't make much difference for we hear no more of this man. There is a reference to a property of Chimham in Jeremiah 41:17 and it is situated near Bethlehem. This, of course, is three centuries later, but it is possible that the place retained the name of the original owner to whom it was given by David.

So David returned with the support of all Judah (v. 42), but of only half of Israel. The divisions between the two halves of the kingdom were by no means healed.

A REFLECTION

Sometimes forgiveness may look like a sign of weakness,
though it is really a sign of strength.

JEALOUSY & UNREST

Some of the details in these verses are not easy to understand, although the main point of them is clear enough. They reveal an intense jealousy between the northern part of David's kingdom and the southern part represented by the tribe of Judah. We have already seen in verses 11 and 12 that the northerners had been the first to suggest that David should now return as king and that David had sent to ask why the Judeans had not yet done so. These were now quick to comply and so he was escorted over the Jordan by 'all the people of Judah' but by only 'half the people of Israel'. Why the other half were not on hand, we do not know. Perhaps the Galileans were too far removed from the scene.

The argument

It is noticeable that the writer uses the terms Israel and Judah to denote the north and south, terms which were commonly used after the division of the kingdoms following the death of Solomon. The Israelites accused the Judeans of 'stealing' David. This is a pretty strong charge seeing that stealing was forbidden in the ten commandments (Exodus 20:15). It may be, however, that here it simply means 'take by stealth': that is, the Judeans had come to take the king home without reference to the rest of the kingdom.

The complaint is first made to David himself (v. 41), though later on in the argument each side addressed the other directly. Does this suggest that it was contested like a legal case before the king as judge? David's part in it is not mentioned again. He gave no answer and made no judgment. At the end, in verse 43, the word 'fiercer' represents a Hebrew word which really means 'hard' or 'difficult', and it is used in this sense in Deuteronomy 1:17 of a law case which is too difficult for the local elders to decide. Perhaps here, too, it means that the Judean arguments were more difficult than those of the Israelites.

But what were the arguments? First, as we have seen, the Israelites accused the Judeans of stepping in without reference to anyone else, as though the king belonged exclusively to them. The reply was that David was closely related to the Judeans, which was true enough. He was a Bethlehemite and he had, after all, been their king for seven years before he became king of Israel as well. They had not received any special favours from the king, so why should the Israelites be jealous and angry? The Israelites countered with the fact that they represented more of the original tribes than Judah. What is perhaps surprising is that they claim only ten shares, not eleven. This perhaps suggests that Benjamin was already seen to be in close alliance with Judah. Alternatively, the writer may have been influenced by what happened later, for when the kingdom finally divided on the death of Solomon, although 1 Kings 12:20 says that only Judah remained with Rehoboam, 12:21 says that Judah and Benjamin were under his control. In any case, the Israelites felt they had a better claim on the king on account of their numbers. The second clause, 'and in David also we have more than you', seems to add nothing, although it is introduced by a word which really means 'moreover', as though a second claim was being made. The early Greek translation had the word 'first-born' in place of 'David'. REB has followed this and then the clause means that the northern tribes were older than Judah, probably referring to the fact that they were the ones who had been brought out of Egypt, had been chosen by God and settled by him in Canaan. On these grounds, therefore, they had a better claim on the king than the Judeans. Then again, they were the ones who had first suggested bringing David back.

The unity of David's kingdom was obviously very fragile, in spite of all the efforts he had made to unite the two halves.

The split widens

The consequence of this dispute was that Sheba took advantage of the situation. He was, in fact, a Benjaminite! He called the Israelites to follow him rather than David and so the kingdom looked ready to fall apart.

A PRAYER

Save us, Lord, from the jealousy which is so destructive. Help us to realize that none of us can possess you. Rather, we are yours.

MORE MURDER

David's return to Jerusalem was somewhat less glorious than it should have been since he was supported only by the Judeans. Nevertheless, he was home. The ten concubines he had left behind were still there, but since they had been used, or misused, by Absalom (16:22) David no longer felt able to use them. Instead he made provision for them, but they had to live as though they were widows for the rest of their lives (v. 3).

Murder in the army

If David was to regain control of the whole kingdom, it was important for him to act quickly, before Sheba could properly establish himself as ruler in the north. He therefore gave orders to Amasa, his new commander (19:13), to get together an army drawn from all Judah, and he gave him three days in which to do it. Unfortunately for Amasa, he was unable to complete the task in the three days and David was not prepared to wait any longer. He therefore summoned Abishai. Joab was in disgrace following the killing of Absalom, and Abishai, his brother, was next in line of command after Amasa. He now had charge of David's personal bodyguard, that group of soldiers who had been with him right from the days when he was fleeing from Saul. These he now regarded as sufficient to deal with Sheba and those whom he had gathered around him.

Not only did Joab's men follow Abishai; so apparently did Joab himself, though no longer in command. Some ten miles north-east of Jerusalem, at Gibeon, where David's bodyguard under Joab had defeated the Israelites under Abner (2:12–17), they met Amasa. Was the large stone (v. 8) erected to mark this earlier victory? It would appear that Amasa was still gathering his forces from this point on the northern border of the Judean territory. Either that or he had been sent by David to follow them after he had returned.

It is not easy to see exactly what happened when Joab and Amasa met. Our text says that Joab's sword fell out, yet he had it in his hand to strike Amasa. The Hebrew text is rather obscure. The best suggestion is that he had, in fact, two swords. One he fastened on his belt under his outer cloak, the other in its sheath. As he went to meet

Amasa the outer one at his right hand fell out of its sheath, leaving Amasa quite unsuspecting. He then pulled Amasa towards him, ostensibly to give him a kiss in greeting, and as he did so he took out the other sword from underneath his cloak with his left hand and struck Amasa with it. Some such deceptive act is clearly meant.

The blow was fatal, messily so! In this way Joab killed his rival and regained control of the army along with his brother, Abishai (v. 10).

Together they pursued Sheba, leaving one man to guard the body of Amasa. His job also was to send Amasa's soldiers after Joab, making it clear that they were on David's side. Naturally, when they saw Amasa dead they stopped to look and wondered what to do next. So, to prevent any hold-up, the soldier dragged him off the road into a field and covered him so that he was out of sight (v. 12). Once more Joab was leading the army to put down a revolt against David.

Once again Joab resorted to violence, partly, no doubt, for selfish reasons. He wanted to regain his position as commander-in-chief. But we should also give him the benefit of the doubt, for he seems genuinely to have wanted to help David. It would have been possible for him to have supported Sheba in retaliation for his demotion but, to his credit, he did not do so. Violent he may have been, and ruthless, but in spite of everything he remained loyal to David. It is this mixture of brutality, cunning and deception with faithfulness to the one he had followed for so long that makes Joab such an interesting character. One minute we can hate or despise him, the next we are bound to admire him. How skilfully the writer of 2 Samuel draws his character!

A REFLECTION

It is characteristic of human beings to act from a mixture of motives. Only Jesus is completely selfless and unreservedly dedicated to his Father.

An UNEXPECTED ENDING

The footnotes in NRSV indicate that the Hebrew text is difficult at this point. However, the difficulties do not seriously affect the interpretation of the passage.

The siege

The town of Abel-beth-maacah is in the very far north of Israel, not far from Dan. So the statement that Sheba passed through all the tribes of Israel would be correct. It is mentioned again only in 1 Kings 15:20 and 2 Kings 15:29 as one of a group of towns in that area captured by foreign kings. It was probably a town of some consequence and easily defended. Beyond that, we know nothing of it. It does mean, however, that Sheba and his men had marched a very long distance, since he was of a Benjaminite family and Benjamin was in the south of Israel. One way of capturing a town so defended was to build a ramp made of earth against the wall of the city. At the same time Joab's men had begun either to batter the walls or to undermine them (REB) but they had not yet been able to make much impression (v. 15).

Another wise woman

This was the second time Joab had met a wise woman. In 2 Samuel 14 he had sought out the wise woman of Tekoa, but here this wise woman made herself known to him to offer him advice. Again, we are probably to think not of any woman who happened to be wise, but of one who was known for her wisdom and who therefore had a position of some standing in the community where she lived. The town had a reputation which had become almost proverbial. There was a saying: 'Be sure to put your question in Abel' and the matter would be settled (v. 18). It does not say to whom the question was to be addressed. It may have been to a priest, which was common enough; but it may have been to a circle of wise people of whom this woman was a descendant.

Speaking on behalf of the inhabitants, she claims that they are peaceable and loyal, seeking only the well-being of Israel. With a telling metaphor she describes the city as a 'mother' of Israel, one who loves, watches over and protects her offspring. Because she uses this metaphor she can accuse Joab of seeking to 'kill' the city, which is what the Hebrew actually says. It was a fitting charge against Joab, whether or not she was aware of all that Joab had done. Maybe his reputation as a 'killer' had already spread even so far north. Moreover, the city is a possession of the Lord, part of the land which belonged to him and which he had entrusted to Israel.

Her plea on behalf of the city was accepted by Joab (v. 20), who was prepared to call off the siege, demanding only that Sheba be handed over as a traitor to the king. The woman's influence in the city was obviously very strong and the people agreed to get rid of Sheba. Cutting off the head and handing it over as a trophy seems to have been not uncommon (see David and Goliath in 1 Samuel 17:54).

So, yet another rebellion in David's kingdom was put down, but how disturbed that kingdom had become since his misconduct with Bathsheba and Uriah. Nothing much is recorded by the writer of Samuel other than the disturbances. He seems anxious to show us the consequences of such wrongdoing even for someone as great as David. The tragedy of the fall of Jerusalem and the exile in Babylon through which he is living can also be traced to the sins of Israel and its kings, in his opinion.

David's inner cabinet

We have now reached a point in the story of David's reign where we can take a rest after the stressful events which have just been recorded. So the writer inserts a paragraph giving details of David's chief officers of state. Joab is back in charge of the army, the whole army, not just the bodyguard. The command of that is given to Benaiah, as in 8:18, though we have heard nothing of him since then. The 'forced labour' would be foreigners who had been taken captive in war and were now employed in various projects. This office was not mentioned in 8:18. Jehoshaphat is still the 'recorder' but there is a new secretary of state, Sheva instead of Seraiah, while David seems to have a personal priest alongside Zadok and Abiathar.

A THOUGHT

Blessed are the peacemakers; they shall be called God's children.

Matthew 5:9

FAMINE AVERTED

The remaining chapters of 2 Samuel seem detached from what has gone before. Chapter 20 ended, as we saw, with a summary. This chapter begins with a event which is said to have taken place some time during the reign of David, but it is not connected with the events in chapter 20. The story of that chapter continues in 1 Kings with events leading to the death of David and the succession of Solomon. Chapters 21—24 therefore form a kind of appendix. In all probability they were added after the division had been made between 2 Samuel and 1 Kings. Nevertheless, they now form part of the book and so must be taken seriously. Whoever placed them there regarded them as sufficiently important to be included in the account of David's reign.

Famine and its cause

At some point in that reign there had been a famine, and famine was generally regarded as being a punishment from God for wrongs that had been committed. It was therefore important to find out what sin had caused the famine and then to do whatever was necessary to put things right. David 'inquired of the Lord', probably through his priest. The answer he received was that there was blood guilt on the family of Saul (v. 1). We have already seen the effects of blood guilt. It demanded that the offended party should repay the offenders, blood for blood or life for life. Unless this demand were met, the balance of relationships would remain disturbed and divine judgment could be expected.

What had happened was that Saul, in his zeal for the establishment of Israel in the promised land, had attacked the Gibeonites and killed many of them. There would have been nothing wrong in that, had it not been for an oath which his predecessor, Joshua, had sworn to the Gibeonites. That story may be found in Joshua 9. Briefly, the Gibeonites had seen what had happened to their neighbours and, in order to avoid a similar fate, had tricked Joshua into making an oath with them that they would be protected. Once the oath was made it was binding for all time. So the Gibeonites, although not of Israelite stock, were able to live among the Israelites in safety. Gibeon was a large town and indeed we learn that there was a shrine to the Lord there (1 Kings 3:4; 1 Chronicles 16:39).

David discussed this matter with them, asking what they demanded in fulfilment of the blood guilt. Serious as their demands may seem to us, they limited them to seven of Saul's sons. Just how they were to be executed is not known. The Hebrew verb is a rare one (used of the dislocation of Jacob's hip). NRSV has 'impale', REB has 'throw down'—the end result is much the same! It is to be done 'before the Lord' and so in fulfilment of the divine obligation laid upon them. It is to take place at Gibeah, which is described as 'of Saul, the Lord's chosen one' in the Hebrew. Such a title is not accorded to Saul elsewhere and we should expect the execution to take place at Gibeon. NRSV has therefore followed a different text, suggested by some manuscripts of the Greek translation.

It would appear that Saul had two grandsons called Mephibosheth. Jonathan's son David spared because of the promise he had made to Jonathan. The other Mephibosheth was one of the seven chosen. His mother mourned his death. The killing took place in the spring, at the beginning of the season of barley harvest, and she stayed with the bodies until the rains came and the famine was over. Probably these were the lighter rains, later in the spring.

When David heard of her mourning he decided to give the bodies a proper burial. In addition he had the bones of Saul and Jonathan disinterred at Jabesh-gilead where they had been buried (2:4) and reinterred them, presumably along with those of the seven grandsons, in the tomb of Saul's father, Kish. So they all rested 'with their father' in the proper manner.

The practice of blood revenge is abhorrent to us. In the ancient world it was a way of restoring relationships which had gone wrong. The New Testament taught the way of free forgiveness and Paul told his fellow Christians in Rome to allow God to take revenge (Romans 12:19). For all that, similar practices have continued until relatively recent times, for instance, in Northern Ireland, where revenge killings have taken place between Catholics and Protestants.

A PRAYER

Help us, Lord, to set aside the desire for vengeance and, in the spirit of Jesus, to forgive.

GIANTS *in the* LAND

This chapter closes with four stories about battles with Philistine giants, all settled by single combat. It is widely held that they are part of Israel's stock of folklore. If they do describe actual events, those events probably took place earlier, since by now the Philistines were no longer a force to be reckoned with.

The giants

All four are described as the descendants of Raphah, known collectively as the Rephaim, the name which is preserved in the REB. These Rephaim were regarded as ancient pre-Israelite inhabitants of Canaan, renowned for their size, hence NRSV's translation 'giants'. Here it is used of the ancestors of Philistines, though, of course, the Philistines were not originally inhabitants of Canaan. Indeed they arrived only after the Israelite tribes had begun to settle there. The fact that the Philistines were identified with this race of giants indicates the view the Israelites had of them as powerful, fearsome warriors.

The first one mentioned was called Benob. The prefixed 'Ishbi' in NRSV probably represents a Hebrew verb which means 'and rested' and belongs with the previous phrase. David was tired and rested. Perhaps this is the reason why the story was put in its present position, it being assumed that because he got tired and needed to rest he was elderly. We have already seen how, on a previous occasion, in the attack which quelled Absalom's rebellion, David was urged not to go with his troops into battle (18:3), though the reason there was different. Here the reason given is that he should not 'quench the lamp of Israel'. In the following chapter, which is also Psalm 18, the Lord is called the lamp of the psalmist. In 1 Samuel 3:3 we read about the lamp that was kept burning throughout the night in the sanctuary at Shiloh and we referred to the injunction in Exodus 27:20 that a lamp should be kept burning in the tabernacle. Perhaps it somehow represented the presence of the Lord there throughout the darkness. On this basis the present passage may mean that if David is killed in battle by the Philistines he will have put an end to the presence of the Lord. However, in Psalm 18 itself (v. 28) it is not the Lord who is the lamp, but the psalmist's lamp is lit by the Lord so that his darkness is lit up. In 1 Kings 11:36, when the kingdom was divided, Rehoboam was promised one tribe 'so that my servant David may always have a lamp before me in Jerusalem'. Here the 'lamp' refers to a descendant of David. In the present passage, therefore, it may mean that if David was killed this would threaten the security of Israel or even his dynasty. Fortunately, good old Abishai came to the rescue again and killed the Philistine.

Another Goliath

The third tale raises an interesting question, since the Philistine giant is named Goliath and, as in 1 Samuel 17:7, the shaft of his spear was like a weaver's beam. This time, though, Goliath was killed not by David but by another Bethlehemite, Elhanan. This looks very much like another, abbreviated version of the same story. In the present context it could hardly be David who killed him since he had not been allowed to go to battle against the Philistines. It seems as though the account of the defeat of the Philistine giant was preserved and handed on by word of mouth in different forms. In 1 Samuel 17 it served its purpose of bringing David to the attention of Saul and was therefore told in greater detail. Here it is simply mentioned along with other similar stories.

How many fingers?

The colourful nature of these stories is shown by this fourth one, of the giant with six fingers on each hand and six toes on each foot. He, too, came from Gath like Goliath. Like Goliath again, he taunted Israel. This time it was David's nephew who killed him.

Taken together, the four stories are meant to demonstrate the complete victory of Israel over the Philistine threat, however great it may have been.

A REFLECTION

Who would true valour see,
Let him come hither…
No lion can him fright,
He'll with a giant fight,
But he will have a right
To be a pilgrim.

John Bunyan, 1628–88

A SONG *of* THANKSGIVING

Before we begin to look at these verses in detail, there are a number of things that need to be said about this chapter as a whole. First, it is almost identical with Psalm 18. The differences between the two are minor and do not affect our understanding of it. Verse 1 of the chapter agrees with the introduction which precedes Psalm 18. This raises the question as to which came first. Did David actually write and sing this psalm, which was then taken up and sung by other kings and finally incorporated into our book of Psalms? Or did the writer of the book of Samuel take an existing psalm which was appropriate to the occasion and place it on the lips of David? There are one or two signs from within the psalm itself which suggest that the latter is probably the case. We shall come to these later.

Second, if this is so, then for what sort of occasion was the psalm originally written? Two suggestions may be made. It may be a victory psalm sung by a king after a successful war. Or it may be that it was sung at an annual festival in Jerusalem, which celebrated the coming of the rains after the long, dry summer that threatened the people, and in which the king, as their representative, symbolically 'died' and was 'raised' again by the Lord.

Whichever of these is correct, our task is to interpret it in its present context, where the writer has put it, and here it celebrated David's many victories over different enemies as he established his rule over Israel.

The rock

The song begins with a recognition that it is the Lord who has placed him where he is (vv. 2–4). Throughout the story of his life we have seen how, again and again, any success of his has been attributed to the Lord. So, with a series of figures of speech, he calls upon God. Our Psalm 18 has an introductory line, 'I love you, O Lord, my strength', and though it is not represented here it would be appropriate for David.

Distress

It needs to be remembered that this is poetry and poetry is meant to appeal to the heart and the emotions even more than to the mind. This is why it uses such vivid figures of speech again. He had been at death's door. Sheol, the place where the dead go, was thought of as having tentacles which reached into life to drag people down into it. Death was a 'trap' which caught people and held them firmly. In such a predicament all a person can do is to call upon God for help. Here in verse 7 is one of the hints that the psalm originated with some king other than David, for it mentions the temple and David had been forbidden to build one. That was a task left to his son. It is possible, of course, to think of God's heavenly temple rather than the one in Jerusalem.

The coming of the Lord

What follows is a vivid description of the Lord coming to help the servant who has called on him (v. 8). The coming of God to his people is not infrequently described in terms of storm, earthquake, thunder and lightning or even volcanic eruption. Similar features are found in Exodus 19:16–19 where the Lord appeared to Moses on Mount Sinai, and Elijah expected to find God in the earthquake, wind and fire when he returned to the same mountain. In fact, though, he found him in the 'sound of sheer silence' instead (1 Kings 19:12). The picture of God riding on a cherub is perhaps derived from the cherubim who sat one at each end of the Ark in later times, and may be identified with the seraphim in Isaiah 6:2, where they are said each to have six wings. The point is, however, that the Lord comes in response to the call of his servant.

Deliverance

His coming means deliverance for the one who calls to him (v. 17). So God had delivered David from his many enemies who had seemed too strong for him. This could be true of Saul and even more especially of the Philistines. Such deliverance is like being led out of a narrow ravine into a broad place where the views are panoramic. It is a good description of what we mean by 'salvation'. And all because God 'delighted in him'.

A PRAYER

Give us confidence, Lord, to call to you when we are in trouble and the faith to believe that you can save us.

A SHORT MEMORY

If David actually composed and sang these words he must have had a very selective memory or else he was exceedingly insensitive. Surely he could not have forgotten the incident with Bathsheba and Uriah? Everything that had happened since, all the troubles he had had to endure, were due to this sin, according to the threat given to him by God through Nathan the prophet (12:10–11). He had not by any means been righteous, that is, he had not fulfilled his obligations to either Bathsheba or Uriah, and certainly his hands were not clean. According to the story as it has been told to us, his greatest achievements had been accomplished before that incident, and up to that point he may well have been able to sing this song; but not now, surely. It seems clear that the writer of 2 Samuel has included the whole psalm, which he knew from his temple worship, without regard to the relevance of this part of it to David's situation.

The Lord's faithfulness

What verses 21–25 celebrate is the righteousness and faithfulness of God. The Deuteronomists of the seventh century, steeped in the teaching of the book of Deuteronomy, of whom this writer was one, believed in a rigid system of rewards for the righteous and punishments for the wicked, and here it is the rewards which are dealt with (see, for instance, passages like Deuteronomy 7:12–16 and 8: 11–20). They were not the only ones to think in this way. Isaiah 1:19–20 expresses the same view and it may be found throughout the Wisdom literature (see, for example, Proverbs 10:6; 11:3 and especially 21:28). It was therefore a view widely held in Israel. All the same, the Israelites were not foolish enough to believe that things always worked out in this way. They knew from their experience, as we do from ours, that sometimes good people suffer and wicked people prosper. The psalmist who wrote Psalm 10 knew this was so, even if he could not understand why and even if he believed that, in the end, this anomaly would be put right (see also Psalm 73). But it is in the book of Job that this apparent failure of the doctrine of rewards and punishments is met head on. Job, the blameless one, suffers the most extreme pain and misfortune and longs for an explanation.

Therefore, passages such as the present one must be understood as setting out what was regarded as proper and as affirming the justice of God. It also serves as an encouragement to do what is right. It calls for humility, which means recognizing our status before God, and it condemns pride, which means thinking that we know best and can manage without God.

Here at verse 29 we are back with words which David could well have spoken, for in the matter of Goliath, and indeed throughout all his adventures, he had attributed his success not to his own skill and power, but to God. In this respect he had shown true humility. God was the light that had lit up the darkness of doubt and uncertainty, enabling him to see the way forward. In Psalm 119:105 it is the 'word' of the Lord which is a lamp and a light for the feet. In this psalm, it is the Lord himself, though it is through his word by priest or prophet that the guidance is given. Not only did God give him guidance; he also gave him strength and power to do things normally beyond him.

On this basis the psalmist can trust the Lord (v. 31). The 'word' of the Lord always proves true. NRSV is not wrong to translate it as 'promise', though 'word' shows the passage's links with Psalm 119 and with the guidance given through priests and prophets. The metaphor in the last line of verse 31 may be a bit mixed, but its meaning is clear. Those who 'take refuge in the Lord', that is, who put all their trust in him, will find him to be their 'shield' or protector.

Altogether this is a psalm which may well be sung in the moment of elation when success has been achieved or when things are going well. It needs to be set alongside other psalms which express the opposite emotions of distress and doubt and sorrow. We should beware of taking one psalm as though it represented the total human experience. Thanksgiving and confidence, however, are appropriate enough at this point in the story of David.

A PRAYER

Lord, your ways are not our ways and we cannot always make sense of things that happen. Make us humble enough to put all our trust in you.

To God *be the* Glory

This last part of the psalm is again appropriate on the lips of David provided we allow for the kind of exaggeration which is permissible in poetry. Verses 26–31 had been addressed directly to God, but now the singer turns again to his fellows and speaks to them about his God. Not for long, however; quite soon, in verse 36, he has turned again to God to address him directly. We should not be surprised at changes like this. They happen in prayer. We want to tell other people, but at the same time feel the need to speak directly to God.

The rock

The God whose way was perfect, whose promise was true and who shielded those who sought refuge in him (v. 31), is none other than the Lord and for the psalmist there is no other. This is not necessarily a confession of theoretical monotheism—the psalmist was not claiming that no other god existed. It is a more immediate statement. For him there is no other god. Only the Lord is the rock which sheltered him and in whom he could feel secure. He has returned to the description of God with which the psalm began (vv. 2–3). Instead of going on to call upon God for help he proceeds this time to recount what God has done for him. The meaning of the second line of verse 33 is unclear. Psalm 18 has a slightly different reading which means 'he makes me walk with integrity' and perhaps something similar should be understood here. Certainly the words used usually have to do with behaviour. However, he goes on from general behaviour to preparedness for battle.

What is important in these verses is the fact that the singer never claims the power to live or fight as his own. It is always given to him by God. David had made similar claims when he had fought against Goliath (1 Samuel 17:37 and 47). On that occasion he had not needed spear or bow or shield, but only his shepherd's sling because it was the Lord's doing. Later, of course, David used the normal weapons of warfare but did not forget that he was dependent upon the Lord. When he defeated the Philistines in the valley of Rephaim he acknowledged that the Lord had given them into his hands (2 Samuel 5:20). In the context of David's life the 'enemies' of verse 41 who 'called upon the Lord' were probably not people like the Philistines, but perhaps those of his own people who had rebelled against him at various times.

That being so, the first line of verse 44 ought to go with the previous verses, for the Hebrew says 'my people' (see NRSV footnote). Psalm 18 simply has 'peoples' and perhaps the writer changed this deliberately to make it appropriate for David.

Israel supreme

But David had also conquered all the smaller nations around Israel and made himself master of that area. Whatever it meant for the psalmist later, as applied to David it could have nothing to do with the great nations such as Egypt or Assyria. The 'foreigners' would be the people of Philistia, Moab, Ammon and Edom who were now under his control.

The final praise

The psalm ends where it began, with the recognition of the Lord as the rock (v. 47). Yet this must never be understood in a static way, for 'the Lord lives'. He not only sheltered his people, but actively went out with them to give them victory. This view of God as alive and active is, of course, central to Old Testament belief. Alive himself, he is the source of all life.

The final verses of the psalm make it clear that it was sung by the king. When it was used in the temple it was the descendants of David who sang it, looking back to their ancestor. Used here in 2 Samuel it is sung by David, looking forward to his descendants who were included in the promise to David in chapter 7. Whatever view we may take about the date of the psalm and its composition, the writer of 2 Samuel was not far wrong in using it to express David's gratitude to God for the achievements of his reign.

A REFLECTION

It is easy, in our success, to gloat over others and forget God's part in it. 'When the Lord your God has brought you into the land that he swore to give to your ancestors... a land with fine large cities which you did not build... take care that you do not forget the Lord.'

Deuteronomy 6:10–12

LAST WORDS

The 'last words' of people are usually regarded as important. If this is their last opportunity to speak, then we should expect them to say something of significance. These expectations are not always met, but our interest in them remains. In the Old Testament we have the last words of Jacob in Genesis 49 and Moses' last words in Deuteronomy 33. It is hardly surprising, therefore, to find here the last words of David.

In fact, they are not quite his last words, strictly speaking, for there are still some events of his life and some words to be recorded in the first two chapters of 1 Kings. Nor are they likely to be the actual words that David spoke. As with the other speeches, this may well have been composed by the writer to indicate what he believed the king to have said as he neared the end of his life.

It has to be said that the Hebrew of this poem is difficult to translate and a comparison of the NRSV and the REB will show where some of the differences of interpretation lie. All the same, the main drift of the speech is clear. After an introduction, the speech itself may be divided into three parts.

The introduction

Verses 1 and 2 use words which remind us of the prophets. The word 'oracle' is rarely used of human messages. It nearly always comes at the end of a prophetic speech where NRSV translates it as 'says (the Lord)' (Amos 1:5, 7, 15 etc). The use of the word here suggests that David's words are, in fact, God's words.

The first three descriptions of David are clear enough; it is the fourth, 'the favourite of the Living One of Israel' (NRSV), which is questionable. REB has followed the traditional interpretation, 'the singer of Israel's psalms', which has given support to the idea that David composed all the psalms. Personally I would prefer 'the delight of Israel's psalms', that is, the one of whom Israel's psalms often speak.

Then the words are said to be inspired by the spirit of God. Although not mentioned as the source of inspiration in most of the prophetic books, the spirit of God is prominent in Ezekiel and in

Numbers 10. When some of the spirit which inspired Moses was transferred to the seventy elders, they prophesied. So perhaps David here speaks as a prophet, passing on the word of God.

Good government

David sees the ideal ruler as being 'righteous', that is, as fulfilling his obligations to his subjects (v. 3). This is how it ought to be. The metaphor he uses is striking. In Israel the sun quickly burns off the morning clouds, and the sun and rain make the grass grow. So the ideal rule makes for prosperity.

The real world

David claims that his own rule has been like this and then reflects on the dynasty he founded. That is to put it badly, for actually it was God who founded it by means of the promise, here described as a covenant or bond, which we met in chapter 7. The Lord is the source of his help and the object of his delight. He will cause it to 'spring up' (where NRSV has 'prosper'). This word is used in Psalm 132:17 for the springing up of David's descendants and probably has the same meaning here. God will ensure his descendants reign after him.

The negative

Verse 6 speaks of the 'godless' (literally, 'Belial'). We have met the 'sons of Belial' before (1 Samuel 1:16; 2:12; 10:27). They are always opposed to God. They are to be dealt with as thorns too prickly to be handled with bare hands, needing to be destroyed.

So the speech moves from David himself as the instrument of God, to his 'house,' which will prosper and to the ungodly who will perish. For the writer, this is what the ideal Davidic kingdom should be like.

A REFLECTION

We look forward to the universal reign of Jesus, the son of David, in which justice is done and is seen to be done, where everyone does what is right and all live in 'shalom'.

The HALL *of* FAME

The medallists

Gold, silver and bronze are awarded to three of David's warriors in this hall of fame. They are mentioned also in 1 Chronicles 11:11, where only two are named and where their names are spelled differently. These are not the commanders of his army, but officers who were specially noted for their bravery and valour. Of them and their exploits we know nothing more than is recorded here.

The first of them managed to kill eight hundred men, probably Philistines, though the text does not say so. Chronicles awards him only three hundred but, since Abishai also killed three hundred and yet was not one of the Three, eight hundred is more likely. It was quite an achievement for one man. The second stood his ground when the rest of the army retreated. He fought until he was so tired that his sword stuck to his hand. When the Israelites came back there was no one left for them to fight; all they had to do was to strip the dead of their arms. The third did much the same in a field of lentils. In each case victory was won over the enemy (v. 12).

What are we to make of these accounts? First, they all took place early in David's life. The last two certainly were engaged in battles against the Philistines who had been finally pushed back into their five cities earlier in his reign (8:1). We must assume that the three were noted for their valour, but, as often happens in cases like this, there may have been some exaggeration. This is apt to happen with stories about heroes which are passed on by word of mouth. The stories improve with the telling.

A joint enterprise

Lower down in the honours list were thirty others, to be named later. Three of these, not the Three already mentioned, went on this expedition. This took place while David was holed up in the cave of Adullam, before he became king. The only occasion on which the Philistines were located in the valley of Rephaim was after David became king and had captured Jerusalem (5:17–25). Either this was another occasion which has not been recorded or the story has become associated with Rephaim in the telling of it. However, the Philistines were clearly in control of much of Judah for they had a garrison in Bethlehem itself.

It is unlikely that there was anything special about the water in Bethlehem (v. 15). It was not a spa or anything like that. The story simply depicts David as longing for his home town and its facilities. He had drunk water from this well in his boyhood and youth. Now it was inaccessible because of the Philistine presence. Hearing this wish expressed, three of his warriors decided to get some of the water for him. They managed to evade the Philistines, got to the well, drew water and returned with it to David.

David's reaction is, at first sight, surprising. Instead of drinking it he poured it out on the ground. It must have looked like ingratitude until he explained his reason. So brave and so loyal had these heroes been that to have drunk the water would have been like drinking the lifeblood which they had risked. Instead he poured it out as an offering to the Lord, a thank-offering for the courage, affection and faithfulness of his men.

We are bound to ask why the writer or editor of 2 Samuel placed these stories here after the last words of David. They look like an afterthought, bits of traditional material for which no place had been found earlier in the account, but which deserved a place in the book. On the other hand, the editor may have wanted to make a point. Could it be that these are meant to illustrate the prosperity of David's life and rule and the downfall of his enemies which had been mentioned in the last words? Again, these verses with their emphasis on the prowess of David's warriors may pave the way for the following chapter in which he took a census to determine the number of men available for the army. The last words had claimed that what David had done was due to the Lord. Now there begins a concern with the numbers of fighting men and their bravery, as though success depended on them. It is always difficult to be sure about the intentions of authors!

A PRAYER

Thank you, Lord, for the loyalty and kindness of friends who try to meet our needs.

The HALL *of* FAME (*continued*)

The runners-up

We have already heard a good deal about Abishai and Benaiah. Both of them have been very active, Abishai in particular, but here they do not qualify for the top places in the list of heroes. Abishai killed only three hundred men! He therefore became the chief of the finalists, the Thirty. As for Benaiah, we have learned that he was in command of the bodyguard of David (8:18; 20:23). Here we are told some of his exploits as an individual. During his outlaw days, David was friendly enough with the Moabites to take his parents there for safety (1 Samuel 22:3), though later, after he became king, he defeated the Moabites and brought them under his control (2 Samuel 8:2). Just when Benaiah killed two of them we do not know. We have not been told of any conflict with the Egyptians (v. 21), so whether this was an isolated incident or took place within some conflict which has not been recorded, we cannot tell. We are not likely to have any confirmation of his killing of the lion in a pit on a snowy day! In spite of all this bravery he still was only a runner-up.

The finalists

Although they are called the Thirty, there are rather more than thirty named here. Verse 39 says there are 37, but even that number is difficult to find from the list itself. The vague phrase 'sons of Jashen', if correct, leaves the number open. There is a parallel list in 1 Chronicles 11 and another in 1 Chronicles 27. Not much is to be gained, for our purpose, by a detailed comparison of these.

One odd feature of this chapter is that Joab is not mentioned at all, as a member either of the Three or even of the Thirty. Did he not perform any acts of personal bravery? Or maybe he was not included because he was commander of the whole army and his position is therefore taken for granted. The grounds on which the Thirty were chosen are not given. We are left to presume that each one did something which qualified him for inclusion. For some reason they were marked out from the rest of David's men.

The list raises some interesting questions to which no definite answers can be given. First, the list appears to relate to the time when David was an outlaw. Verse 13 of this chapter clearly places the incident about the water of Bethlehem at the time when he was based in the cave of Adullam. Further, at the end of this list in verse 39 we find Uriah the Hittite, the husband of Bathsheba, and so the list must belong to a period prior to his death and, most probably to the outlaw band. Yet when we read the stories of that period we were given no indication of any structure of this kind. Admittedly this is not a description of the organization of the band, but a grading of their exploits. Nevertheless, we might have expected some hint of this earlier. In 1 Chronicles 11 the list is given immediately after the capture of Jerusalem, indicating those who helped to make him king. Second, how did the writer obtain this list? Remember he was writing some four hundred years after the events and it is very unlikely that a list in such detail would have been handed down by word of mouth. If it was a written source he was using, then when was this written? It could hardly have been during David's period in the Negeb. We should have to assume that it was written some time after David became king, as suggested by 1 Chronicles 11. We learned in 20:24 that there was a Recorder in David's court and it is possible that he kept a record not only of contemporary events but also of past achievements by individuals. 1 Chronicles 27 mentions the same names in a passage about the organization of David's army. This, too, may suggest that it was an official court list of some kind.

It is possible, therefore, that this is a record from later in David's reign, listing the famous people up to that time. The writer of 2 Samuel clearly wanted this to refer to the Negeb period and so at the very end, in order to make his point, he added the name of Uriah the Hittite. But why should the writer wish to include this list at this point in his story? Again we have to ask whether it was just an afterthought or whether the emphasis on the prowess of individuals at this point in the story was meant to indicate that, in spite of the admission of reliance on God in the previous chapter, there was, towards the end of David's reign, a growing concern with human ability which culminated in the taking of the census in the next chapter.

QUESTIONS

How important is it to be enrolled in the hall of fame? What are the dangers in a graded list? What makes for greatness in God's eyes?

The CENSUS

In the book of Chronicles, this event follows directly the story of the Philistine giants which was recorded in 2 Samuel 21:18–22. It may be as well, therefore, to glance again at the end of chapter 21.

Checking the resources

The central fact here is that David ordered and carried out a census of his people to find out what resources were at his disposal, particularly as far as the army was concerned. This was obviously considered as inadvisable or even wrong, not only by Joab but by the writer as well. There doesn't appear to us to be much wrong with assessing resources. In the New Testament the king who sat down to count the cost before embarking on any expedition was regarded as wise (Luke 14:31–32). So why did it appear so wrong here? We have mentioned before a tradition which has become known as the Holy War tradition. We saw it at work in the story of David and Goliath, where David fought with the minimum of armour in order that it may be seen that it was the Lord who gave the victory (1 Samuel 17). At the time of the exodus from Egypt, Israel was told that all they needed to do was to be still; the Lord would fight for them (Exodus 14:14). In Judges 7 Gideon started with an enormous army against the Midianites but it was gradually reduced to three hundred men so that they could not claim victory for themselves, but would have to acknowledge that it was given to them by God. Later on, the prophets will say that it was wrong to rely on the strength of arms or on allies to the exclusion of God (Isaiah 31:1). Remarkably Joab, the realist, the practical soldier, questions the need to know how many men are available. Whether his protest was prompted by faith in the Lord or by confidence in his armed forces and his satisfaction with them, we cannot tell.

The writer is also very uneasy with the idea and found it difficult to attribute it to David. In order to avoid saying that it was David's idea, he had to go quite a long way round.

Since David was inspired by God, then it must be the Lord who had planted the idea in his mind. But why should the Lord plant a bad idea in David's mind? It must be for some reason and that must be so that he could punish Israel for carrying through the idea. But why should he want to punish Israel? It must be because they had sinned against him and made him angry. There the matter stops. So, the anger of the Lord was kindled against Israel and he incited David to do this wrong thing.

Then there is the 'again'. On what previous occasion had the Lord been angry with Israel? All we can say is that there was a famine in Israel according to 21:1 and famines were usually attributed to the anger of God and seen as punishment for wrong. There the wrong was the unresolved blood feud. In the present instance there is no indication of what they had done wrong. The Chronicler deals with the matter differently. He says it was Satan, the adversary, who incited David. The writer of 2 Samuel could not fall back on this because he believed that God alone was responsible for what happened.

The census

The count of manpower took nine months and twenty days. This is understandable, for it meant going through all the towns and villages to determine the numbers. They seem to have started across the Jordan in the south and gradually worked their way north and then west and finally down south to the Negeb. The description indicates the size of David's kingdom. Never was it larger than this.

All Israel

There is one other significant point in these verses. David was told to go and count the people of 'Israel and Judah' as though they were still separate entities, and when the numbers are reported in verse 9 the numbers for the two peoples are given separately. Of course, the writer may have been reflecting thoughts from his own time. But if this really were so in the time of David, and towards the end of his reign, as the position of the story suggests, it indicates that the unity was fragile, as we have seen before.

A REFLECTION

We should be thankful that, in Jesus, God has shown us how he deals with our wrongdoing differently, by forgiving us through the cross.

REWARD *for* ERROR

This would be a perfectly straightforward account were it not for what has gone before. For this writer, God rewards the righteous and punishes the wrongdoer. David has done wrong and therefore must be punished. So far, so good. This is what we should expect. But if we are to take verse 1 at face value, then God told David to take the census so that the people should be punished. In this case it is hardly fair to blame David; he was only doing as he was told. Yet now he admits that he has sinned and been very foolish. How can he have sinned when he has been obedient to God? Some punishment of the people is understandable because that was why God told David to take the census, but why should David admit to guilt?

It really does look as though this is a story about David's desire to take a census and evaluate his resources, and verse 1 is a way of shifting the blame from him on to the people who needed to be punished. Once the task was completed David realized what he had done, confessed his sin and sought the removal of his guilt from the Lord. When he confessed to foolishness he meant not just silliness. Foolishness in the Old Testament always carries with it the idea of moral wrongdoing.

Multiple choice

This time (v. 11) God's word came to him through Gad and not through Nathan as in chapter 12. He, too, was a prophet who had been with David for a long time. In fact he was with him right from the start. When David first went to the cave of Adullam it was Gad who advised him to leave and hide in the forest (1 Samuel 22:5), but we have not heard of him since then until now. Nor do we hear of him again. However, now he speaks to David a word from God in answer to his plea that his guilt should be removed.

The offering of three options is a familiar narrative device and the writer may well have been influenced by this in the way he tells this one. Though there was a choice of punishment, punishment there had to be. These three were the conventional forms of punishment. They occur together in Amos 4:6–11, Jeremiah 24:10 and Ezekiel 5:12. Sometimes all three are threatened for everyone; in Ezekiel each is threatened for part of the people. Here a choice was given, but David allowed God to decide, though he apparently ruled out enemies, since these would be 'human hands' (v. 14). He is prepared to do this because he is aware of the great mercy of God. He had already had experience of this after his affair with Bathsheba. There, too, the penalty had been commuted and his life was spared, though his child died.

That mercy is shown consequently, in so far as the punishment chosen by God was not carried out in full. True, seventy thousand people died of the plague, but God called a halt as the 'angel' reached the capital, Jerusalem (v. 16). The word 'angel' really means 'messenger'. Angels play some part in Old Testament affairs, but always as messengers of God and in no way independent of him. Indeed it is little more than saying that God appears and speaks. They have no separate identity, no name until the latest pages of the Old Testament. The nearest parallel to this story in in Exodus 12:23 where the 'destroyer' passes over the threshold to bring the plague upon the Egyptians but is not allowed to enter the houses of the Israelites.

It is stories such as this which show how Israel came to believe that Jerusalem would always be safe from disaster, a belief which had, of course, been shattered by the time our writer was at work.

We are told precisely where the pestilence stopped because the writer wants to tell us about this special place, the threshing-floor of Araunah. Before he does so, however, he adds another note about David. Although he was encouraged to take the census in order that the people might be punished, he now claimed it was his fault only and he was ready to take the blame and the punishment for it. Don't be misled by the sheep; they are his people over whom he is the shepherd-king.

REMEMBER

Jesus, the son of David, did actually lay down his life for his sheep and saved us from our sins.

A PRICE WORTH PAYING

We are not sure of the whereabouts in or near Jerusalem of the threshing-floor of Araunah. David was told to 'go up' and so we assume it was on higher ground. It would need to be, so that the wind could catch the grain as it was lifted into the air and blow away the chaff. Araunah was a Jebusite, one of the people who occupied Jerusalem before it was captured by David and who were allowed to stay on there afterwards. He was still permitted to own his own piece of land in the city.

The purpose of the purchase of the threshing-floor was not just so that David could build an altar there. It was so that he could offer there a sacrifice to the Lord which might persuade him not only to halt the pestilence but to end it altogther.

The deal done

As was customary, Araunah prostrated himself before the king as any subject would. There were certain conventions for meeting royalty just as there are today. The language also is court language, with Araunah calling himself 'your servant'. It would be unusual for him to use his own name, as in verse 23, and, since in Hebrew the word 'Araunah' is very similar to the word for 'lord', it is possible that originally it read 'my lord's servant', the normal form of expression.

Was there perhaps a note of anxiety about Araunah's question? If so, it was soon put at rest. David wanted to buy the threshing-floor. He respected the rights of Araunah and did not simply take possession of it, as some kings would have done. We are reminded of the later occasion when King Ahab wanted a plot of land from one of his subjects and similarly refused to take possession of it when Naboth refused. Jezebel, from a different culture, did not understand this Israelite way and had Naboth killed to get it (1 Kings 21). It illustrates well the fact that the Israelite king was no despot, but was subject to the same laws as his people—ideally, at least.

No doubt Araunah was as anxious as the king to avert the plague. He was therefore prepared to give the king what he wanted without payment. Not only so, he would add to his gift the oxen and the fuel for the sacrifice. It would mean that he would lose completely the ability to thresh his corn. If he also threshed other people's for them, then it would mean that he was willing to give up his livelihood. But that was better than giving up his life. Still, it was a generous offer.

The offer was refused and David insisted on paying for the ground and oxen. It is difficult to know the price of land in Jerusalem at that time but it was probably a fair, if not generous, price. David's reason for doing this has become a well-known saying. He would not offer a sacrifice that cost him nothing. It would not have been a sacrifice in our more modern sense of the word since he was not giving up anything of great value. But also we have seen that David claimed that he alone had sinned (v. 17). Therefore it was right that the sacrifice should properly be his and not someone else's.

The sacrifices he offered were not sin- or guilt-offerings, as prescribed in Leviticus 5 and 6. They were whole offerings, in which the whole animal was burnt on the altar as a gift to God, and peace- or shared-offerings, in which part was offered on the altar and part eaten by the offerer and his family or friends as a means of confirming relationships.

The whole book of 1 and 2 Samuel began with Elkanah offering shared-offerings at the shrine at Shiloh; it ends with David offering them in Jerusalem at the threshing-floor of Araunah. This was an entreaty, an acted prayer, a supplication, rather than any kind of payment to God. It was answered and the plague stopped.

So end the books of Samuel, but not the life of David. The nature of his death and the question of the succession remain unanswered. For that we have to read on into the books of Kings. We shall glance at these as a postscript.

A PRAYER

Help us, Lord, to be like the better side of David, and, when we fail, to be humble and honest enough to confess it. May our offering of worship and service be sincere, whatever the cost.

POSTSCRIPT:
The STRUGGLE *for* POWER

It seems a pity to leave the story of David where 2 Samuel ends. There is still a little more about his life to be learned, and the question about the succession, which has occupied some of the previous sections, has not yet been answered. It cannot have been easy to decide where to draw the line between 2 Samuel and 1 Kings. The difficulty lies in the fact that Solomon was acclaimed king before David had died. So a decision had to be made whether to end 2 Samuel with the death of David or to begin 1 Kings with the 'coronation' of Solomon. The editors of the work decided on the latter.

The human hot water bottle

David was already an old man. We are not told his age, but later we learn that he reigned for forty years all told. His age was obviously affecting his circulation and no matter what bedding was provided he was still cold. His courtiers hit on an excellent idea for keeping him warm. They provided him with the most beautiful teenage girl they could find. She was to sleep with him and keep him warm. Perhaps they also thought he would be rejuvenated! Alas, sexual relations were out of the question.

This only serves to introduce the real theme. Who would succeed David? The sons who were born to him while he was king at Hebron obviously had a very good claim on the throne. Of those, however, Amnon was dead; so too was Absalom, who had been David's favourite. The next in line was Adonijah and he was still very much alive. For very different reasons, Solomon was also a candidate. His mother was Bathsheba, a favourite wife, whose first son, born as a result of the adultery, had died, but whose second son, born soon afterwards, was also called Jedidiah, 'Beloved of the Lord', because the Lord loved him. That strong hint in 12:24–25 marked him out as special.

These two, then, were the contenders, and the 'trouble within his own house' (12:11) came to a head. Each had his backers. David's two oldest companions, Joab and Abiathar, supported Adonijah

(v. 7). All through the story so far, these two have been absolutely loyal to David. It is true that relations between David and Joab had been strained at times, especially when Joab had killed Absalom, but nevertheless he was still commander-in-chief and his loyalty to David never wavered. So Adonijah had strong support. On the other hand Benaiah, who was now in command of the bodyguard, and Zadok, who appears as David's priest after the capture of Jerusalem, and Nathan the prophet who had advised David and had criticized him at the time of his adultery, all supported Solomon, as did Bathsheba, his mother, naturally (v. 8).

With David now too old to function properly as king, some decision was necessary. Adonijah, with the backing of Joab and Abiathar, set himself up as king without letting the other side know anything about it. Nathan heard of it and contacted Bathsheba at once. She was sufficiently in David's favour to be able to approach him and tell him what had happened. The plan was for her to do so and then for Nathan to confirm it. She was to say that David had sworn to her that her son would succeed him (v. 17). We have not heard about any such oath but that does not mean that Bathsheba was inventing it. He may have done so or he may not.

A PRAYER

Save us, Lord, from seizing power at the expense of others.
Make us content to be 'servants of all' (Mark 9:35).

The FINAL SCENE

The coronation

Consequently Solomon was now officially and publicly acclaimed king before Adonijah's claim could be recognized. The event is described in 1 Kings 1:38–40. Later, another entered Jerusalem riding on a donkey to be acclaimed 'Son of David' (Matthew 21:8). All the other side could do was to forget about their claim. Adonijah himself was afraid of what Solomon would do to him and so he went and clung to the horns of the altar, protuberances on each corner. There he could claim asylum (v. 50). Solomon promised him safety provided he behaved himself in future.

David's last words

We have already heard David's last words in 2 Samuel 23, but here further last words are addressed directly to Solomon. Those in 2 Samuel 23 had spoken of David's own just rule and of God's promises of a 'house' or dynasty to succeed him. Knowing that death was near, he now charged his son to keep the commandments of God and again recalled the promise which had been given to him in chapter 7. The dynasty was to continue in Solomon and his sons and, provided they were obedient, it would continue 'for ever'. The problem for Solomon himself and for all the following kings was just here. They found obedience difficult and very often failed. Our present writer sees the dynasty as dependent on obedience and, at the time he was writing, there had been too much disobedience by the Israelite and Judean kings, so it had come to an end.

David had one other piece of advice for Solomon. The sons of Barzillai, who had helped him at the time of Absalom's rebellion, were to be kept safe and to keep their place at court. Shimei, who had cursed David but then retracted it, was to be put to death in due course. The most striking thing, though, is that David said the same about Joab (v. 6). He was clear-minded enough to know that Joab, for all his loyalty to David, would not necessarily be the same with Solomon, especially as he had supported Adonijah, but also because of the blood guilt he had incurred by killing two army commanders, against David's orders.

The death of David

So this great king died. He had reigned for forty years. Even if this is used as a round number, he had certainly reigned for a long time. There were flaws in his character. He tended to have favourites to whom he gave preference. He was perhaps less than decisive about his successor. He never got over his adultery and its effects. Yet, in spite of these failings, he reigned well and handed on to his son a kingdom of considerable size and strength. It was a united kingdom even if the cracks still showed from time to time. The writer of the books of Samuel does not gloss over the weaknesses, but still sees him as a great king of Israel whom most of his successors failed to match. Now that the line had come to an end, people could begin to look forward to God's gift of a new David to rule Israel

A PRAYER

Lord, help us to learn the lessons from your word, to see what is wrong and avoid it, to see what is right and do it.

NOTES

NOTES

NOTES

NOTES

NOTES

NOTES

NOTES

THE PEOPLE'S
BIBLE COMMENTARY

VOUCHER SCHEME

The People's Bible Commentary (PBC) provides a range of readable, accessible commentaries that will grow into a library covering the whole Bible.

To help you build your PBC library, we have a voucher scheme that works as follows: a voucher is printed on the last page of each People's Bible Commentary volume (as above). These vouchers count towards free copies of other books in the series.

For every four purchases of PBC volumes you are entitled to a further volume FREE.

Please find the coupon for the PBC voucher scheme overleaf.

All you need do:

- Cut out the vouchers from the last page of the PBCs you have purchased and attach them to the coupon.

- Complete your name and address details, and indicate your choice of free book from the list on the coupon.

- Take the coupon to your local Christian bookshop who will exchange it for your free PBC book; or send the coupon straight to BRF who will send you your free book direct. Please allow 28 days for delivery.

Please note that PBC volumes provided under the voucher scheme are subject to availability. If your first choice is not available, you may be sent your second choice of book.

THE PEOPLE'S BIBLE COMMENTARY

VOUCHER SCHEME COUPON

TO BE COMPLETED BY THE CUSTOMER

My choice of free PBC volume is (please indicate your first and second choice, as all volumes are supplied subject to availability):

❑ 1 and 2 Samuel

❑ Psalms 1—72

❑ Nahum–Malachi

❑ Mark

❑ Luke

❑ John

❑ 1 Corinthians

❑ Revelation

Name: . . . .

Address: . . . .

. . . .

Postcode: . . . .

TO BE COMPLETED BY THE BOOKSELLER

(Please complete the following. Coupons redeemed will be credited to your account for the value of the book(s) supplied as indicated above. Please note that only coupons correctly completed with original vouchers will be accepted for credit.):

Name: . . . .

Address: . . . .

. . . .

Postcode: . . . .

Account Number: . . . .

Completed coupons should be sent to: BRF, PBC Voucher Scheme, Peter's Way, Sandy Lane West, OXFORD OX4 5HG

Tel 01865 748227
Fax 01865 773150
Registered Charity No. 233280

THIS OFFER IS AVAILABLE IN THE UK ONLY
PLEASE NOTE: ALL VOUCHERS ATTACHED TO THIS COUPON MUST BE ORIGINAL COPIES.